CiTY·SMaRT™

Berkeley/Oakland

John Weil

**AVALON
TRAVEL**
publishing

CiTY•SMaRT: Berkeley/Oakland
1st edition

John Weil

Published by
Avalon Travel Publishing
5855 Beaudry St.
Emeryville, CA 94608, USA

Printing History
1st edition— August 2000
5 4 3 2 1

Please send all comments, corrections, additions, amendments, and critiques to:

CiTY•SMaRT™
AVALON TRAVEL PUBLISHING
5855 BEAUDRY ST.
EMERYVILLE, CA 94608, USA
e-mail: info@travelmatters.com
www.travelmatters.com

ISBN: 1-56261-514-9
ISSN: On file with the Library of Congress

Editors: Suzanne Samuel, Ellen Cavalli, Chris Hayhurst
Graphics Editor: Bunny Wong, Erika Howsare
Graphics Assistance: Kim Marks
Production: Amber Pirker, Melissa Tandysh
Design: Janine Lehmann
Cover Design: Suzanne Rush
Maps: Mike Ferguson, Mike Morgenfeld, Allen Leech

Front cover photo: © John Elk III—University of California, Berkeley, CA
Back cover photo: © John Elk III—Lake Merritt, Oakland, CA

Distributed in the United States and Canada by Publishers Group West

Printed in the U.S. by Publishers Press

CONTENTS

MAP CONTENTS

Restaurants, hotels, museums and other facilities marked by the
♿ symbol are wheelchair accessible.

See Berkeley and Oakland the CiTY·SMaRT™ Way

The Guide for Berkeley and Oakland Natives, New Residents, and Visitors

In *City•Smart: Berkeley/Oakland*, local author John Weil tells natives things they never knew about their city. New residents will get an insider's view of their new hometown. And visitors will be guided to the very best Berkeley and Oakland have to offer—whether they're on a weekend getaway or staying a week or more.

Opinionated Recommendations Save You Time and Money

From shopping to nightlife to museums, the author is opinionated about what he likes and dislikes. You'll learn the great and the not-so-great things about Berkeley and Oakland sights, restaurants, and accommodations. So you can decide what's worth your time and what's not; which hotel is worth the splurge and which is the best choice for budget travelers.

Easy-to-Use Format Makes Planning Your Trip a Cinch

City•Smart: Berkeley/Oakland is user-friendly—you'll quickly find exactly what you're looking for. Chapters are organized by travelers' interests or needs, from Where to Stay and Where to Eat, to Sights and Attractions, Kids' Stuff, Sports and Recreation, and even Day Trips from Berkeley and Oakland.

Includes Maps and Quick Location-Finding Features

Every listing is accompanied by a geographic zone designation that helps you immediately find each location. Staying in the Oakland Marriott in downtown Oakland and wondering about nearby sights and restaurants? Look for the Oakland label in the listings, and you'll know that statue or café is not far away. Or maybe you're looking for the Chapel of the Chimes. Along with its address, you'll see a South Berkeley/North Oakland label, so you'll know just where to find it.

All That and Fun to Read, Too!

Every City•Smart chapter includes fun-to-read (and fun-to-use) tips to help you get more out of Berkeley and Oakland, city trivia (Did you know that 14 streams once flowed through Berkeley?), and illuminating sidebars (for interesting information about the music, theater, and dance series known as Cal Performances, for example, see page 189). And well-known local residents provide their personal "Top Ten" lists, guiding readers to the city's best restaurants, attractions in the East Bay, and more.

BERKELEY/OAKLAND ZONES

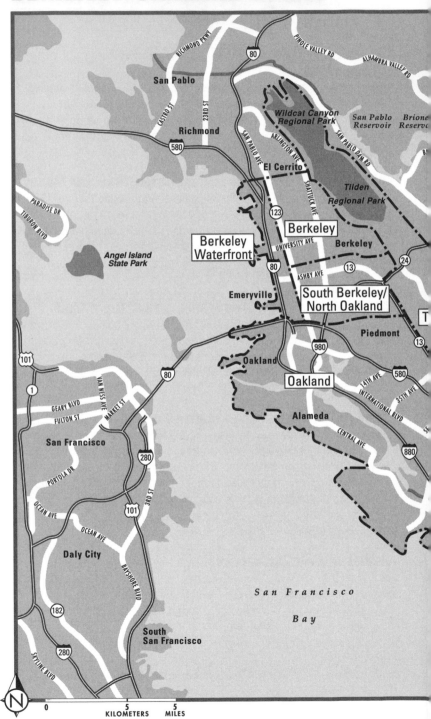

BERKELEY/ OAKLAND ZONES

Berkeley (B)
Covers the University of California campus, downtown Berkeley, North Berkeley, parts of Albany, and most of the residential areas in the Berkeley Hills.

Berkeley Waterfront (BW)
Covers Emeryville and Berkeley west of San Pablo Avenue, including the neighborhoods along Fourth and Tenth Streets.

South Berkeley/ North Oakland (SB/NO)
Covers Rockridge in North Oakland, the hills near Claremont, and Berkeley neighborhoods south of campus, including Elmwood.

Oakland (O)
Covers nearly all of Oakland, including Jack London Square, Downtown Oakland, and Lake Merritt, plus Alameda and Piedmont.

The Hills (H)
Covers the parkland of both Oakland and Berkeley, including Tilden and other East Bay Regional Parks, plus most of the residential areas in the Oakland Hills.

Saxon Donnelly

1

WELCOME TO BERKELEY AND OAKLAND

There are no cable cars with hour-long lines. You won't find ashtrays shaped like Alcatraz. And don't bother hunting down package tours. Unlike their famous neighbor at the other end of the Bay Bridge, Berkeley and Oakland haven't been turned into theme parks. An independent-minded traveler can still discover things here, such as a wide-angle view of the Golden Gate, a Sunday morning overflowing with gospel music, or possibly the best baguette west of Paris.

Berkeley, with its unique combination of brains, beauty, and bohemia, is like no other city in the United States. The University of California is a magnet for some of the best minds in the world, the best bookstores, and the best performers. Any day of the year, on or off campus, you can sit in on lectures, readings, concerts, plays, dances, recitals, and coffeehouse debates. Conversation is the number-one civic pastime, and right on its heels is food. A renaissance in American architecture took place in Berkeley in the first decades of the twentieth century. Today, despite years of fire, earthquakes, and modern architects, a rich sampling remains in the city's bucolic neighborhoods. Yet 10 minutes away from all this urbanity you can windsurf along the edge of the bay or bike and hike up, down, and around the rolling hills and their postcard panoramas.

Oakland has always played brawn to Berkeley's brain. It's a real, sometimes gritty, working city. But there's an urban romance about it when you look closely. This city hasn't turned its past into a parking lot. You can see a show at a glamorously restored movie palace, then spend the night in a Victorian bower. California history can be savored in detail in an extraordinary roof-garden museum. The view along the water at Jack London Square is of loading cranes that loom high over the *shore like 10-story equestrian statues. Breakfast has a more adventurous flavor when you're sitting in a café surrounded by trucks unloading fresh fruit harvested from nearby San Joaquin Valley.*

Combined, Berkeley and Oakland offer the churchlike serenity of redwood groves and the visual, mental, and gastronomic stimulation of a sophisticated city. And on occasion—thanks to small seismic tremors—you might be treated to an extra jolt of excitement.

Getting to Know Berkeley and Oakland

The long stretch of land opposite San Francisco and the peninsula is known as the East Bay. Officially it is called Alameda County. Berkeley and Oakland are its chief cities. They share the same hills, the same sea plain, and the same freeways, if not the same mindset.

A few areas within these cities have preserved their political independence. The island of Alameda, directly across from the Oakland waterfront, bears a striking resemblance to a small town in Kansas. Piedmont is a gated community without the gates, a debutante enclave in the Oakland Hills. Emeryville, just south of the Berkeley waterfront, was once a small and tough industrial city. But then it became an art district, evolved into a high-tech business center, and succumbed to the sprawl of the mall. Oakland and Berkeley dominate the region, though, and almost everything of interest can be found within their city limits.

Berkeley and Oakland History

The First 26,800 Years

San Francisco Bay was just another primordial valley until the Pacific, swollen with water from melting glacier sheets, rose and flooded it 15,000 to 25,000 years ago. The warming climate sparked the growth of oak and redwood groves on the eastern side of the new bay.

When the first Native Americans arrived, around 1200 B.C., they found a kind of paradise. The bay and the streams that fed into it were rich with life, and the forests were populated by deer, bears, and small animals. Thanks to an almost ideal climate and few threats from neighboring tribes, the Costanoan Indians, also known as the Ohlones,

Oakland City Center

Todd Jokl

TIP Local papers are a good source of what's doing: Fridays and Sundays, the East Bay editions of the *San Francisco Chronicle and Examiner* and the *Oakland Tribune* have listings of events. Other alternatives include the *East Bay Express, The Berkeley Monthly, Urban View, Berkeley Daily Planet, San Francisco Weekly,* and *Bay Guardian.* You'll find them available for free in vending racks around town. For campus activities, check the UC Web site at www.berkeley.edu/calendar.

led a Stone Age life. Acorns practically fell into their laps. Mussels could be harvested at the water's edge.

This idyll ended abruptly with the arrival of Spanish soldiers and missionaries. Portola discovered San Francisco Bay in 1769. Three years later, the governor of Alta California, Pedro Fages, marched a troop inland from Monterey across Contra Costa county to the edge of the bay where Oakland now sits. No missions or military settlements were built. Instead, the Spanish forced the Ohlones to the mission in San Jose. Within a decade, disease had all but destroyed the Indians.

Luis Maria Peralta, one of the soldiers who had accompanied Portola on his explorations, retired in 1820 and was granted a vast ranchero— 44,800 acres extending from San Jose to Oakland. For a brief period the ranchero prospered, but the Spanish, like the Indians before them, were unprepared for the next wave of Californians.

Boom Towns
The first Yankee settlers arrived in the area in the 1830s. Much like their Spanish predecessors, they barely paid lip service to local authority. They came, they saw, they squatted.

Peralta's heirs proved no match for Yankee entrepreneurs like Horace Carpentier, who sold lots and mapped out streets he didn't own. The overpowered Peraltas tried to resist, but Carpentier tied them up in court. Legal fees impoverished them. A law enacted in 1868 finally gave all Yankee owners legal title to the property they had claimed.

The last half of the nineteenth century witnessed a steady evolution of the East Bay from wildlands to civilization, a process accelerated by the 1849 discovery of gold elsewhere in California. Farms flourished and small factories opened, although grizzly bears still strolled into town. The first newspaper set up shop in 1854. By 1855 regularly scheduled ferry service ran to San Francisco, and in 1863 a steam railroad carried passengers along Broadway to the ferry landing.

But this development was nothing compared to what happened with the completion of the Central Pacific Railway on September 6, 1869. The 1860 population of around 9,000 shot up to 24,237 by 1870. Hotels and restaurants sprang up along Eighth, Ninth, and Washington Streets in Oakland. A

BERKELEY AND OAKLAND TIME LINE

1200 B.C.	Costanoan and Ohlones tribes arrive.
1772	Pedro Fages, the governor of the Spanish colony of Alta California, marches inland across Contra Costa to the bay.
1820	Peralta, a retired general, is granted a 44,800-acre rancho between San Jose and Oakland.
1830s	Yankee settlers arrive in droves.
1849	Gold is discovered elsewhere in California; Oakland becomes a way station for miners, and the East Bay hills are deforested to build San Francisco.
1850s	Squatters settle along the Berkeley shoreline.
1852	Oakland is incorporated by the State Legislature.
1853	The first Berkeley wharf is built.
1869	The Central Pacific Railroad is completed and Oakland becomes its terminus.
1870s	The industrial boom begins.
1871	Mills College opens in Oakland.
1873	The first UC Berkeley commencement takes place.
1878	Berkeley is incorporated as Ocean View.
1894	Oakland railway workers join the national Pullman strikes.
1903	Electric streetcar routes are created with the Key System.
1906	Oakland becomes a haven for 150,000 San Francisco earthquake refugees.
1923	A fire scorches 130 acres and destroys 584 buildings in Berkeley.
1934	The East Bay Regional Park District is established.
1936	The Bay Bridge is completed.
1964	Berkeley becomes the first U.S. city to desegregate its schools.
1969	Governor Reagan dispatches the National Guard to occupy People's Park on the Berkeley campus.
1972	BART, a subway linking the East Bay to San Francisco, opens.
1973	Berkeley's Neighborhood Preservation Ordinance is passed.
1989	The Loma Prieta earthquake, 7.1 on the Richter scale, brings down Cypress Freeway and damages 1,200 buildings.
1991	The Hills Firestorm on Sunday, October 20, results in 25 deaths and 3,354 homes lost.
1999	Former California governor Jerry Brown becomes mayor of Oakland.

Railroad tracks on Shattuck Avenue in downtown Berkeley, 1892

sandbar on the edge of the city was removed, and the port became a shipping hub.

The heady economic activity of the 1870s transformed Oakland into a working town, a city built by immigrants from Germany, Italy, Ireland, China, and many other countries. Labor conditions were abysmal. One laborer, Jack London, worked at a cannery here when he was 15 and often put in 36-hour shifts. He became, not surprisingly, a lifetime socialist (and a famous writer). In 1894 Oakland railroad workers joined the nationwide Pullman strike, blocking streets and creating Oakland's reputation as a strong union town.

Racial diversity has been a part of Oakland from the beginning. Many African American porters on the Union Pacific's Pullman cars settled and raised their families in the area. Oakland's first African American Methodist Episcopal Church opened in 1858. Its first black newspaper was founded in 1892. Chinese people who had sailed to California to work on the railroads moved to Oakland and wound up fishing for shrimp along the estuary. Discriminatory laws forced them to live in a small area downtown, though, and hiring biases kept them out of the factories.

Berkeley Ups Its IQ

Berkeley, or Ocean View as it was called then, experienced growth, but not at the same velocity as Oakland. It began as a cluster of small farms and lumberyards near the bay, but it was destined for bigger, brainier things. In 1866 trustees from the College of California in Oakland, on a mission to find a new site, visited the hills above Ocean View. One of the trustees, musing on the impressive scene before him, recited some favorite lines of poetry by the seventeenth-century British bishop George Berkeley: "Westward the course of the empire takes its way." On the spot the decision was made to name the school after the bishop. Seven years later, the struggling institution held its first commencement.

At the end of the century, the East Bay was transformed again, this time by real estate brochures. Developers touted the area as a garden suburb for San Francisco merchants and their families. Rococo resort hotels opened along the beach in Alameda. One of the early suburbs was along Lake Merritt, a former marsh. Electric streetcars along the Key Route whisked commuters to the newer, faster ferryboats.

An additional 150,000 San Franciscans involuntarily visited Berkeley and Oakland following the 1906 earthquake and fire. Damage here was minimal—mostly broken glass and fallen chimneys. Many of the visitors opted to stay. Oakland's population jumped from 67,000 in 1900 to 150,000 only 10 years later.

With the opening of the Panama Canal, the region's economic expansion took another leap. By World War I, Oakland was home to iron and auto plants, paint companies, and a shredded wheat factory, among others. During the '20s the urbanization of the hills continued despite a setback on September 17, 1923, when a grass fire set off by a high-tension wire resulted in a conflagration in North Berkeley that covered 130 acres and destroyed 584 buildings.

Radical Changes

Berkeley, fundamentally a one-industry town, was somewhat buffered from the Depression by its university. Oakland took a harder hit. Jobless men lived in pipes at the foot of 19th Street; dockhands, many of whom unionized after the war, staged a bloody strike in 1934.

Things began to turn around with the opening of the San Francisco-Oakland Bay Bridge in 1936. With its proximity to the Pacific, Oakland expanded enormously during World War II. The demand for workers exploded, and this era marked a dramatic expansion in Oakland's black population.

But the economic adjustment following the war was rough. With the ascendance of the automobile, residents and businesses headed farther out to the suburbs. The tracks of the Key Line were pulled up. The bustling downtown emptied. Even today the city hasn't fully recovered.

Berkeley had a more controversial role in mid-century events. The Atomic Age was partly created here. Physicists such as Ernest Lawrence and Robert Oppenheimer developed their research in the campus cyclotron and in the nation's first radiation lab. Nervousness over Communist infiltration infected these labs and the campus itself. During the McCarthy era, professors were required to take loyalty oaths.

TRIVIA

Berkeley has always been ahead of its time politically. It voted for women's suffrage in 1911—the same year it elected the country's first socialist mayor, J. Stitt Wilson.

Erika Howsare

Lake Merritt

A small but vocal opposition became the seed that, a decade later, gave birth to a radically reinvented Berkeley, the site of the free speech movement in 1964. Antiwar demonstrations continued throughout the Vietnam conflict. An attempt to turn a half-block of University land into People's Park in 1969 prompted Governor Reagan to call in the National Guard and tear gas protesters on campus and along Telegraph Avenue.

The Civil Rights movement, too, had a profound effect on Oakland. It was here in 1966 that the Black Panther Party was formed. But as an indication of how compatible the city's ethnic groups had become, no race riots took place here during the '60s.

Revitalization followed revolution. The Bay Area Rapid Transit system (better known as BART), which linked the area to San Francisco, opened in 1972. Berkeley halted the destruction of its architectural heritage with the Neighborhood Housing Ordinance in 1973. Oakland took the same steps to preserve its historic downtown. World-class museums were opened in both cities. But for pumping up civic pride, nothing could match the addition of Oakland's own major-league sports franchises. Loyalty runs strong and deep here for the Athletics, the Raiders, and the Warriors.

The end of the twentieth century has been a reminder that no matter how ambitious city planners are, Mother Nature always has the last word. Although its epicenter was miles away, the Loma Prieta earthquake of October 1989 caused the collapse of the elevated Cypress Freeway and killed 41 people. And then, just when the cities were beginning to recover from that disaster, a brush fire in the Oakland and Berkeley hills on October 20, 1991, left 25 people dead and destroyed more than 3,300 homes and 450 apartments.

Now both cities are moving beyond recovery. A new freeway has been built. Homes in the hills have been rebuilt. And respect for the area's past

Chinatown wares

is growing, too. Historical societies and preservation groups protect the cities' pasts. It's an obvious irony that the years of neglect have left hundreds of extraordinary buildings intact.

The People of Berkeley and Oakland

"Diverse" is the politically correct but paltry description usually given to the population of the East Bay. At last count, 120 different languages and dialects were spoken here. Even a few founding families who came here in the middle of the last century have resisted the siren song of suburbia.

African Americans, who first came here to find jobs during World War II, have stayed; and today, while West Oakland is mostly black, they reside in every neighborhood in the city. Spaniards may have been here more than two hundred years ago, but the current Hispanic influx is a recent phenomenon. Today Mexican Americans represent the largest, but not the only, block of Latinos. Many residents from Central America also live here. International Boulevard in East Oakland has dozens of blocks of shops and restaurants catering to Ecuadorians, Peruvians, and El Salvadorans. Although Chinatown is clearly defined, Asian Americans live everywhere. And Oakland officials report an influx of gay couples moving from San Francisco, looking for less nightlife and more lawn.

Despite the oceanlike waves of new citizens, population figures have remained somewhat stable. Asians and Hispanics make up a growing percentage of the population, whereas African Americans constitute less and less. The official breakdown of minorities in Oakland is: African American, 42.8 percent; non-Hispanic white, 23.3 percent; Asian Pacific Islander, 14.2 percent; Hispanic, 13.9 percent. In Berkeley it's non-Hispanic white, 58 percent; African American, 18 percent; Asian Pacific Islander, 14 percent; Hispanic, 8 percent. Oakland calls itself the most integrated city in the United States, and all groups participate actively in running the city.

In political terms, Berkeley doesn't have a lot of diversity. There are 6,501 registered Republicans versus 46,409 Democrats. If a political dividing line exists in Berkeley, it is the perceived schism between people who live in the flatlands near the bay, an area once dubbed "The People's Republic of Berkeley," and the hill dwellers (who, despite having million-dollar homes, are often former radicals themselves).

Berkeley is a young city, too. More than 35 percent of the city's population is under the age of 25, largely because of the presence of UC Berkeley. But the students are, in general, less vociferous than they used to be. Today you're more likely to find evangelists and Young Republicans than Maoist revolutionaries in UC Berkeley's Sproul Plaza. Berkeley's live-and-let-live policies also draw footloose teenagers from across the country to Telegraph Avenue where they loll in pierced splendor. For years, the city has tried to discourage them and yet respect their civil rights. To date, nothing has worked.

The Shakes

Of course, one crack can be found in the East Bay paradise. It runs along the northern edge of Oakland and Berkeley, parallels Highway 13, then cuts across campus right under Memorial Stadium and the UC Cyclotron. It's better known as the Hayward Fault—one of California's major geological fissures. Because it has experienced no major movements for several years, scientists say there's a 28 percent chance it will become active in the next three decades.

Hardly a year passes without some sort of seismic activity in the East Bay. The tremors are usually mild shocks that jolt people from their sleep or knock canned vegetables off grocery store shelves. But even a quake centered miles away, such as the 7.1 Loma Prieta in 1989, can have devastating effects here.

It sounds scary, but people here don't lose sleep over it. It's like Oklahomans living with tornadoes or Floridians living with hurricanes. Nevertheless, a large emergency network is in place. Many people have reinforced their homes and have backup food and medical equipment stashed in their gardens. But the truth is, the greatest danger from tremors is that posed by postquake fires.

For all their diversity, these cities are still medium-size. Oakland's population is 388,100. Berkeley's is 104,700. They are more affluent than they may look to the untrained eye. Berkeley's average household income in $55,200; Oakland's is $53,400. The population is well educated, too. Almost 72 percent of Berkeley's adult residents have attended college.

Just a slight hint of a rivalry exists between these two cities. Oaklanders think of themselves as a little more urban and realistic than their sometimes-utopian neighbors. But one thing that residents of both cities have in common is tremendous local pride.

Weather

Given the wacky shifts in global climactic conditions over the past few years, the weather anywhere is hard to predict. Nevertheless, it is pretty safe to say that the East Bay is a paradigm of temperate climate. When it comes to weather, Oakland ranked number one in the country in Prentice Hall's *Places Rated Almanac.* It never snows. The end of summer may be dry and warm (dangerous conditions for wildfires), but air conditioner sales are nil. The real summer weather occurs in the fall. During the calendar summer months, fog rolling in from the Golden Gate keeps things as

Weather

The figures listed below are for Berkeley. Oakland's differ by a fraction of a degree in either direction.

	Average High	Average Low
January	57	44
February	60	46
March	61	47
April	63	48
May	66	51
June	69	53
July	70	54
August	70	55
September	72	56
October	70	53
November	62	48
December	56	44

Annual Precipitation: 25 inches

Average number of days with rain: 40

cool as refrigerated Chardonnay. Unwarned tourists can be seen shivering in their shorts and T-shirts.

Dressing in Berkeley and Oakland

In an area with a troupe of public nudists, it's hard to dress wrong. The population is inured to eccentricity, from the tie-dyed, tattooed denizens of Telegraph Avenue to pony-tailed male senior citizens. Even for a dinner at Chez Panisse or a ballet at Zellerbach Hall, you don't need a tie. If a style pervades here, it's ethnic, like Balinese earrings or mud-print jackets. Winter nights get wet and chilly, so dress for the cold. In summer, when the fog rolls in, you'll want long pants, a sweater, and a windbreaker.

When to Visit

Something's always going on. Time your visit so that it coincides with an As, Raiders, or Warriors game or a Mark Morris dance performance at Zellerbach Hall. Winter offers a schedule of rich indoor cultural activities. Spring brings the city outdoors, and brilliantly blossoming gardens make the Chamber of Commerce's claim that these cities are Mediterranean no smug boast. Summer, when most of the student body is gone, is quieter around the university—parking is easier, waits at restaurants are shorter. Each August, a buzz fills the air when students return and UC sports and intellectual activities—as well as the weather—heat up. If you're looking for a predictably ideal time of year to visit, come in September.

Calendar of Events

JANUARY
Jack London Birthday Celebration on Jack London Square

FEBRUARY
Asian Lunar New Year in Chinatown

MARCH
Oakland Museum White Elephant Sale near the Oakland Airport; Old-Fashioned Easter at Dunsmuir House

APRIL
Secret Gardens of East Bay; Estuary Boat Show in the Oakland Estuary; Cal Day on the UC Berkeley campus

MAY
Cinco de Mayo Celebration in downtown Oakland; California Wildflower

Show at the Oakland Museum; Festival of Greece at the Greek Orthodox Cathedral of the Ascension in Oakland; Berkeley Folk Festival in various locations

JUNE
East Bay Open Studios in various locations; Live Oak Craft Fair in Live Oak Park in Berkeley; Crown Beach Sandcastle Contest in Alameda

JULY
Berkeley Kite Festival in Cesar Chavez Park; Jewish Film Festival at the UC Theater; Scottish Highland Games at Dunsmuir House

AUGUST
Dragon Boat Races in the Oakland Estuary; Chinatown Street Fest

SEPTEMBER
Black Filmmakers Hall of Fame Awards at the Paramount Theater; "How Berkeley Can You Be?" Parade on University Avenue; Italian Festa on Jack London Square; Solano Stroll on Solano Avenue; Oakland Blues & Jazz Festival

OCTOBER
Black Cowboys Parade on Broadway; Indigenous People's Day (replaced Columbus Day); Halloween on the Square on Jack London Square; Boo at the Zoo festival at Knowland Zoo

NOVEMBER
Berkeley Artisans Holiday Open Studios; Tree Lighting Festival on Jack London Square

DECEMBER
Christmas at Dunsmuir; Lighted Yacht Parade on the Oakland Estuary; Zoo Lights at the Oakland Zoo; Telegraph Avenue Street Festival in Berkeley; Christmas Revels at the Scottish Rite Temple in Oakland; Dickens Holiday Faire in Jack London Village

For updated activities in Oakland, visit the city Web site at www.oakland-chamber.com or stop at the Jack London Square Visitors Center. For Berkeley, go to www.visitberkeley.com or call the Visitor Information Hotline at 510/549-8710.

Business and Economy

Ever since Yankee cargo ships docked at Long Wharf, the East Bay has been an economic engine. The ruboff from nearby Silicon Valley's long-running boom hasn't hurt at all. The Bay Area economy is now the country's fourth largest. The potential for high tech hardly seems to be tapped. Pacific Rim markets are just beginning to come into their own.

Oakland long ago eclipsed San Francisco as a commercial port. Maritime operations, including 29 deepwater berths and 31 container cranes, occupy 680 acres on the city's western shore. The port handles more than $25 billion in imports and exports and is now the fourth most active port in the United States. The bulk of the trade—66 percent—is with Asia.

But Oakland isn't all shipping. Clorox is headquartered here, as is Dreyers Ice Cream, Kaiser Permanente, and high-tech operations such as Pangea. And the city still has room to grow. Whole blocks downtown have been renovated and are waiting for tenants.

The most striking economic makeover has been in Emeryville, a town wedged between Oakland and Berkeley. Once home to mostly iron foundries and brickyards, today it's the site of out-on-the-edge companies such as Sybase, AskJeeves, and Chiron.

Berkeley is thought of as a one-industry town: the brain industry. But that isn't quite the case. West Berkeley, located near the bay, is home to a smattering of manufacturers (Bayer, for instance). Even Fantasy Studios, which produced films such as *Amadeus* and *The English Patient,* chose Berkeley over Hollywood. And retail, especially on Fourth Street, draws shoppers from all over the Bay Area.

Still, the University of California dominates everything. It has 11,400 employees working in its offices, classrooms, labs, and institutes for ad-

The annual "How Berkeley Can You Be?" parade

John Solomon

vanced studies. Lawrence Lab alone employs 3,100 people. A lot of tomorrow's business titans are born at UC. The Haas Graduate School of Business is ranked among the top 10 in the country. The city serves all these thoughtful folks with more than 60 bookstores and 34 movie screens.

People pay a price for living here, though. The Bay Area ranks as one of the most expensive places to live in the United States. California state income tax tops out at 9 percent here, and the local sales tax is 8.25 percent. Property taxes in Oakland are at 1.18 percent of assessed value. In Berkeley it's slightly worse: 1.22 percent.

Visitors often experience sticker shock. A dinner for two with wine and tip can easily reach $80. A hotel room with a view of the bay can put you back more than $200. For years, reporters have tried without success to discover why the gasoline here is always among the most expensive in the United States.

Typical Prices

Daily newspaper:	25¢
Average dinner for two:	$35
Hotel room (double):	$85
Five-mile taxi ride:	$12
Movie ticket:	$8
Bus ticket:	$1.35
Double espresso:	$2

Housing

The only people not shocked by the cost of living in the East Bay are other people in the Bay Area. To them, Oakland and Berkeley are still relative bargains.

Both cities were "built out" 50 years ago. Tract housing is nonexistent. Only Emeryville has seen a significant increase in residential construction in the last few years, and most of this has occurred in multi-unit dwellings. Local officials have made new low-income housing a budget priority.

The median price for a home here is around $235,000. The "flats" offer mostly single-family homes in the $265,000 range. Lofts, which are becoming more common in former industrial zones, range from $250,000 to $300,000 depending how close to completion they are. Landmark homes in the Arts and Crafts style of

Preservation Park

Todd Jokl

Top 10 Reasons I Wouldn't Live Anywhere But Oakland

By Jerry Brown, Mayor of Oakland and former Governor of California

1. Lake Merritt
2. Le Cheval Restaurant
3. Paramount Theater
4. Oakland A's
5. Arizmendi Bakery
6. Oakland Ballet
7. Farmers' Market in Jack London Square on Sundays
8. Parkway Theater
9. Mexicali Rose Restaurant
10. The East Bay Symphony

early-twentieth-century architects such as Bernard Maybeck and Julia Morgan sell for $500,000 and up. The priciest areas are right where you'd expect them to be—where the views are. It's not uncommon to find million-dollar homes in the Northside Hills, around the Claremont Hotel, and above Oakland in Piedmont.

Renting is a touchy issue in Berkeley. Tenants are so active as a political force that a Rent Control Board is required to adjudicate disputes. Its proceedings are of such widespread interest that they are televised every week on Berkeley cable channel 25. There are 24,455 rental units in Berkeley. The median monthly rent for an apartment is a steep $638.

Schools

Berkeley is a college town, so there's an indigenous preoccupation with education at all levels here. Parents torment themselves over getting their kids into the best schools, and they have plenty of choices: Oakland has 81 public schools and 53 private ones; Berkeley has 15 public and 14 private schools. These schools include some specialized institutions such as Ecole Bilingue, where most classes are taught in French; and Crowden School, where the core curriculum is all music. Tuition can give you pause. Oakland's Head-Royce School runs $15,000 a year.

There never seems to be a dull moment in Oakland's public schools. A few years ago the proposed Ebonics program made it into Jay Leno's *Tonight Show* monologues. Piedmont High made it onto the program, too,

Crime Story

Oakland, similar to any big city, has its mean streets. But its reputation as crime-ridden is inflated. Downtown Oakland, in statistical terms, is actually one of the safest places in the Bay Area. And the City Center BART station is five times safer than the one in the bedroom suburb of Concord.

when a national audience heard the winners of their annual Leonard J. Waxwing Memorial Bird Calling Contest.

Berkeley schools were integrated in 1968 and although busing is not used as extensively now, a remarkably balanced enrollment has been maintained ever since. Berkeley High is a mixed bag of remedial students, multicultural programs, and future Ivy League graduates. It also offers more extramural sports than any other school in the country.

But the ubiquitous presence of college students makes the East Bay feel like one big campus. Nearly one-fifth of the local population—more than 100,000 people—attends college at any given time. You can see them as they hurry along Telegraph Avenue weighted down beneath backpacks, printing term papers at copy stores and turning coffeehouses into study halls.

Although most of the world hears the word "Berkeley" and thinks of UC, other institutions of higher learning are located here as well. Mills College, which was built for women only in 1871, lies in a bucolic setting off Highway 13 in Oakland. Laney College is a commuter junior college near downtown Oakland. Samuel Merritt and Holy Names Colleges are in groves of academe high in the hills. The California College of Arts and Crafts, founded in 1907, has expanded its fine arts programs to include cutting-edge computer graphics.

Even Berkeley is not just UC. It's also home to Vista Community College and, on Northside, the Graduate Theological Union. But the 170-acre University of California at Berkeley, with its 21,000 undergraduates and 9,000 graduates, is master of the academic universe here. Admission is fiercely competitive. Even the scruffiest student pedaling down Bancroft Way is likely to have had a 4.0 average in high school. Students from every state and one hundred countries worldwide attend UC. Departments such as Mathematics, English, and Chemistry are regularly ranked among the top in the United States, and the school's distinguished faculty includes seven Nobel laureates. The university offers 100 graduate programs, 400 degree programs, 7,000 course offerings, 150 research groups, and 8 million books in 18 libraries. In short, it's huge.

Todd Jokl

2

GETTING AROUND BERKELEY AND OAKLAND

Even if you are directionally challenged, you should find getting around Berkeley and Oakland to be fairly easy. These cities are not big: Berkeley is just 18 square miles and Oakland is 52 square miles. And because they are pedestrian cities, if you do happen to lose your way, you're likely to find someone who can help. In addition, numerous helpful landmarks are located in the area. The hills are always to your east and San Francisco Bay is always to your west. Oakland's downtown high-rises are clearly visible from miles away. And the Sather Tower, rising from the UC Berkeley campus, serves as a beacon day and night.

The general layout of this area is uncomplicated. Both cities are part of one long sweep of curving shoreline that has moved steadily west as the bay has filled in. Slightly more than half of each city is situated in this coastal plain area, also known as "the flats." The mix of residential and industrial areas sprawls from city to city with such continuity that you'd never know where Berkeley ends and Oakland begins without the city limit signs.

The region's "hills," as they're known—site of the pricier residential districts with the most coveted views—rise slowly, then steeply. The hills are the one place where it's easy to get lost. Roads twist and turn as they follow the ridges and canyons. When you get to the top, you are in mostly open space—the East Bay Regional Parks system.

Berkeley and Oakland Layout

Both Berkeley and Oakland are laid out in grid patterns along the flatlands and waterfront, but the grids of each city are completely distinct and go in different directions. Seventh Street in Oakland, for example, has nothing to do with Seventh Street in Berkeley. Oakland's main street, which connects the waterfront to the hills, is Broadway. In Berkeley, it's University Avenue.

Some major streets in the flats break the grid. Telegraph and San Pablo Avenues radiate northward from Oakland City Hall. Adeline cuts across Oakland from Shattuck to MacArthur. Claremont Avenue spikes off Telegraph Avenue and winds into Claremont Canyon.

When main streets cross city lines, the numbering often changes. Driving along San Pablo Avenue, for example, the street numbers jump from 4700 to 5700 when you cross 53rd Street. And the numbers on Telegraph Avenue leap from 3200 to 6000 when you cross 66th Street.

Where the streets start climbing into the hills, the easy-to-follow grid geometry is lost. On the north side of Berkeley, Euclid Street, which twists and turns up to Tilden Park, is the closest thing to a main street going east. South of the UC campus, Tunnel Road takes you up to Highway 13. In Oakland, the main routes into the hills are Broadway Terrace, Moraga Avenue, Park Boulevard, Lincoln Avenue, and Redwood Road. They also end up at Highway 13, which starts in Berkeley and curves all the way south to Highway 580. Despite the mazelike tangle of the smaller hill roads, it would be difficult to get completely lost on them. All you have to do is head west and you'll eventually get back to town.

Public Transportation

The East Bay has had an extensive public transportation system for a long time. In fact, commuters have taken the train to San Francisco since the early 1900s. Today, thanks to that tradition, Berkeley and Oakland lack the

A BART train at MacArthur station

TIP

Your parents probably told you never to get into cars with strangers. But thousands of people do just that every morning at the casual carpool pickup locations around Berkeley and Oakland. Drivers then get to take carpool lanes to the bridge and don't have to stop to pay tolls on their way to the city. Riders are dropped off around the Transbay Bus Terminal in downtown San Francisco.

oppressive car congestion that plagues other California cities. In fact, if you had the time, you could get around entirely by using public transportation and your own two feet.

Trains

It's often possible to get to downtown San Francisco faster from the East Bay than from other parts of San Francisco. All you need to do is hop on BART, the Bay Area Rapid Transit system. The downtown Oakland BART station is only eight minutes from San Francisco's Embarcadero Station via a sleek set of tracks beneath the bay. It's also possible to take BART from the East Bay to Powell Street Station, which is just a couple of blocks from the Union Square theater and shopping district; or to the Civic Center, which is only two short blocks away from the San Francisco Opera and Symphony. BART trains also connect to San Francisco's Muni streetcar system, which in turn provides transportation to all of the city's surrounding neighborhoods.

BART is also a fairly convenient way to get around the East Bay. There are four stations in Berkeley and seven in Oakland. BART can take you to downtown Oakland, but it leaves you 10 blocks from Jack London Square. Similarly, you can take it to downtown Berkeley, but not to the waterfront. From the East Bay, trains continue north to Richmond, east to Contra Costa and Pleasanton, and south to Fremont and Dublin.

Every BART train includes maps that make transferring easy, and during the day you'll almost never have to wait longer than 10 minutes between trains. Trains run from 4 a.m. to midnight Monday through Friday, 6 a.m. to midnight on Saturdays, and 8 a.m. to midnight on Sundays and holidays. Ticket fares vary by distance, but they are always reasonable. To go from downtown Berkeley to the Coliseum, for instance, costs $1.65. You can purchase tickets at machines in BART stations. In theory, the ticket machines are child's play. The fares to various destinations are posted, and

TRIVIA

The builders of the Bay Bridge intended that when construction costs were paid for by tolls, it would be free. Yeah, right.

*Interior of the Amtrak station
at Jack London Square*

you simply feed in your money and punch in the fare you want to pay. But in reality, the machines can be finicky. If your dollar bills are old or wrinkled, the machine may just spit them out, so carry crisp bills.

Oakland Air-BART is the shuttle bus from the Oakland Airport to the BART station at the Coliseum. It leaves every 7 to 10 minutes and costs two dollars. Purchase tickets in the station at the airport before boarding the bus.

During the week, parking at BART stations can be hard to come by. You have to get there very early—before the commuters. And parking in most neighborhoods adjacent to BART isn't an option. Unless you have a neighborhood permit, only two-hour parking is allowed. If you plan to rely on BART frequently during your stay, choose accommodations that are within walking distance of a station.

Buses

Although streetcars no longer run in the East Bay, AC Transit buses can take you anywhere in the business and residential sections of Oakland and Berkeley. AC Transit has 148 routes. These are not express buses. Number 51, for example, travels from downtown Oakland to Rockridge, to the UC campus, and down to the Berkeley waterfront, and stops in numerous places along the way. Locals use them heavily, especially students. If you don't have a lot of time, you may want to get around some other way.

Fares are $1.35 for adults and teens and 60¢ for seniors, the disabled, and youths aged 5 to 12. Most buses are wheelchair accessible. AC Transit also operates routes to and from San Francisco during commute hours. For specific route information, call 510/817-1717.

Electric cars can be rented at the Ashby BART station. An EV1 costs only six dollars an hour with a three-hour minimum. Call 510/849-4973 for more information.

Oakland locals may have finally gotten over expatriate novelist Gertrude Stein's stinging comment that, as far as the city is concerned, "there is no there there." A plaque has been placed in the middle of the spiffy City Center Court that simply says, "there." A flag flying atop the Tribune Tower proclaims the same thing.

Taxis

A cab can be hailed at any reasonable hour at the Oakland Airport and at many East Bay BART stations—especially the one in downtown Berkeley—during commute hours. The drop fee is two dollars; after that it's two dollars per mile. The fare from Oakland Airport to the UC Campus is around $30. Two of the major taxi companies are Yellow Cab, 510/317-2200; and Veteran's Cab, 510/533-1900.

A slightly more economical way to get to the airport is by shuttle. A shuttle trip from the UC campus to the Oakland Airport costs around $22. The only real drawback is the fact that these vehicles pick up and drop off other passengers, so you may have to wake up extra early to make sure you don't miss your flight.

Ferries

Before the Bay Bridge was built and before the BART subway was tunneled, people from the East Bay rode ferries to and from San Francisco. Today a daily commuter service (for people, not cars) still runs from Alameda and Jack London Square to Pier 39 and the Ferry Building in San Francisco, but far fewer people use it. You can make connections in San Francisco for boats to Alcatraz and Angel Island. Twelve weekday and six weekend departures leave from the terminal at Clay and Embarcadero. The journey to San Francisco takes you right under the Bay Bridge and past Yerba Buena and Treasure Island.

This 20- to 30-minute trip is a magical experience night or day, even in the fog and rain. One-way tickets cost $4.50 each for adults and children. On board the ferry, a small concession sells juice and coffee in the morning and drinks and snacks in the evening. For the latest schedule information, call 510/522-3300.

Alameda Gold Coast

Marty Forsyth

Neighborhood Watch

Architectural treats stud the East Bay's residential neighborhoods. A few areas are especially worth noting. Almost all of these neighborhoods were built 70 to 100 years ago.

The Gold Coast: *At the turn of the twentieth century, Alameda was an ornate Victorian resort. Approximately three thousand Victorian homes are still scattered across the island. But the most fabulous concentration is an eight-block strip of manicured mansions, including three by Julia Morgan, the architect of San Simeon. Two streets not to miss are Grand and St. Charles. The Tilden Mansion, at 1031 San Antonio, is Italianate at its giddiest. (Alameda)*

Greenwood Common: *In general, modern architecture hasn't been kind to the East Bay, but this intriguing property on the north side of the UC campus is an exception. Once a dairy farm, it's now a park-like area held in common by owners of mid-twentieth-century Bauhaus/Japonesque classics. The homes are all quite serene and rational, at least compared to Maybeck's fantasies nearby. (Berkeley)*

La Loma and Buena Vista: *You cannot find a more pure expression of the Arts and Crafts style than in this neighborhood north of the UC campus. Most homes are in the shingled-chalet style of architect Bernard Maybeck. His masterpiece, the Lawson House at 1515 La Loma, is brilliantly designed of reinforced concrete. Farther up, at 2800 Buena Vista, is the classic Temple of the Wings, where Isadora*

Driving in Berkeley and Oakland

Freeways

Five major freeways criss cross the East Bay area. After years of rebuilding in the aftermath of the Loma Prieta earthquake, they are all up and running—at least in theory. The signage can be confusing and the traffic gruesome.

Highway 880 follows the eastern edge of the bay from San Jose to the Oakland International Airport to the Bay Bridge. Highway 80 also follows the rim of the bay from the Bay Bridge and along the Berkeley waterfront, eventually ending up in Lake Tahoe. No matter what time of day you drive

Duncan danced and which a member of the Getty family has restored. (Berkeley)

Peralta and 10th Street: Even locals rarely venture into these sketchy blocks near the Oakland West BART station. Yet although paint is peeling, porches are sagging, and the population is poor, its collection of elegant Italianate homes is unmatched. (Oakland)

Pleasant Valley Court: Some '50s horrors are located on this tuning fork-shaped street off Pleasant Valley Road, but its several dozen '20s bungalows are fascinating variations on the same charming design. The home at 4408 is poetry in bricks. (South Berkeley/North Oakland)

Roble Road: This sylvan, stately fantasy of early-1900s realtors is across the street and up Tunnel Road from the Claremont Hotel. Behind hedges and lichen-covered walls, but easily visible, are romantic woodland estates, mostly in the Spanish Colonial style. (South Berkeley/North Oakland)

Rose Walk: Another early-1900s storybook fantasy, this classical cement staircase rises gracefully up a hillside near the Berkeley Rose Garden. It's flanked by 10 seductively charming Arts and Crafts and Spanish Colonial residences. (Berkeley)

Seaview Avenue: All of Piedmont is upscale, but this block between Hampton and Mountain is the ultimate Ralph Lauren fantasy. Tudor and Spanish palazzos sit poised amidst some of the area's most magnificent gardens. It's Beverly Hills with a bay view. (Oakland)

it, the congestion on 80 along the Berkeley waterfront to the bridge is reminiscent of Los Angeles at its worst.

Highway 580, beginning at the Bay Bridge, cuts across the eastern edge of Oakland before continuing on to Pleasanton and the San Joaquin Valley toward Stockton. It also leads to Highway 24, which shoots across South Berkeley through the Caldecott Tunnel to valley communities such as Concord and Orinda in Contra Costa.

Highway 13 rides the top of the Oakland Hills in a journey from South Berkeley to Highway 580. It's a rolling road with lush foliage and is blessedly free of traffic.

During the morning and late afternoon, all the roads that lead to the Bay Bridge become very slow as they approach the span. If you want to get to

A Pleasant Valley bungalow

San Francisco more quickly, have at least two passengers in your car so you qualify as a carpool. You'll get your own lane and can zip right through the toll plaza without paying a cent. Carpool lanes operate Monday through Friday from five to ten in the morning and from four to six in the afternoon.

City Streets

Even with stoplights, during commute hours surface streets will generally get you where you want to go faster than a freeway. All the major north/south roads, such as Telegraph, Broadway, and San Pablo, will take you straight from Berkeley to Oakland. If you want to check out the Berkeley/Emeryville waterfront instead of getting gridlocked on Highway 80, take Frontage Road.

Oakland doesn't suffer from much congestion. Parts of Berkeley, on the other hand, can get pretty jammed. Downtown rarely gets crowded, but Telegraph Avenue near the university and College Avenue near Ashby get clogged on the weekends.

Getting to and from the university from the south side of Berkeley is slow going. Tunnel Road, particularly, becomes jammed during both commutes. To avoid the traffic on College Avenue, take a parallel street such as Benvenue or Hillegass.

TRIVIA

The Mr. Popularity Award in Berkeley has to go to Martin Luther King, Jr. He has a civic center, a park, a street, a swim center, and a junior high school named after him.

Lower University Avenue is often bottlenecked. Try Hearst Avenue, two blocks north, instead. Similarly, Ashby Avenue off Highway 80 is rough during commute hours. Alcatraz Avenue used to be a good alternative, but now even that route is getting busy. The best advice is to do your driving during noncommute hours.

Residential neighborhoods have tried to reduce speeding, and you'll find speed bumps and barriers throughout the city. Slow down unless you want to crack an axle. The Berkeley Police Department reports that the most frequent accident sites are at Shattuck and University and at Ashby and Sacramento, so be advised.

Parking

Parking is plentiful in downtown Oakland and near Jack London Square. At Oakland City Center, lots charge 85¢ an hour. Parking in Berkeley, on the other hand, can be frustrating because many of the lots around the university require UC stickers. Some of the city's downtown and campus lots use an antiquated system in which you must fold up dollar bills like origami and squeeze them into miniscule slots. Others take only quarters, and still others take nothing at all (anti-meter guerrillas have decapitated them). The latest innovation is single meters that cover five spaces. Whatever you do, try not to park illegally. Tickets will set you back about $20.

Biking in Berkeley and Oakland

You might think that with such a huge student population and the area's reputation for being friendly to the environment, people on bikes would rule the roads, but that's not the case. Rather, if you bike on the "flats,"
you essentially put your life on the line. Although city planners talk a lot about providing bike lanes, so far only a few streets have them for a few blocks. Plans to build a bike overpass across Highway 80 in Berkeley are in the works. Considering the speed with which these proposals are implemented, you shouldn't hold your breath.

Activism is everywhere in Berkeley

Karena Dacker

Bicycles are allowed on BART; however, some stringent regulations are enforced, especially during commute hours. For example, bikes are not permitted in the first car of a train, and on other cars they're only allowed in the rear. Many AC Transit buses provide racks for bicycles.

Air Travel

The Bay Area is served by airport terminals in San Francisco, San Jose, and Oakland. Not every carrier flies into Oakland International Airport, but you'll be best off if you can make arrangements to land there. Why? For one, San Jose International Airport is simply too far away. Second, San Francisco International Airport can be a zoo and occasionally gets shut down because of heavy fog or strong winds. Finally, in Oakland, conditions are far more favorable: Weather-related delays are much less likely; there are only 362 daily flights, so you won't have to put up with endless taxiing; and, for anyone flying in from a West Coast city, flights are often cheaper than those to San Francisco. In addition, Oakland is relatively small and blessedly convenient. You don't have to deal with miles of Kafkaesque terminals, shuttles, and moving sidewalks that tend to make air travel such a pain these days. There are only two terminals, and you can be off your plane and out the front door in minutes, no matter where your gate is located.

All the major rental-car companies are available right outside the terminals. Door-to-door shuttle service will take you anywhere in the East

Top 10 Reasons I Live in Berkeley and Not in Washington, D.C.
By Elizabeth Farnsworth, Chief Correspondent, *The News Hour with Jim Lehrer*

1. The cool wind off the Pacific that blows through the Golden Gate, east across the bay, and up Alcatraz Avenue into our neighborhood.
2. Star Market, a neighborhood store that stocks just about everything you might need and is still remembered for extending credit to customers during the Depression.
3. Bay laurel in the hills.
4. Local bookstores like Cody's, where poets often read.
5. The Elmwood Theater and its quirky choice of films.
6. Ubiquitous jasmine that perfumes our days and nights.
7. The kindness of my neighbors.
8. The Berkeley Public Education Foundation, which raises private money for public schools.
9. Local baseball—both Little League and the team at UC.
10. Living on the edge of the continent, which means being on other edges, too.

Bay or San Francisco. Some of the better shuttle companies are Bayporter Express, 510/864-4000; BayShuttle, 415/564-3400; and BayArea Connection, 510/215-2098. If you plan to get around by public transportation, you can catch buses to the Coliseum BART station, which arrive every 10 minutes, at the entrances to both terminals.

If you'd rather fly in or out of Oakland without having to sit next to a total stranger, charter jet flights are offered by Kaiser Air, 510/569-9622. They recommend that you make reservations three weeks in advance of your departure. They're located at North Field, a few miles east of the main terminal off Doolittle Drive.

Major Airlines Serving Oakland
Alaska Airlines, 800/252-7522
America West, 800/235-9292
American Airlines, 800/433-7300
CityBird, 888/248-9247
Continental Airlines, 800/523-3273
Corsair, 800/677-0720
Delta Airlines, 800/221-1212
Martinair, 510/568-9441
Southwest Airlines, 800/435-9792
United, 800/241-6522
USAir, 800/428-4322

Train Service

A good argument can be made that transcontinental trains, such as the Union Pacific in 1869, put Oakland on the map. Hundreds of acres of tracks are still centered around the Port of Oakland, where freight from the Far East is unloaded and shipped across the country. Amtrak stops at two locations: in Oakland, a few blocks from Jack London Square (510/238-4306); and in Emeryville (510/450-1080). If you arrive on the Zephyr from Chicago, your only stop will be in Emeryville. Both stations are small but dramatically modernized versions of the great glass and iron terminals of the early nineteenth century.

Bus Service

A Greyhound bus terminal is located at 2103 San Pablo Avenue in Oakland (510/834-3213) in a scruffy building that was built in 1918. Despite its appearance, you can make connections from here to just about anywhere.

David Fenton

3

WHERE TO STAY

Berkeley and Oakland are not on the well-beaten tourist path. You won't find any lap-of-luxury, five-star hotels. Nor will you find any major bargains; in fact, the area has only one YMCA (which passes as a youth hostel), and tent and RV camping is restricted to one park. And although chain hotels are located around Oakland International Airport, they're convenient only for people doing business close to the runways. Expect to stay at older, homier accommodations that run the gamut from a grandly restored, early-twentieth-century resort to a Moroccan fantasy hotel to rumpled bed-and-breakfasts run by the eccentric spouses of local professors. And expect to pay because the area is one of the most expensive in the country.

You could try several places on or near the bay and be lulled to sleep by distant foghorns, but most are blandly modern. For local charm, choose a place in downtown Berkeley near the UC campus. Or go to the North Berkeley foothills or South Berkeley. Or snuggle into one of the many B&Bs scattered throughout Oakland. Some places are faded, and some places are funky, but all give you a taste of actually living here.

Price rating symbols:
$ **$50 and under**
$$ **$51 to $75**
$$$ **$76 to $125**
$$$$ **$126 and up**

BERKELEY

Hotels

BANCROFT HOTEL
2680 Bancroft Way
Berkeley
510/549-1000
$$$

Long before hippies and beatniks, Berkeley was a humming bohemia. This landmark 22-room Craftsman-style hotel, built as a women's club in 1924, elegantly recalls that lost era. The trellised exterior and the lobby, with its elaborately carved paneling, colored windows, and lampshades inscribed with Latin verses, re-create the slightly medieval feel of the Arts and Crafts era. The smallish rooms also have the heavy furnishings of that period. Try to get a room on the third floor facing the bay. A continental breakfast is served next to the library, and more coffee and a livelier atmosphere are available next door at Caffe Strada. On the west side is the excellent UC Art Museum. Across the street is the UC Law School. This richly atmospheric hotel makes you feel like sitting down and reading one of Henry James's later novels. (Berkeley)

THE BEAU SKY HOTEL
2520 Durant Ave.
Berkeley
510/540-7688
beausky@beausky.com
$$$

In 1994, when the owners of this 1911 girls' boardinghouse decided to do some remodeling, they apparently wanted to make it wildly extravagant. They painted the front a crisp white. They arranged some amazingly ornate pieces, such as glass and ceramic Art Nouveau bouquets and plush love seats, in the tiny lobby. They installed a Cajun restaurant named Café Orleans (which serves guests complimentary continental breakfasts). But then they must have run out of money. The 20 rooms are rather large but unremarkable, clean but dull. The whole place faces a sidewalk streaming with students going to and from Telegraph Avenue. The place has a soupçon of seediness about it, which some people used to call "European." (Berkeley)

BERKELEY CITY CLUB
2315 Durant Ave.
Berkeley
510/848-7800
www.berkeleycityclub.com
$$$

This Moorish palace was designed by Julia Morgan, the same architect who built William Randolph Hearst's castle at San Simeon. The six-story, 42-room fantasy, which is still used as a private club, is rich with Arts and Crafts ornamentation. To get a

The Bancroft Hotel

Jennifer Suttlemyre

BERKELEY

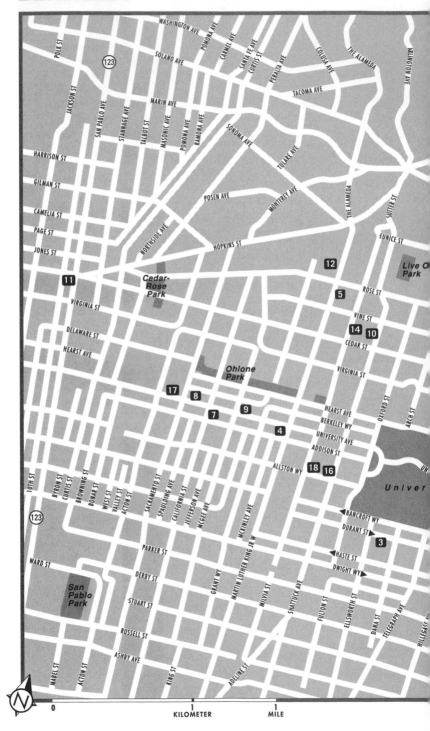

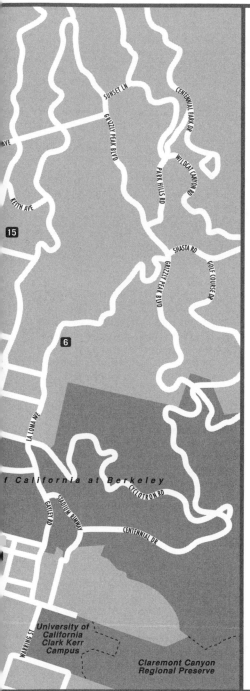

Where to Stay in Berkeley

1. Bancroft Hotel
2. The Beau Sky Hotel
3. Berkeley City Club
4. Berkeley Travelodge
5. Bonita Studio
6. Brown Shingle
7. Campus Motel
8. Capri Motel
9. Flamingo Motel
10. The French Hotel
11. Golden Bear Motel
12. Hannah-Roy House
13. Hotel Durant
14. North Berkeley B&B
15. Oxford Place
16. The Shattuck Hotel
17. Travel Inn
18. YMCA

sense of this romantic landmark, wander around the quiet first two floors, past the exotically tiled indoor pool, the dining room with its majestic ceiling and ceramic rosettes on the wall, and the verdant patio, a miniature paradise. Admittedly, the hotel is a bit tired. Few changes have been made in 75 years: the rooms retain a '40s decor, and some of them are still in the process of getting TVs. In any case, ask for a room on the fourth to sixth floors, which offer the best views of the bay or the campus. A fairly large continental breakfast is served in the dining room. Lunch and dinner are also available, although the food can't compete with the architecture. & (Berkeley)

THE FRENCH HOTEL
1538 Shattuck Ave.
Berkeley
510/548-9930
$$$
This establishment is really an espresso bar with a hotel attached. The funky café is its heart and soul and *echt* Berkeley—especially from seven to nine at night when the neighborhood crowd spills out to the sidewalk tables and the din of intellectual discussion is, well, truly French. Breakfast is complimentary here for guests. The hotel itself is a tiny sliver, just 18 rooms on three floors. The rooms, however, are larger than you'd expect, with

modern furnishings. For instance, instead of drawers there are high-tech wire baskets. Each room has a south-facing balcony, unfortunately overlooking the parking lot of Andronico's supermarket. No matter, though, for its location—in the heart of Berkeley's Gourmet Ghetto—is what counts. Right across the street is Chez Panisse, the restaurant run by California cuisine's founding mother, Alice Waters. & (Berkeley)

HOTEL DURANT
2600 Durant Ave.
Berkeley
510/845-8981
www.hoteldurant.com
$$$
Berkeley alumni, a fiercely nostalgic lot, swear this hotel hasn't changed in 30 years. They may be right. Its six floors and 140 rooms were built in 1928. Photos of scenes from campus life over the past one hundred years adorn the walls. The décor recalls the old days, too. The entry is Hollywood Spanish with a tiled floor and wonderful coffered ceilings. The rooms are serviceable and seem unchanged from times past. But you'll definitely know what year it is across the lobby in Henry's Public House. Henry's Café is fairly quiet, but the bar, with 32 brews on tap, gets pretty insane during football weekends. The bar's colorful history centers on a hostage/murder

Yes, you can spend the night on the UC campus. Occasionally, rooms become available at the **Men's Faculty Club** (510/540-5678) and the **Women's Faculty Club** (510/642-4175). Prices range from $54 to $85 for a double and include a continental breakfast. Both facilities are coed.

incident that happened here a decade ago. Understandably, the staff doesn't like to talk about that. & (Berkeley)

THE SHATTUCK HOTEL
2086 Allston Way
Berkeley
510/845-7300
$$$

If you like movies, then this hotel may be your place. Twenty-three screens are located within a few blocks of this downtown hostelry. Otherwise, it's a fairly typical businessman's hotel, circa 1910. The 175 rooms are reasonably spacious with dark, English-style furniture. The lobby has been gently updated. It doesn't have the feel of a lovingly restored landmark, although the new owners have promised big changes. If anything, you know you're in Berkeley when you see the great posters of David Lance Goines, a popular artist here in the '70s and '80s who updated the graphics of the Arts and Crafts movement. The dining room, which serves lunch and a complimentary breakfast for guests, is nothing special, but a few years ago it was a hip, downtown hotspot. Knowing Berkeley, it could get popular again anytime. & (Berkeley)

Bed-and-Breakfasts

BONITA STUDIO
1420 Bonita Ave.
Berkeley
510/525-6416
$$$

This pleasant B&B is located on a street decked out with turn-of-the-last-century charmers. But as you enter the garden studio of this circa-1900 residence, you step down into a large room that is completely contemporary—a clean, open, brightly lit space that Martha Stewart would be proud of. The furnishings are simple; the kitchen area, an ad hoc setup of microwave and hot plate. The bathroom is huge and beautifully marbled. The floor sports radiant heat. The owner is a contractor who recently took down a dying redwood in the small garden, brought in a portable sawmill, and, out of the lumber, built a lovely, jasmine-draped deck with portico. Now she's working on a spa. How many B&Bs have you visited where a half-bottle of Russian River Chardonnay awaits your arrival? Sure beats a mint on your pillow. (Berkeley)

BROWN SHINGLE
1514 La Loma Ave.
Berkeley
510/848-6385
www.brownshingle.com
$$$

It's hard to imagine a more enchanting neighborhood than the 1500 block of La Loma. Across the street from this B&B is a collection of storybook homes, including three by Maybeck, the master of Arts and Crafts style. The Lawson property, in particular, is a real jewel. As if that wasn't enough, the back of this 1924 shingled house faces a sweeping cinemascope view of the entire bay, from Oakland to Richmond. Three of the four guestrooms offer this panorama, and two have their own private bathrooms. The master bedroom includes a small, charming sun porch. A continental breakfast is served in the small dining room. The interior of this bed-and-breakfast, however, is not particularly distinguished. It has a homespun clutter with motley oak furniture and old quilts. It might remind you of a professor's slightly disheveled style. (Berkeley)

HANNAH-ROY HOUSE
1328 Josephine St.
Berkeley
510/525-2265
$$$

The restoration of this 1896 Brown Shingle-style farmhouse in a typical North Berkeley neighborhood was obviously a labor of love. It is finely detailed, with rich paneling, historic photos on the wall, and stained-glass windows, but it's not at all fussy. This house is no antique shop. The two-room bed/sitting suite on the second floor is sunny and comfortable and can sleep three. Its back door opens to a deck with a partial bay view through a small redwood grove. In addition, a laundry alcove is provided. The convivial owner serves breakfast upstairs, but guests are free to wander into the cozy downstairs living room or slip out to the bougainvillea-draped back deck to dine. If you're out there, check out the hot tub—it's private enough to be clothing-optional. (Berkeley)

LA POSADA GUEST HOUSE
Berkeley
510/548-8658
fax 510/548-6528
laposada@hooked.net
$$$

The proprietor of this B&B didn't want her address listed in this book. From the street (which is just a few blocks northwest of the UC campus), this rambling, shambling 1920s clapboard home is quite lovely. Rose, jasmine, and potato vines arch over the driveway, but inside, it's wild. The traditional house has been cut up into eight jigsaw puzzlelike rooms, each with its own bath and kitchenette, including microwave. The furnishings look pretty makeshift, but that doesn't seem to bother any of the visiting professors who encamp here for months and, sometimes, years at a time. A tented patio in the front garden is equipped with lounge chairs. For unexplained reasons, this B&B is popular, and reservations (a two-night minimum) are required well in advance. (Berkeley)

NORTH BERKELEY B&B
1517 Milvia St.
Berkeley
510/849-0649
www.bbonline.com/ca/
northberkeley
$$$

The garden is amazing: black bamboo, rhododendrons, huge white magnolias, delicate pieris, camellias, a massive two-story trellis festooned with wisteria and clematis. This small but serene woodland dream invites you to just sit and quietly unwind during your stay at this completely renovated, shingled B&B. One unit in the main house

---

For a list of bed-and-breakfasts in the area, call 510/548-7556.

The North Berkeley B&B

house with antimicassars on tired mohair sofas and tatterdemalion furnishings. Kitschy old art hangs on the walls, but don't be disheartened. The bedrooms upstairs are clean and spare with cast-iron beds, quilts, plenty of light, and a lovely bay view off the front deck. The bathrooms are from the '20s but are nicely maintained. You can enjoy breakfast (try the homemade apple cakes) on the sun porch, which overlooks the wildest garden you've ever seen, filled with strange sculptures, piles of tools, Buddhas, and a rusting xylophone. In the back is a newer cottage/studio with its own kitchen. (Berkeley)

Motels

BERKELEY TRAVELODGE
1820 University Ave.
Berkeley
510/843-4262
$$$
This motel is as close as you can get to UC without actually enrolling. It's a mere 10-minute jaunt through downtown to the west campus entrance. Nattily nautical with blue-trimmed white buildings, its 30 well-kept although typically motel-modern rooms belie its age. The accommodations are slightly larger than other motels in the neighborhood, and it's the only one with a real mix of kings, queens, and doubles. You get your own coffeemaker and a complimentary copy of *USA Today.* (Berkeley)

CAMPUS MOTEL
1619 University Ave.
Berkeley
510/841-3844
$$
Why this 23-room motel has a big

includes two bedrooms and a spacious sitting area. A private cottage, bathed in sunshine that filters through the skylight, is nestled at the back of the garden and sleeps up to four. This cottage also includes a separate kitchen with a beautiful (and working) stove from the '40s. Both accommodations are simple and slightly Asian in décor. Breakfast is left on trays outside your door. Should all this privacy and serenity make you restless, the gourmet stores, restaurants, and coffeehouses on Shattuck Avenue are just a short stroll away. & (Berkeley)

OXFORD PLACE
1151 Oxford St.
Berkeley
519/599-0089
www.bbonline.com
$$$
Get down and get funky at this ramshackle bed-and-breakfast in a 1908 Craftsman home on Berkeley's cottagey north side. The main floor resembles a well-worn rooming

Rooms become scarce during football weekends in the fall (especially if the Big Game against Stanford is being played in Berkeley) and at graduation in May, so reserve one well in advance if you're planning to visit during these times.

sign advertising that it's air-conditioned is anybody's guess. Berkeley rarely heats up enough to need it. Designed in that familiar mid-century Spanish-Colonial style, this small motel is cleaner and spiffier than a lot of its neighbors. A few of the rooms even have reproductions of antique furniture. No microwaves or coffee machines are available, but you do get cable TV. And this busy commercial neighborhood has Laundromats and restaurants within a block or two. (Berkeley)

CAPRI MOTEL
1512 University Ave.
Berkeley
510/845-7090
$$
Similar to most of the accommodations on University Avenue, the prices at this 26-room, family-run establishment drop up to 20 percent in the winter. It's in good shape, considering that it's more than 50 years old, but you may wish that the cleaning crew wasn't so generous with their ammonia cleansers. A 7-Eleven is located across the street, and a microwave and cable TV are included in every room, so you independents are in luck. (Berkeley)

FLAMINGO MOTEL
1761 University Ave.

Berkeley
510/841-4242
$$
It's painted hot pink, of course, with bright chemical-green indoor/outdoor carpeting. Inside this 29-room, two-story, typical '50s motel, the ambiance can be kind of borderline. The facilities are basic, a little worn at the edges, and a little musty—just a bed, dresser, TV, and shower. If you've always wanted to stay where one of Raymond Chandler's on-the-lam characters stayed, this motel should fit the bill quite nicely. (Berkeley)

GOLDEN BEAR MOTEL
1620 San Pablo Ave.
Berkeley
510/525-6770
$$
If you were scouting locations to film a movie set in a 1950s California motel, this one would do just fine. It has that LA-Spanish feeling—red tile roofs; a long, covered porch; a few small bungalows in back, but more important, it hasn't gone to seed. Its 43 rooms are plain but squeaky clean. It's a long, eight-block walk to BART from here, and the campus is three times farther. No meals are served, but you're right across the street from Alice Water's cozy Café Fanny, and a sushi restaurant is practically at your front door.

Unlike almost all of the motels in this part of town, pets are allowed, but it will cost you five dollars extra. (Berkeley)

TRAVEL INN
1641 University Ave.
Berkeley
510/848-3840
$$

The roses and bougainvillea are a nice touch in the parking lot, although what those picnic tables are doing in the middle of all that cement is a mystery. You'll find 41 well-kept rooms in this aging University Avenue motel. You'll also find that you have a choice of bath or shower, as well as laundry facilities and coffee available every morning in the office. You could pick up dinner at Andronico's deli directly across the street. This place is a bit confusing to find because it sports three signs—Travel Inn, California Motel, and Superior Motel. (Berkeley)

YMCA
2001 Allston Way
Berkeley
510/848-6800
$

The location is convenient—just a block away from the downtown Berkeley BART station—but the place is dark and disheveled. If you arrive after 10 p.m., the doors will be locked. There are shared bathrooms on every floor and a common kitchen off the lobby. Bed linen is provided. This facility is the closest thing to a student hostel in the whole area, and with such cheap prices, it fills up early. You can make reservations ahead of time. Every guest has to be over 18. & (Berkeley)

BERKELEY WATERFRONT

Hotels

FOUR POINTS SHERATON
1603 Powell St.
Emeryville
510/547-7888
$$$

This place gets points for trying to rise above its location in the middle of a mall parking lot. The marbled lobby and terracotta planters give the Four Points Sheraton the aura of a sophisticated boutique hotel. It's small enough (153 rooms) to allow the staff to give you as much attention as you want, which includes providing laundry and dry-cleaning services. The rooms aren't huge, but they were recently remodeled and are well maintained. Get one above the fourth floor for a tiny balcony and a panoramic view over the highway to the bay. Other amenities include a small pool and workout center. The Compass Café serves breakfast and dinner, but the restaurant is actually a Pizza Hut. & (Berkeley Waterfront)

HOLIDAY INN BAY BRIDGE
1800 Powell St.
Emeryville
510/658-9300
$$$$

Thanks to the spectacular front-row view of the Bay Bridge, this otherwise cookie-cutter corporate hotel will cost you. But it's still half the price of a similar San Francisco hotel room with a bay view. Be sure you ask for a room above the fourth floor, or you may find yourself looking straight into an office complex. Plenty of amenities include a fitness center and jogging path out to the waterfront. The Greenery

BERKELEY WATERFRONT

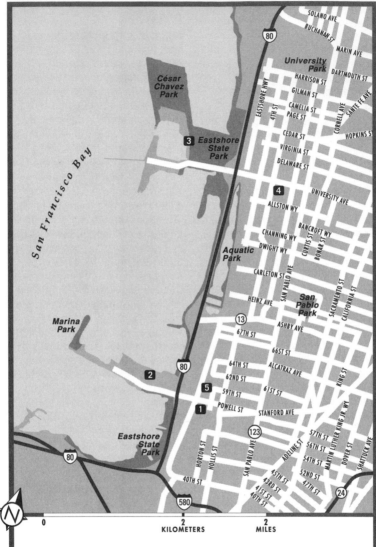

Where to Stay at the Berkeley Waterfront

1. Four Points Sheraton
2. Holiday Inn Bay Bridge
3. Radisson Hotel Berkeley
   Marina
4. Ramada Inn
5. Woodfin Suite Hotel

Restaurant serves generic but decent breakfasts, lunches, and dinners. A shuttle is available to take you to BART or to the shops, restaurants, movies, and clubs of Emery Bay, but the shopping center is so close, you could stretch your legs and walk to it. Prices drop slightly on winter weekends. & (Berkeley Waterfront)

RADISSON HOTEL BERKELEY MARINA
200 Marina Blvd.
Berkeley
510/548-7920
$$$
This hotel amidst the mass of masts of the Berkeley Marina offers the most pure and direct view of the Golden Gate Bridge from any place in the Bay Area. Be sure you specify your interest in a waterside room on the second or third floors. Otherwise you're liable to feel like you're in a run-of-the-mill 375-room hotel that could be anywhere. The lobby and rooms are crisp and light but conventional, designed mostly for business clientele. The Bay Grill's breakfast, lunch, and dinner menus are nothing special, but each meal comes with a world-famous view at no extra charge. On Friday and Saturday nights you can dance to live rock music. The hotel offers a free shuttle to the North Berkeley BART, or you can head in the other direction and out into the bay. (Hornblower yachts, which sail daily to and from San Francisco's Fisherman's Wharf, offer splendid bay dinner cruises six times a year.) & (Berkeley Waterfront)

WOODFIN SUITE HOTEL
5800 Shellmound St.

Emeryville
800/237-8811
$$$
This waterfront hotel, with a lineup of incongruous palm trees out front, is scheduled to open in Fall 2000. The upper stories of the baby-grand hotel will supposedly give guests a closeup view of I-80 and, beyond it, the Bay Bridge. The management is even promising a view of the Golden Gate. You can rightly assume you will find the homelike amenities usually available at suite hotels like this—separate living rooms, full kitchens, and considerable space to entertain or spread out your spreadsheets before the next day's business meeting. Expect all of the technical support demanded by today's e-commerce crowd, plus a good splash of suburban elegance. & (Berkeley Waterfront)

Motels

RAMADA INN
920 University Ave.
Berkeley
510/849-1121
$$$
This establishment may be the only Ramada in the country that serves Ethiopian food. You'll find it in the Chibbo Bar & Grill, which also offers live entertainment Wednesday through Sunday. It's also the only motel on University Avenue with a pool. The rooms are just slightly bigger than other motels up the street, and they do have tiny balconies, but the carpeting is buckling and the general aroma is of disinfectant. No matter how you look at it, it still resembles an upscale penal institution. & (Berkeley Waterfront)

The Legacy of Maybeck and Morgan

Two architects, Bernard Maybeck (1864-1957) and Julia Morgan (1872-1957), are largely responsible for the unique and beautiful city you see today. Maybeck was a model bohemian in the early part of the twentieth century. He studied at the Ecole des Beaux-Arts in Paris and began working in the Bay Area in 1892. His best-known work is probably the Palace of Fine Arts in San Francisco. What he built in Berkeley tends to be more eccentric, slightly medieval, and with a craftsman's eye for detail. The First Church of Christ Science on Durant Avenue, built in 1910, is a National Landmark. It is a mix of Byzantine, Gothic, and Japanese influences, and yet somehow all of these disparate flavors work perfectly. His other buildings, whether Spanish or Tudor or Craftsman in style, all have a deeply romantic, sometimes rustic, streak.

Julia Morgan is best known as one of America's first women architects and the creator of William Randolph Hearst's massive ego trip at San Simeon. She also studied at the Ecole des Beaux-Arts. In Berkeley, her architectural repertoire includes more than 60 homes, as well as her Moorish fantasy on Durant Avenue, the Berkeley City Club. The spectacular Greek Theatre and dramatic Hearst Mining Building on the UC campus are also her designs. Like Maybeck, Morgan was consummately skilled at working in a variety of historical and cultural styles.

Together Morgan and Maybeck benefited from the generous patronage of William Randolph Hearst's mother, whose name, Phoebe Apperson Hearst, is inescapable on the UC campus. For her, they combined forces on the richly neoclassical Hearst Gymnasium for Women.

The Berkeley Architectural Heritage Society is a rich source of material about the remarkable buildings here. Their offices are right across the street from the Berkeley City Club at 2813 Durant Avenue, or you can call them at 510/841-2242.

SOUTH BERKELEY/
NORTH OAKLAND

Hotels

CLAREMONT RESORT
41 Tunnel Rd.
Oakland
510/843-3000
$$$$
This splendid 1915 hotel is a grande
dame in tennis shoes. Towered and
turreted, it is perched, in bridal-
white grandeur, in the Oakland Hills,
replete with jaw-dropping views of
San Francisco Bay (at least when
the fog rolls away). The resort's 22
acres include 10 tennis courts and
a full exercise/spa center with two
Olympic-size pools. You can bliss
out with everything from a full-body
aloe mask to a deep-tissue massage. The rather ordinary rooms become stunning at night when San
Francisco spreads before you like a
cache of loose diamonds. The food
at Jordan's Restaurant is fine but,
again, can't match the view. The

The Claremont Resort

Marty Forsyth

Terrace Room has evening dancing,
including swing night. If you're feeling too relaxed and pampered, you
can always remind yourself that the
Hayward Earthquake Fault lies just
a few hundred yards away. &
(South Berkeley/North Oakland)

Bed-and-Breakfasts

BELROSE HOUSE
BED-AND-BREAKFAST
2744 Belrose Ave.
Berkeley
510/845-7454
$$$$
This street is graced by some of
Berkeley's most classic and historic
homes. This residence, although elegant and refined, is not one of
them. It was built after World War II
and is basically a sumptuous example of '50s suburbia. There is a small
studio with a bathroom downstairs,
while upstairs there are two larger
rooms. The one on the east side can
get noisy. The master bedroom is
decorated with wicker furniture and
has French doors leading out to a
large deck. Breakfast, with rolls
from the nearby Bread Garden bakery, is served in the bright kitchen,
which looks out through an enormous lemon tree to one of the few
residential swimming pools in
Berkeley. Be warned that Belrose is
the main southern entry to the UC
campus, and the traffic can be bru-
tal. (South Berkeley/North Oakland)

DEAN'S BED-AND-BREAKFAST
480 Pedestrian Way
Oakland
510/652-5024
$$$
Say you want to go on a Zen retreat,
but you want your own swimming
pool heated to a therapeutic 85 de-

SOUTH BERKELEY/NORTH OAKLAND

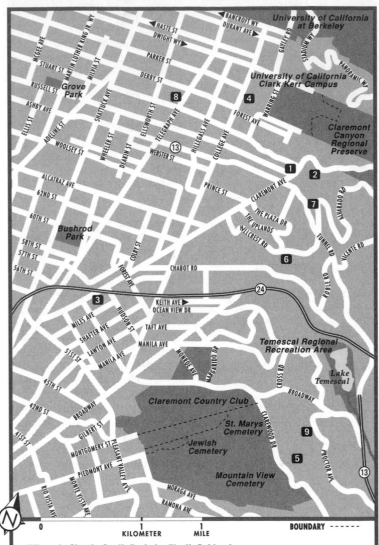

Where to Stay in South Berkeley/North Oakland

1. Belrose House Bed-and-Breakfast
2. Claremont Resort
3. Dean's Bed-and-Breakfast
4. Elmwood House
5. The Hills B&B
6. M's Bed-and-Breakfast
7. Mary's Bed-and-Breakfast
8. Rose Garden Inn
9. Tudor Rose

grees, a kitchenette, and 60-channel cable TV. This 1906 property, squeezed in an ivy-covered alley in a busy neighborhood just off Highway 24, fits all your requirements. It has a tiny but exquisite garden with streambeds and rock fountains and bonsai. Make sure you get the little Japanese pavilion, which has a sitting room/bedroom, bathroom, and a kitchenette stocked with what you need to make your own breakfast. Although this place is within walking distance of the Rockridge BART station and the hip boom of College Avenue, it is quite serene. It's the kind of bed-and-breakfast that comes with peace of mind included at no additional charge. (South Berkeley/North Oakland)

ELMWOOD HOUSE
2609 College Ave.
Berkeley
510/540-5123
$$$

The passion for saving Berkeley's rich architectural inheritance is vividly demonstrated in this 1902 home, which is situated just a few blocks from the campus. The current owner, Steve Hyske, laughingly claims he knows more about the families that have lived here during the past century than he knows about his own. On the walls are original floorplans and family photos. The rooms are decorated with a mixture of old furnishings, including some especially fine Mission pieces. The house has four cozy bedrooms, two of which share a bath. The dark redwood paneling gives the place a moody, mysterious aura. A small garden in the back is nice but is overlooked by some hideous student apartments. Breakfast is not served, but several coffeehouses are lo-cated a few blocks away. (South Berkeley/North Oakland)

THE HILLS B&B
1547 Harbord Dr.
Oakland
510/547-0652
$$$

All the homes in this hilly North Oakland neighborhood are variations of the colonial/ranch style so admired by Beaver Cleaver's family. This large, contemporary apartment is on the bottom floor of one of these houses. The stairs leading down are quite steep and, in wet weather, slippery. The two spacious rooms face west and have a tree-lined view of the bay. This place can easily sleep four. The main bedroom is cheery and comes with plenty of closet space. The living room has a sofa bed, working fireplace, small deck, TV, VCR—the works. The bathroom is clean and up to date. The owners leave juice, breads, and coffee so that you can make your own breakfast as they head off to work. Discounts are available for longer stays. (South Berkeley/North Oakland)

M'S BED-AND-BREAKFAST
262 Hillcrest Rd.
Berkeley
510/654-0648
$$$

"I don't like schedules," Mary Leggett, the bubbly hostess of this 1911 English Tudor, makes very clear. She lets her guests check in and out on their own and have free rein in this small but inventively redesigned home in the Claremont District. The walls are richly sponged the color of persimmons. Charming antique touches include a working pump organ. The three bedrooms are snug

TRIVIA

The property on which the **Claremont Hotel** was built was won in 1910 in a game of dominos.

nests, one of which comes with its own bath and shower. The other two rooms share a bathroom with a large Jacuzzi. A fruit-laden continental breakfast is served in the kitchen, but guests often like to enjoy theirs outside on the flower-filled deck, which has a hot tub and south-facing view of Oakland and the bay. It also, unfortunately, overlooks the roar of Highway 24. (South Berkeley/North Oakland)

MARY'S BED-AND-BREAKFAST
47 Alvarado Rd.
Berkeley
510/848-1431
$$$
The 1991 Berkeley/Oakland Hills Firestorm destroyed much of the neighborhood above the Claremont Hotel. Fortunately, the mansion-lined street on which this bed-and-breakfast is located was spared. The B&B is a gracious 1911 home with gleaming hardwood floors and three rooms on the top story. Its owner, a former antiques dealer, has decorated it with a loving hand and a tasteful eye. The two larger bedrooms provide treetop panoramas of Berkeley and, beyond, the bay. Breakfast, which includes homemade breads, is served in the classic dining room downstairs. Wander a mile or so up Alvarado Road to tour the neighborhood, which has been almost completely rebuilt since the fire. Highlights include some uncanny duplicates of the historic homes that used to be

on this street, as well as a few startling examples of contemporary design. The fantastic views will make you see why most of the owners chose to rebuild here. (South Berkeley/North Oakland)

ROSE GARDEN INN
2740 Telegraph Ave.
Berkeley
510/549-2145
$$$
In the '60s, Berkeley rebels advocated "Flower Power." This homey inn, a few blocks from the buzz of "Telegraph," is probably not what they had in mind. It is a nonstop display of floral wallpaper, carpets, chintz, lace, china, and art. Most flowery of all is a sweet, meandering, rose-filled English garden. The rooms are in five turn-of-the-century mansions (the original owners were two brothers who paved most of the sidewalks in Berkeley and Oakland) that were lovingly restored, beginning in 1979. Most of the frilly and comfortable rooms have fireplaces but not a lot of closet space. The staff provides a continental breakfast and afternoon tea in the greenhouse. Always charming, the inn gets busy over the weekend with private parties. It is at its peak in April and May, when the garden explodes. &
(South Berkeley/North Oakland)

TUDOR ROSE
316 Modoc Ave.
Oakland

510/655-3201
$$
Firefighters managed to stop the horrendous 1991 Firestorm just across the street from this plain brick and stucco '50s home. The hilly neighborhood, completely rebuilt with larger homes, feels considerably more crowded than it used to be. But the single unit here is cozy with deep-piled carpet, a working fireplace, and a wall-length window with a view of Mount Tamalpais, which towers to the north of the Golden Gate. The owner is a confessed Anglomaniac, and the spacious chamber is sprinkled with tea cups, Paddington bears, and pub menus. A sofa opens for an additional guest. The room has its own kitchen, and guests are free to partake of juice, milk, coffee, scones, and muffins at their leisure. The sunny, double-decked garden is lovely, but you have to traipse through the family's quarters to get there. (South Berkeley/North Oakland)

OAKLAND

Hotels

CLARION SUITES LAKE MERRITT HOTEL
1800 Madison St.
Oakland
510/832-2300
$$$$
This neighborhood on the west side of Lake Merritt is a few blocks and about 60 years removed from downtown's new high-rises. Most of the surrounding apartment houses, as well as this six-story, 75-year-old hotel, have a worn-at-the-edges, old-Hollywood, romantic

feel to them. The Lake Merritt Hotel's 51 warrenlike suites are immaculate. The best suites come with views of the lake and its diorama of joggers, sailboats, and waterfowl. The charming Terrace Room restaurant serves lunch and dinner and hosts live jazz on Thursday nights. ♿ (Oakland)

OAKLAND MARRIOTT AT CITY CENTER
1001 Broadway
Oakland
510/451-4000
www.marriott.com
$$$$
If you're nervous about staying in downtown Oakland, this 21-story, 483-room fortress will calm you down. The teal and cream color scheme and the marbled lobby with its bustling bellhops and phone banks are reassuringly familiar to any corporate business traveler. Make sure you get a room above the 16th floor on the west side for a wide-screen view of the bay. The hotel is part of the sprawling Oakland Convention Center, so expect to see a lot of guests checking their pagers. You're also likely to run into pro sports teams that are in town to do battle with the local stars. If you're in the mood for a less-pressured reality, stroll across the street to the country's third-largest Chinatown and the turn-of-the-last-century charms of Old Oakland. ♿ (Oakland)

WASHINGTON INN
495 10th St.
Oakland
510/452-1776
www.thewashingtoninn.com
$$$
This handsomely remodeled 1913

DOWNTOWN OAKLAND

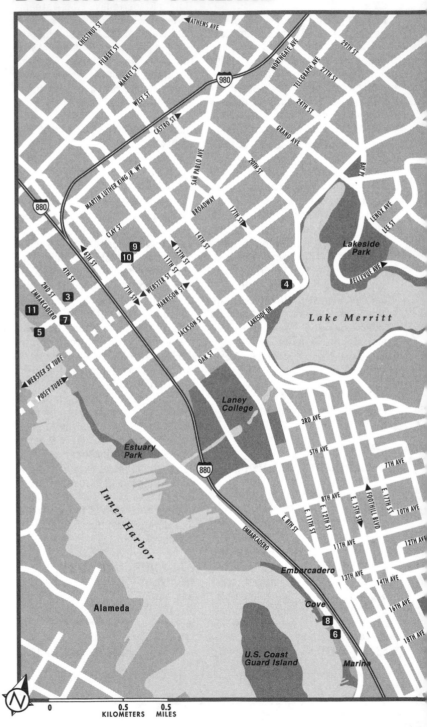

Where to Stay in Downtown Oakland

1. Bates House
2. B&B on Fairmount
3. Best Western Inn at the Square
4. Clarion Suites Lake Merritt Hotel
5. Dockside Bed & Boat
6. Executive Inn
7. Jack London Inn
8. Motel 6
9. Oakland Marriott at City Center
10. Washington Inn
11. Waterfront Plaza Hotel

BOUNDARY - - - - - -

hotel appears to have been lifted directly from a cowboy movie. Small and snug, it's loaded with late-nineteenth-century charm—not the froufrou Victorian kind, but the more rugged brick-and-wood-paneled version. Its 47 rooms on four narrow floors are clean and spare with just a few Early-American and English antiques (as well as cable TV and modem hookups). Not surprisingly, the south-facing rooms have the best light. The lobby houses the 495 Restaurant and Café, which offers a full breakfast buffet on weekdays (the cost of which is included in the room price). If you don't have to get up early the next day, try the chicken marinated in vermouth. ♿ (Oakland)

WATERFRONT PLAZA HOTEL
10 Washington St.
Oakland
510/836-3800
www.waterfrontplaza.com
$$$$
This small, standard-issue, commercial hotel is situated in the heart of Jack London Square and next to the landing for the San Francisco Ferry. Perched three stories over the Oakland Estuary, the rooms are what you'd expect—efficient and clean—

Top 10 Favorite Things About the East Bay
by Jon Carroll, columnist for the *San Francisco Chronicle*

1. The **Peace Grove,** located about three miles in from the trailhead at Inspiration Point, with its wooden plaques, many of them half hidden, and the strange stone circle at the top of the hill beyond it.

2. The **Bay Wolf Restaurant** because Michael Wild has the best taste in literature of any restaurant owner I know.

3. The **view from I-580** just as it descends onto the Bay Bridge Toll Plaza.

4. **Codys**—the old one on Telegraph—because it's so important and cared for so lovingly.

5. The strange **elf village** at Spruce and Hearst in Berkeley.

6. **Allen Temple Baptist Church,** where I am permitted to participate in another culture.

7. The **Smoke House,** for its memories, and because its burgers are unlike any creations anywhere.

8. The walk around **Lake Chabot.**

9. The **Grand Lake** cinema.

10. Sundays in **Oakland Chinatown.**

TOP TOP TOP TOP TOP TOP TOP TOP TOP TOP TOP TOP TOP TOP TOP

but the water views are unobstructed. Rooms 232 and 332, both equipped with balconies, have the best sight lines up the Alameda shoreline to San Francisco. Even the small pool includes a wonderful view of the water. The hotel is favored by businesspeople, so don't be surprised to find sales meetings in progress in the lobby. The hotel's restaurant, Jack's Bistro, serves breakfast, lunch, and dinner. It specializes in Italian food but also offers a large selection of fish and nouvelle California dishes such as vegetarian napoleons. & (Oakland)

Motels

BEST WESTERN INN AT THE SQUARE
233 Broadway
Oakland
510/452-4565
$$$
This 102-room motel, set just a couple of blocks off Jack London Square, gets points for trying. They've taken a typical motel and tweaked it just enough for it to be tasteful. The rooms are quiet, spare, and comfortable. The building is too far from the estuary to have views, but an enormous patio has a large *Melrose Place*-style swimming pool in the center. A continental breakfast is complimentary in the adjacent Buttercup coffee shop, which is a real '50s throwback. You can also get lunch and dinner there. & (Oakland)

EXECUTIVE INN
1755 Embarcadero
Oakland
510/536-6633
$$$
Canadian geese have been spotted

swimming in the small pool of this 149-room motel on the estuary, a few miles south of Jack London Square. Beyond that, the main attractions are the waterside rooms. They cost $14 more than the ones facing the freeway, but they include their own balconies and greener, less-industrial views. The rooms are simple and the whole place is pretty generic, although a faint effort has been made to endow it with a nautical theme. A fireplace in the lobby really works, and the library is stocked with actual books. Continental breakfast is offered in a downstairs reception room that turns into a bar on weekday evenings. You can take in the view from inside or at tables on a grassy strip outside. Shuttle service is available to the Oakland airport and Jack London Square. & (Oakland)

JACK LONDON INN
444 Embarcadero West
Oakland
510/444-2032
$$$
The good points are that this inn is conveniently located just across from Jack London Square, it has a pool, and there's a pool table in the macho Moe's Bar. Its rooms are plain but clean, and the 24-hour coffee shop looks as if it was lifted straight out of the '50s. Other than that, it's hard to get excited about this 110-room cinderblock inn. & (Oakland)

MOTEL 6
1801 Embarcadero
Oakland
510/436-7428
$$
The only food you'll find is out of the vending machines, and the 96

GREATER OAKLAND

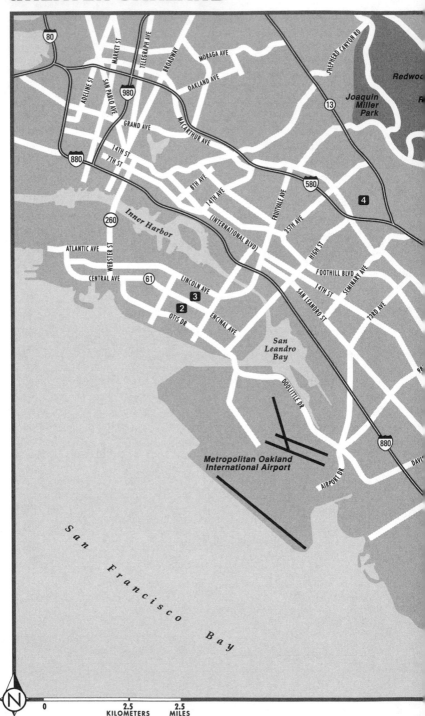

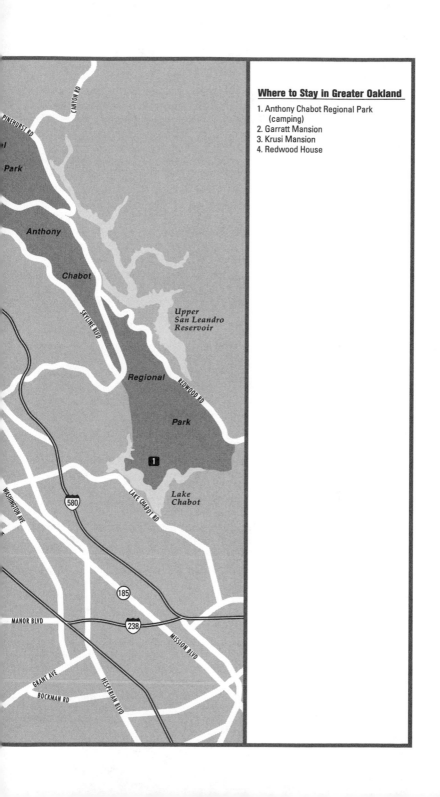

Where to Stay in Greater Oakland

1. Anthony Chabot Regional Park (camping)
2. Garratt Mansion
3. Krusi Mansion
4. Redwood House

rooms are nondescript, but this motel puts you right on the Oakland Estuary, just two miles away from Jack London Square. And it does have a few surprising charms: The grounds, for instance, are well maintained and include a small pool with water jets that allow swimmers to get a workout. And the accommodations back up against a waterfront park with picnic tables. At one end of the park is the San Antonio Fishing Pier. At the other end is a small marina, all white and blue with cabin cruisers and sailboats. The bell-like ring of rigging in the wind can be therapeutic. If you decide to stay here, be sure to ask for directions. Getting here from the interstate can be confusing. &. (Oakland)

Bed-and-Breakfasts

BATES HOUSE
399 Bellevue Ave.
Oakland
510/893-3881
$$$
This bed-and-breakfast bears no relation to Hitchcock's famous motel, but a kind of drama does go on inside this gracious 1907 home. Victoriana and Orientalia run wild. Its high-ceilinged rooms are decorated in a deliriously over-the-top style. Prints, kimonos, fans, and Balinese puppets cover the walls. The four bedrooms are crammed with delicate antiques, so klutzes might want to pass on staying here. The small garden is a good effort, but it's exposed to the street and looks out on a neighborhood of mostly dull apartments. If you want greenery, stroll two blocks to the rambling park along Lake Merritt. Continental breakfast is served. (Oakland)

B&B ON FAIRMOUNT
640 Fairmount Ave.
Oakland
510/773-7726
$$$
In an ungentrified neighborhood of Craftsman-style houses, this 1907 restored residence is about as homey a place as you can hope to stay in Oakland. Even though the B&B is 29 stairs from the street, host Nancy Lovejoy lives up to her name, and her ebullience makes it worth the climb. The three guestrooms are large and uncluttered, old fashioned but not fussy. The "Charlie's Queen" room has the best view, but it's painted in an eye-popping turquoise. An unusually generous breakfast is served in the crisp, light kitchen overlooking an organic garden. If you're lucky, you might get Nancy's custard-bread pudding. Tea aficionados can enjoy a hot cup and fresh scones in the afternoon in the small but bright upstairs sunroom. (Oakland)

DOCKSIDE BED & BOAT
77 Jack London Square
Oakland
510/444-5858
www.boatandbed.com
$$$$
Enjoy your own private yacht without the work of actually sailing it. These luxurious sailboats and cabin cruisers are docked at the new Jack London Marina. They're big—up to 54 feet in length—and some sleep six. The decks and staterooms are spacious (one of the former owners was seven feet tall) and handsomely appointed. And despite the hundreds of boats docked nearby, the yachts feel private. You'll probably want to start

your stay by chilling a bottle of champagne and watching the lights dance along the water. You'll be offered a continental breakfast, but if you want anything else in the way of food, you'll have to use the microwave. Better yet, just walk to the other end of the dock and enjoy dinner and a movie or go to a jazz club in Jack London Square. (Oakland)

GARRATT MANSION
900 Union St.
Alameda
510/521-4779
garrattm@pacbell.net
$$$

If Victorian architecture is like gingerbread, then Alameda's Gold Coast neighborhood is a pastry shop. One of its treasures is this stately colonial revival home built in 1893. Its lobby is full of intricately carved redwood and beveled glass. A grand staircase leads up to a second-floor balcony, where small orchestras once entertained guests. The seven rooms are frilly, but not excessively so, and graced with comfy, overstuffed sofas and antiques. The spacious attic rooms are especially charming. The magnificent home is full of welcoming details such as extra parlors where guests can find books, magazines, board games, and even chocolate

chip cookies. It is the only B&B around that offers a full breakfast. If you like to start your mornings with fresh-squeezed juice, baked apple pancakes, sausages, coffee, and tea, try this place. (Oakland)

KRUSI MANSION
2033 Central Ave.
Alameda
510/864-2300
kmansion@dnai.com
$$$

Embroidered pillows, chenille bedspreads, Bauer pottery, inlaid wooden pictures, old suitcases, Hawaiian memorabilia, and early-twentieth-century photography are just a few of the things that the owners of this 1888 Victorian home collect. You'll find these delights downstairs in the dining room (where an expanded continental breakfast is served) and the redwood-columned parlor, and upstairs in the three guestrooms. A gracious country feeling pervades the lovingly restored rooms, especially in the bowerlike Rose Room. All rooms come with fastidiously restored bathrooms. The entrance is impressively flower-laden, and if you ask nicely, the hosts may show you their dazzling kitchen. Everything would be perfect if it weren't for all those stucco apartment houses in this east-end Alameda neighborhood. (Oakland)

REDWOOD HOUSE
4244 39th Ave.
Oakland
510/530-6840
$$$

This house has the highest room you can get in the Oakland Hills. And if you're planning to spend time in the East Bay Regional Parks, it's a smart choice. Owner Don Taylor has taken a conventional 1938 home in a remote suburb and decorated it to within an inch of its life. A junglelike wall of lovebirds and parakeets greet you at the entrance. There are two bedrooms and a particularly dazzling bathroom, where you can sit in a marble-wrapped Jacuzzi and watch the sun slip into the Pacific. Each Christmas and Easter the place is given an additional dose of lights and glitter. Breakfast is continental and served in the formal dining room. This bed-and-breakfast is half antique store, half garden shop, and wholly unique. (Oakland)

THE HILLS

Campgrounds

ANTHONY CHABOT REGIONAL PARK
Enter through Marciel Gate off Redwood Rd.

510/631-1684
www.ebparks.org
$
Seventy-five sites are available here in the southern area of the Oakland Hills, but you should still be sure to reserve one ahead of time, especially in the summer, because they fill up fast. Only 12 sites have full hookups for RVs. The remaining sites offer restrooms and hot showers, water fountains, picnic tables, and barbecue pits. The sites vary widely in degrees of privacy, shade, and views, so be specific about what you want when you make your reservation. You must walk in to 10 of the sites; the rest are accessible by car. Fees are $15 per night, plus a single $6 reservation charge. Visits are limited to 14 days. Bring a sweater—even in the summer. The days may be warm and toasty, but the nights can get pretty cold and foggy. (Hills)

Marty Forsyth

4

WHERE TO EAT

Berkeley is to "foodies" what Rome is to Catholics. Nearly 30 years ago, the renaissance of American cuisine began in the Chez Panisse kitchen of Alice Waters, the godmother of California cuisine (which is actually quite French and Italian). Since then, chefs under the tutelage of Waters have gone forth and shared the culinary delights found in fresher, locally produced foods prepared in simpler, yet more imaginative, ways. Today you won't find a major city in the country that doesn't have one of Waters's disciples cooking there.

The Chez Panisse revolution also created a much more discerning population of local restaurant-goers. A significant percentage of East Bay residents can name at least five kinds of lettuce and identify which brand of sea salt is the best. Appropriately enough, restaurant standards are high here, whether you are having French or California/Asian fusion. The area's international population has encouraged a global range of cooking. The density of Chinese restaurants is higher, of course, in Oakland's Chinatown, but you can find ethnic restaurants all across the East Bay. And when paying your bill, you'll happily find that bargains can be had here.

Because food is such an all-consuming interest in Berkeley and Oakland means you'll invariably find coffeehouses that offer the perfect decaf double espresso, bakeries with 30 kinds of artisan breads, gourmet supermarkets, and, because of its geographic proximity to Napa and Sonoma, a selection of wine that's on a world-class level. Surprisingly, Berkeley and Oakland have only a handful of restaurants on the bay. Numerous vegetarian restaurants but no real steakhouses are located here.

Restaurants come and go, even the seemingly established ones listed here, so call first before showing up. And interesting new restaurants are always opening. Ask at a restaurant you like for another recommendation. This chapter begins with a list of restaurants organized by the type of food each offers. For details about each restaurant, consult the pages that follow—dining spots are listed alphabetically within each geographic zone. Dollar-sign symbols indicate how much you can expect to spend per person for an entrée.

Price rating symbols:
$ **$10 and under**
$$ **$11-20**
$$$ **$21 and up**

All restaurants listed accept credit cards unless otherwise noted.

American
Autumn Moon (O), p. 79
Fatapple's (B), p. 62
Fat Lady (O), p. 82
LJ Quinn's Lighthouse (O), p. 87
Oakland Grill (O), p. 87
Oaktown Café (O), p. 88
Pyramid Brewery (BW), p. 70
Rockridge Café (SB/NO), p. 77

Barbecue
Doug's (SB/NO), p. 74
Everett & Jones (O) p. 82, (B) p. 82

Breakfast
Bette's Oceanview Diner (BW), p. 66
Café Fanny (BW), p. 68
Mama's Royal Café (O), p. 87
Rick & Ann's (SB/NO), p. 77
West Side Bakery Café (BW), p. 72

Burmese
Nan Yang (SB/NO), p. 76

Cajun/Creole
Gingerbread House (O), p. 83
Gulf Coast Grill & Bar (O), p. 83

California
Café Rouge (BW), p. 68
Chez Panisse (B), p. 61
Chez Panisse Café (B), p. 62
Garibaldi's (SB/NO), p. 74
JoJo (O), p. 86
Jordan's (SB/NO), p. 75
Lalime's (B), p. 63
Nava (SB/NO), p. 76
Rivoli (B), p. 65
Santa Fe Bar & Grill (B), p. 65
Santa Fe Bistro (B), p. 65
Townhouse Bar & Grill (BW), p. 71

Cambodian
Battam Bang (O), p. 79
Cambodiana (B), p. 61
Phnom Penh House (O), p. 88

Chinese
Jade Villa (O), p. 83
Peony (O), p. 88
Shen Hua (SB/NO), p. 77
Trader Vic's (BW), p. 71
Xanadu (BW), p. 72

Deli
Saul's (B), p. 65

Ethiopian
Asmara (SB/NO), p. 72
Blue Nile (SB/NO), p. 74

French
Bistro Viola (BW), p. 66
Citron (SB/NO), p. 74
La Note (B), p. 63
Obelisque (B), p. 76
Soizic (O), p. 89
Thornhill Café (H), p. 91

Fusion
Christopher's (B), p. 62
Ginger Island (BW), p. 68

Italian

Bay Wolf (O), p. 79
Bucci's, (BW), p. 68
Caffe 817 (O), p. 79
Giovanni's (B), p. 63
Italian Colors (H), p. 90
Mazzini (SB/NO), p. 75
Old Spaghetti Factory (O), p. 88
Oliveto (SB/NO), p. 77
Spettro (O), p. 89
Venezia (B), p. 66

Indian

Ajanta (B), p. 57
Breads of India (B), p. 60

Japanese

Kirala (SB/NO), p. 75
O Chame (BW), p. 70
Uzen (SB/NO), p. 78

Korean

Hahn's Hibachi (O), p. 83
Sam Won Kai Bi (O), p. 89

Laotian

Dara (B), p. 62

Mexican

Christopher's Nothing Fancy (BW),
   p. 68
La Estrellita (O), p. 86
Picante Cocina Mexicana (BW), p. 70

Middle Eastern

Britt Marie's, (B), p. 60
La Mediterranee (SB/NO), p. 75

Noodles

Long Life Noodle Company (B),
   p. 64

Pizza

Zachary's (SB/NO), p. 78 (BW),
   p. 79

Seafood

Kincaid's Bayhouse (O), p. 86

Skate's (BW), p. 71
Spenger's (BW), p. 71

Spanish

César (B), p. 61

Thai

Plearn (B), p. 64

Vegetarian

Café Intermezzo (B), p. 60

Vietnamese

Le Cheval (O), p. 86
Vi's Vietnamese (O), p. 90

BERKELEY

AJANTA
1888 Solano Ave.
Berkeley
510/526-4373
$-$$

Here's culinary ambition on an epic scale. This modest, and deservedly popular, Indian restaurant creates mild dishes that hail from northern India as well as spicy entrées influenced by southern India cuisine. The menu changes monthly, but tender lamb-rib chop in yogurt and the aromatic tandoori salmon remain as staples of this North Berkeley establishment. Chicken, beef, and lamb are marinated in heady blends of traditional spices, but this place is also a field day for vegetarians. If you'd like, call as much as a month in advance and get a newsletter that lets you know what they're serving when you visit. The food may be hot—you can take your choice of five degrees of heat—but be prepared to cool your heels. Waits of up to half an hour at dinner are not unusual on the weekends. Lunch and dinner daily. (Berkeley)

BERKELEY

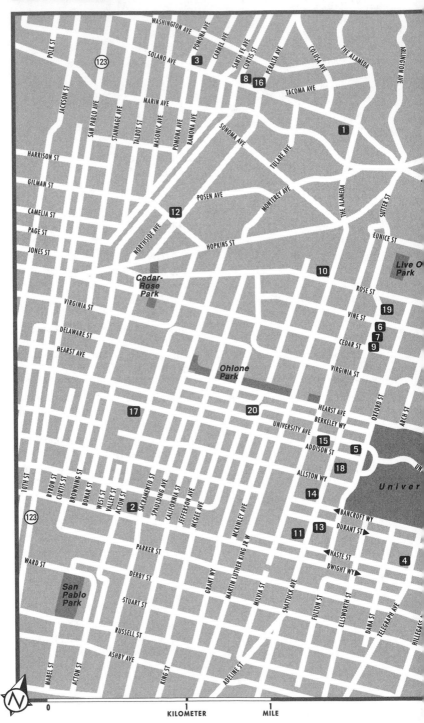

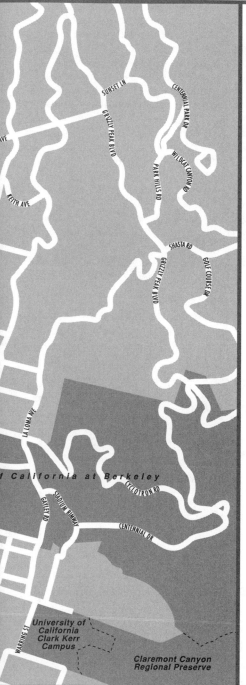

BOUNDARY - - - - - -

BREADS OF INDIA
2448 Sacramento Ave.
Berkeley
510/ 848-7684
$

The scene outside this storefront restaurant can get as crowded as a Bombay sidewalk, but don't let the sign mislead you: It's not a bakery (although the kitchen has recipes for 160 different breads). The menu of gourmet curries spans the subcontinent. The dishes, which vary every night, are noted by region and are described in complete detail, including some of their health benefits. The spice level is sensuous without causing palate panic. The griddle-cooked breads are a small extra charge but well worth it. Lunch Mon-Sat; dinner nightly. &
(Berkeley)

BRITT MARIE'S
1369 Solano Ave.
Berkeley
510/527-1314

$-$$
In this yuppie-free local favorite, you'll find lunch and dinners with a slight leaning toward the Middle East. Appetizers such as the smooth *taramolsata* or the garlic-roasted eggplant go nicely with the dark-seeded homemade breads. Entrées read like a veritable United Nations cafeteria menu—pork schnitzel, prawns in coconut milk, duck roasted with caraway seeds, lemon-roasted chicken. The desserts seem imported from your childhood; the rich chocolate cake is but one example of the nostalgic lineup. The wine list is short but features a nice sampling from all the major California North Coast valleys. The small space is well worn, comfortable, and funky. Lunch and dinner daily. & (Berkeley)

CAFÉ INTERMEZZO
2442 Telegraph Ave.
Berkeley
510/ 849-4952

The Café Scene

*Who are all these people hanging out day and night at the dozens of local coffeehouses? At **Mediterraneum Caffe** (2475 Telegraph), street poets, grad students, and aging hippies rail against "The System." **Peets,** at 2124 Vine Street, is circled by shmoozers, despite its lack of seating. The atmosphere is more civilized at Peets' Fourth Street branch, with its large sidewalk patio. **Roma** (College and Ashby) is frequented by mostly students eyeing each other from behind their laptops. Oakland is catching up fast. **Café Temescal** (4920 Telegraph) is cool, art-filled, and quiet. Downtown in a former service station, the **Urban Blend** (33 Broadway) is high-tech hip.*

$

Whatever happened to sprouts? Anyone with memories of grazing on those sweet green grasses will find themselves reliving their youth at this hugely popular student hangout in the heart of Telegraph Avenue. You don't get a lot of choices here, but the portions are massive. The veggie salad is a small haystack of avocados, beans, carrots, tomatoes, cucumbers, and, of course, sprouts. The sandwiches are whole meals contained by thick slices of homemade honey wheat bread, focaccia, or French rolls. Sodas, beer, wine, and various espressos are available, including some house specials like the Rock Climber, made from iced espresso, soy milk, and honey. And the prices fit the tightest student budget. Lunch and dinner daily. &. (Berkeley)

CAMBODIANA
2156 University Ave.
Berkeley
510/843-4630
$-$$

Don't let the mustard and turquoise walls or white bread with mayo condiments scare you away. The food here is excellent. Seafood, meat, and poultry are all available with a choice of intriguing sauces. Naga Princess sauce is mostly spicy tamarind, lemongrass, and coconut milk. Ginger Blossom sauce is dark and tangy with garlic, lemon, and soybeans. For spicier tastes, there's Mekong House Boat sauce with garlic, lime juice, chile, and sugar. Lamb and quail are done particularly well, but don't leave town without trying the smoky eggplant. Lunch weekdays; dinner daily. &. (Berkeley)

CÉSAR
1515 Shattuck Ave.
Berkeley
510/883-0222
$

A lot of people who eat out these days make a meal of appetizers only. This stylish tapas bar that Berkeley intellectual hipsters use as their clubhouse caters to this trend. If you thought Spanish food was under-seasoned, then this place should change your mind fast. You can usually choose from about a dozen tapas (ranging from four to six dollars each), such as roasted grapes and ham, smoked salmon, or peppered salt cod. The selection changes daily. If you're still hungry, there are *bocadrillos,* offbeat baguette sandwiches, as well as a few desserts. The wine list is full of novelties, especially rosé wines for people who don't drink rosé. Open 3-midnight daily. &. (Berkeley)

CHEZ PANISSE
1517 Shattuck Ave.
Berkeley
510/548-5525
www.chezpanisse.com
$$$

After almost 30 years and countless imitators, this landmark still shines, although it wears its cult status modestly. The setting is intimate, on the bottom floor of a narrow Arts and Crafts-style home. Don't expect chandeliers and velvet drapes or atlas-size menus. Every night one menu fixe is served (with either a French or Italian twist), and every night it offers something different. The salads are pristinely organic—many diners say it's like tasting lettuce for the first time. Entrées may include lamb, poultry, seafood, or beef, but the kitchen is especially adept with game. The seasoning is added with a light hand, using the freshest rosemary or the most ethereal saffron broth. The best desserts are usually fruit from local farms, a simple and unadorned tartlet, or a patisserie-perfect *profiterole*. The wine list is rich in unusual French and California wines. The prix fixe rises as the week goes on, from $39 a person on Monday to $69 on the weekend. Dinner only; reservations required well in advance. ♿ (Berkeley)

CHEZ PANISSE CAFÉ
1517 Shattuck Ave.
Berkeley
510/548-5049
$$

You can say you've been to Chez Panisse without maxing out your gold card. Upstairs from the culinary landmark is the humming Café, whose kitchen operates with the same subtle philosophy as the one below. The prices are still high, but two can eat upstairs for the price of one down below. The menu changes constantly. Seafood, such as the sea bass, is always good here. Game is a specialty, such as duck breast with roasted artichokes. Dessert can be as creative as an apple and pear frangipane tart or as simple as a plate of tangerines and dates. Make reservations early (nine in the morning) on the day you intend to go. Lunch and dinner Mon-Sat. (Berkeley)

CHRISTOPHER'S
1501-A Solano Ave.
Berkeley
510/525-1668
$$

Christopher's is the latest reincarnation of one of the city's first fusion

restaurants. The new design gives you the sense of being in one enormous kitchen—you can watch cooks turn out a Mexican rock shrimp and green papaya *chimichangette*. It's doubtful you could find a more exhilarating appetizer anywhere than the smoked garlic/pepper oyster martini. The cinnamon rack of lamb is also a good bet, and the spicy Chinese lamb is even better. The dishes are all over the map, but the kitchen pulls it off. Some unusual California wines are featured. If in doubt about what to eat or drink, ask the well-informed staff—and trust their recommendations. Brunch weekends, lunch weekdays, dinner nightly. ♿ (Berkeley)

DARA
1549 Shattuck Ave.
Berkeley
510/842-2002
$

Fresh and down-to-earth, Lao cuisine is simpler and less sweet than Thai food. This cluttered and somewhat tacky, homey restaurant serves both if you'd like to compare and contrast. The seafood is good and not particularly spicy, especially the catfish in yellow curry and the prawns in red. The award-winning crunchy papaya salad is a joy. Lao desserts are great treats. Try the fried bananas in coconut sauce or fresh mangoes with sticky rice and coconut milk. In good weather, sit outside. Lunch and dinner daily. (Berkeley)

FATAPPLE'S
1346 Martin Luther King Jr. Way
Berkeley
510/526-2260
$

The University of California isn't the

Café Culture

tomato-drenched spaghetti; this one still is. Highlights include the buttery garlic bread; fresh, warm focaccia; and plenty of crusty pizzas with your choice of about 20 different toppings. The calzones are great, especially the Greek version with feta cheese. You can choose lighter dishes, but if you're going to try the pasta Alfredo or carbonara, you'd better bring your biggest appetite. The wines, appropriately enough, are pretty bold. Lunch and dinner daily. & (Berkeley)

LALIME'S
1329 Gilman St.
Berkeley
510/527-9838
www.lalimes.com
$$

Less a restaurant than a love feast, this cherished neighborhood institution attracts regulars more frequently than alumni to the Big Game. The seasonal menu is all over the map—Italian, French, Moroccan, Indian. The combinations are always inventive, such as Portobello mushroom fritters with aioli. Everything is seasoned beautifully, if a little on the light side. The kitchen is especially creative with such vegetarian dishes as brioche stuffed with smoked goat cheese and caramelized shallots. Fresh fish and pork are almost always on the menu, and you can be fairly sure of finding game here, such as smoked quail or venison. The homemade sorbets are a knockout. Dinner daily. & (Berkeley)

only institution in Berkeley. This restaurant in a quiet North Berkeley neighborhood is one, too. Located in a cool, dark, high-ceilinged room with pictures of Jack London on the walls and a trompe l'oeil library, Fatapple's serves salads and sandwiches, but the burgers draw the crowds. The one-third-pound hamburgers are the most beloved in town. At six or seven at night there can be a serious wait. If you'd rather avoid the crowd, try breakfast—all of the great pastries are made fresh in Fatapple's bakery next door. Or order take out—the entire menu is available to go. Breakfast, lunch, and dinner daily. & (Berkeley)

GIOVANNI'S
2420 Shattuck Ave.
Berkeley
510/843-6678
$$

Once upon a time, Italian restaurants were darkly lit, with checkered tablecloths and heaping plates of

LA NOTE
2377 Shattuck Ave.
Berkeley
510/843-1535
$$

Top 10 Places To Eat

By Alice Waters, owner/founder of the world-famous Chez Panisse Restaurant

1. **Berkeley Farmers Market** every Saturday (Milvia and Center) and Tuesday (Derby and Martin Luther King Jr. Way)
2. **Chez Panisse Restaurant and Café**
3. **The Cheeseboard**
4. **Café Fanny,** for breakfast and coffee
5. **Mazzini**
6. The meat market at **Café Rouge**
7. **Picante,** for their tacos and homemade tortillas
8. **Acme Bread Co.**
9. **Kermit Lynch Wine Merchant**
10. **Ajanta, Breads of India,** and **Vik's** (4th St.) for Indian food

In warm weather, when you're sitting at La Note amid the lavenders on the terrace, Berkeley could almost pass for a town along the Mediterranean. Inside this restaurant, French songs fill the air, the walls are painted the colors of Provençe, and the tables are tiny. Aptly, the food is generally southern French, but breakfast has been Americanized. For lunch, try baguette sandwiches or a fresh ratatouille; for dinner, check out the stews or seafood. Lunch and breakfast daily; dinner Fri-Sat. ♿ (Berkeley)

LONG LIFE NOODLE COMPANY AND JOOK JOINT
2261 Shattuck Ave.
Berkeley
510/845-6062
$

Jook is a kind of noodle pudding, and although in Asia they like it plain, you'll probably prefer it with ginger and tofu puffs or barbecued pork. This is just one of the noodle dishes in this spiffy downtown restaurant with high ceilings and huge windows. Although the cooks use beef, chicken, seafood, and even quail eggs, most of the 18 noodle dishes can be made for vegetarians. This spot is one of a chain whose owners are betting that noodles are the next big thing. With a place like this, they may be right. Lunch and dinner Mon-Sat. ♿ (Berkeley)

PLEARN
2050 University Ave.
Berkeley
510/841-2148
$

A lot of people here swear that Plearn has the freshest pad Thai in the Bay Area. In fact, everything that comes from their woks is recommended, as well as the remarkably light spring rolls and sharply marinated beef and duck with baby corn and pineapple. The kitchen does wonderful things with peanuts in both spicy curries and cool mint or cucumber ones. A light dessert is the Thai version of custard pudding made with taro and coconut cream. Lunch and dinner Mon-Sat. & (Berkeley)

RIVOLI
1539 Solano Ave.
Berkeley
510/526-2542
$$

Every possible square inch of charm has been squeezed into this jaunty bistro. The copper-topped bar at the entry, a lush but tiny glassed-in garden, and a menu rich in locally raised meat and produce make Rivoli a busy, reservations-recommended restaurant. Although the offerings change every three weeks, some dishes such as crisp Portobello mushroom fritters with aioli and a stellar Caesar salad are standards. Entrées are classics of California cuisine with a slight leaning toward Italy. Freshness is the mantra, whether the dish is a lightly grilled halibut or a tenderly seasoned pork loin. The star of the dessert list is the kitchen's interesting take on a hot-fudge sundae. Dinner daily. & (Berkeley)

SANTA FE BAR & GRILL
1310 University Ave.
Berkeley
510/841-4740
www.santafegrill.com

$$-$$$

A former train station, this California-style restaurant looks like a hacienda but has the feel of a supper club. Although the menu changes nightly, chances are you'll run across the garlic-roasted risotto or delicate grilled-squash pizza. Fresh salads are guaranteed; the restaurant has a lettuce and herb garden out in back. Other specialties, prepared in the gleaming wood grill and oven, include juicy pork chops, steaks, and racks of lamb. Although located on a busy stretch of University Avenue, the outside eating area is quite relaxing. Lunch weekdays, dinner nightly. & (Berkeley)

SANTA FE BISTRO
2142 Center St.
Berkeley
510/841-4047
$$

The bistro's red walls, tiled floor, and industrial lighting look smart. So do the customers—professors, and students with generous parents. More California than French, this restaurant offers an interesting selection of salads. The beef and risottos are decent, but you'd be wiser to stick with the fish or chicken. Try the tender halibut with saffron rice or the crisp and juicy spit-roasted chicken. Dessert highlights include some strikingly original homemade ice creams and sorbets. Lunch is less pricey but more crowded. At dinner the soft lights make it one of the few romantic spots downtown. Lunch and dinner daily. & (Berkeley)

SAUL'S RESTAURANT
& DELICATESSEN
1475 Shattuck Ave.
Berkeley

510/848-3354
$

A corner of Brooklyn in the heart of Berkeley? Who knew? A crowd always forms at the small deli up front, where you can take out just about anything on the menu. Classics range from thick egg creams to pickled herring, kippered salmon, and smoked fish. You might wish the pastrami and corned-beef sandwiches were a little thicker and spicier, or the matzoh-ball soup a little saltier, but the eggs with lox and onion are perfect. & (Berkeley)

VENEZIA
1799 University Ave.
Berkeley
510/849-4681
$$

Ordinarily, you might not want to eat beneath someone's laundry line. But what's hanging is mostly lingerie, and it's all part of the atmosphere here, a re-creation of a piazza near the Grand Canal. The fare is not really that Venetian or theatrical. The clams baked with oregano and Parmesan is a good starter, and *fritto misto* (mixed fried veggies) is a good choice, too. The kitchen excels with fish and chicken. The pastas are well done, too, because they're not weighted down by heavy sauces. The menu changes every week. Weekend evenings are packed; reservations recommended. Lunch and dinner daily. & (Berkeley)

BERKELEY WATERFRONT

BETTE'S OCEAN VIEW DINER
1807 Fourth St.
Berkeley
510/644-3230
$

On Sunday mornings, young, arty, academic couples who've just spent the night together line up to wait an hour or more for breakfast at this small, shiny diner, a Berkeley institution since 1982. It's American home cooking at its freshest and most comforting. Eggs come in any style; one of the fancier options is a fluffy omelet of goat cheese and croutons. The lox scramble with hash browns on the side is a winner, as are the soufflé pancakes, especially the apple-brandy ones. Breakfast is served from 6:30 until 4 every day with a slightly different menu on Sundays. Lunch consists of mostly sandwiches, from simple grilled cheese to pasilla chile chicken. The Reuben and the meatloaf are classics. Too hungry to wait? There's a Bette's Take-Out next door. You can also pick up her packaged mixes such as pancakes and scones to make at home. Breakfast and lunch daily. & (Berkeley Waterfront)

BISTRO VIOLA
1428 San Pablo Ave.
Berkeley
510/528-5030
$$

This eatery is just what the West Berkeley fog belt needed: a hearty Parisian bistro that gets better with each course. The onion soup and garlicky snails and frogs' legs are decent appetizers, but the entrées are splendid. The grilled chicken is tender, served with savory potatoes and goat cheese. A sweet, smoky beet reduction works perfectly on steak. The *frites* are thin and crisp. Classic desserts include crème brûlée and chocolate mousse, but the real prize is a sublime Gorgonzola cheese sweetened with honey and truffle oil. This cuisine may be

BERKELEY WATERFRONT

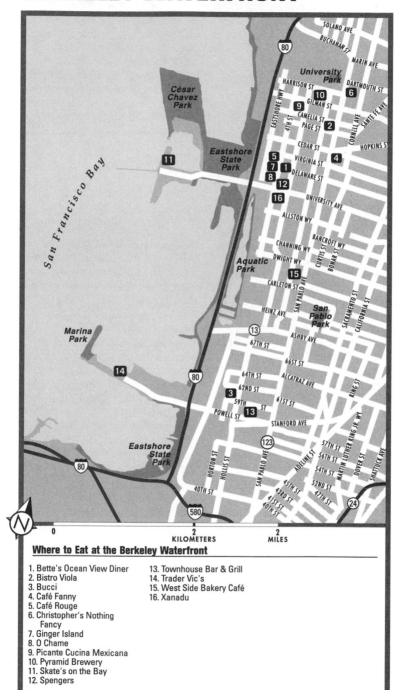

Where to Eat at the Berkeley Waterfront

1. Bette's Ocean View Diner
2. Bistro Viola
3. Bucci
4. Café Fanny
5. Café Rouge
6. Christopher's Nothing Fancy
7. Ginger Island
8. O Chame
9. Picante Cucina Mexicana
10. Pyramid Brewery
11. Skate's on the Bay
12. Spengers
13. Townhouse Bar & Grill
14. Trader Vic's
15. West Side Bakery Café
16. Xanadu

French, but don't expect an elaborate evening; the presentation is as simple as the décor. Lunch and dinner daily; brunch Sun. & (Berkeley Waterfront)

BUCCI'S
6121 Hollis St.
Emeryville
510/547-4725
$$

The designer of this Italian restaurant had a major postmodern moment with this warehouse space. You can tell by the neon wall sculptures and a pair of clear plastic Doric columns lit from within. It's wild. The menu is considerably more traditional, and the portions are generous. Among the notable dishes are the antipasti plate with its paper-thin, pungent *braseola,* and the wonderfully tender grilled chicken. The pastas are hearty and old-fashioned and come with thick tomato sauce. The best bets are the tasty thin-crust pizzas; standouts include the Timpone with fennel sausage and carbonara with pancetta in a creamy egg custard. For a really memorable dessert, try the warm bread pudding with rum-butterscotch sauce. Lunch Mon-Fri, dinner Mon-Sat. & (Berkeley Waterfront)

CAFÉ FANNY
1603 San Pablo Ave.
Berkeley
510/526-7664
$

This tiny café bar was built by Chez Panisse's founder, Alice Waters. With the aroma from the Acme bakery next door filtering in through the minimalist-style space, you might think you are in a back-road café on the Loire. Breakfast is simple and light, from buckwheat crepes to poached eggs with prosciutto. The levain toast enhances everything and makes for great sandwiches. Have an espresso and a crunchy *tuiles aux amandes* for dessert. You can stand at the bar or, better yet, sit at one of the terrace-side tables outside under an arbor (unfortunately placed adjacent to a parking lot). Breakfast and lunch daily. & (Berkeley Waterfront)

CAFÉ ROUGE
1782 Fourth St.
Berkeley
510/525-1440
$$

This open, warm, romantic, and noisy space is another favorite of Berkeley's hip-oisie in the bustling Fourth Street *quartier.* The ambiance is reminiscent of a supper club; you expect a jazz quartet to start riffing any minute. But eating is the entertainment here. Start with a selection of fresh oysters, and move on to such exceptional main courses as the golden spit-roasted chicken or the lamb braised with olives. Portions are fairly generous, for California. Desserts are decent; the vanilla citrus crème brûlée is better than most of the other selections. You could have a great time just sitting at the gleaming bar and ordering from the impressive collection of wine (try the offbeat ones from Oregon and Corsica). Many bottles are less than $20. A worldly choice of whiskies, cognacs, and grappas awaits you, too. Lunch daily, dinner Tues-Sun. & (Berkeley Waterfront)

CHRISTOPHER'S NOTHING FANCY
1019 San Pablo Ave.
Albany
510/526-1185
$

This small, cheery Mexican restaurant is not as modest as it sounds. If freshness counts, then this place has a lot to boast about. The chicken fajita salad is crisp, and the asparagus enchilada, Portobello mushroom burrito, and various wraps are light. Expect to eat your way through the lemony guacamole in record time. Try an Agua Jamaicas, a refreshing, cool hibiscus-blossom juice and wild-berry purée. A few Mexican beers are also offered. The prices are astonishingly low, considering the variety of dishes available. Open daily. ⅍ (Berkeley Waterfront)

GINGER ISLAND
1820 Fourth St.

Berkeley
510/644-0444
$$

Hey, mon, this place is the reggae of restaurants. In the heart of buzzing Fourth Street, Ginger Island celebrates the tingling pleasures of—what else?—ginger root. Take, for instance, a bona fide ginger ale, calamari in ginger sauce, and ginger cake with orange cream. The entrée menu, however, extends far beyond ginger; in fact, this restaurant offers the city's best example of Asian fusion. Try the witty variation of French fries using yam and taro, or the juicy yellowfin tuna burger. Portions are large. Check to see if they're having one of their $20 prix fixe weeks—a

The Late Show

After 10:30 the people of Berkeley and Oakland are usually at home with a good book, but a few restaurants and pubs keep their kitchens warm for you.

Au Coquelet, *2000 University, open until 1*
Ben & Nicks, *6512 College, open until 11 Thursday and Friday*
César, *1515 Shattuck, open until midnight*
Everett & Jones, *126 Broadway, open until midnight*
Giovanni's, *2420 Shattuck, open until midnight on the weekends*
Jack London Inn Coffee Shop, *444 Embarcadero West, open all night*
Mexicali Rose, *701 Clay, open until three in the morning*
Pyramid, *901 Gilman, open until midnight on weekends*
Spats, *1974 Shattuck, open until 11*
Spengers, *1919 Fourth, open until 11:30*
Sun Hong Kong, *389 Eighth, open until three in the morning*
Triple Rock, *1920 Shattuck, open until midnight*

good deal. When the weather's good, the roof rolls back and the space is transformed into a tropical festival. But even in a downpour, on a busy night it still feels like a party. Lunch and dinner daily. ♿ (Berkeley Waterfront)

O CHAME
1830 Fourth St.
Berkeley
510/841-8783
$
Hearty meals of soba and *udon* noodles entice the hip and the hungry (and budget-minded) to this soothing Japanese restaurant on trend-setting Fourth Street. It looks like an elegant cave, with its glowing lights and creamy etched walls. The food is amazingly subtle, and everything is flavored with a delicacy that demands that you slow down and taste the tender grilled shiitake, the translucent sashimi, and the light-as-air burdock root and tofu dumplings. The more expensive entrées—non-Japanese items such as steak and salmon—are treated with similar attention. A cup of warm, velvety sake goes beautifully with everything. Lunch and dinner Mon-Sat. ♿ (Berkeley Waterfront)

PICANTE COCINA MEXICANA
1328 Sixth St.
Berkeley
510/525-3121
$
Don't be intimidated by the fact that this restaurant is owned by Alice Waters's relatives. You'd never know it. The Cocina is a sprawling, cafeteria-like space with a smattering of Mexican folk art. You order your dinner—mostly popular south-of-the-border favorites—at the counter and receive a mountainous portion of food made with the freshest ingredients. And everything comes at an amazingly low price. Interesting dishes include chicken in red mole with onion cilantro relish and plenty to satisfy vegetarians or vegans. Brunch weekends, lunch, and dinner daily. ♿ (Berkeley Waterfront)

PYRAMID BREWERY
901 Gilman St.
Berkeley
510/528-9880
$-$$
This beer hall is almost German in its proportions, but its architecture is pure high-tech cool. The lighting is wild. Huge portions are the rule; examples include the hefty burgers on sourdough and the fish and chips. You can eat happily on appetizers, including jalapeño poppers and crispy onion rings—or just drink beer. The actual Pyramid Brewery, where 10 different ales are brewed, is on the other side of the restaurant's wall-length window. If you're curious, you can take

TIP

Hallelujah!—it's brunch. Sundays from 10 to 4, Geoffrey's Inner Circle (410 14th Street) throws a gospel brunch with a soul-food buffet and either recorded or live gospel singers. The price is just $17 a person.

one of the twice-daily tours of the brewery. Lunch and dinner daily; open until midnight on weekends. 🛇 (Berkeley Waterfront)

SKATE'S ON THE BAY
100 Seawall Dr.
Berkeley
510/549-1900
$$-$$$

Sometimes those big, corporate restaurants get it right. Named after the skate fish (which no longer survives in the bay), this cousin of Kincaid's in Jack London Square offers considerably more than a dead-on dazzling view of the Golden Gate. The housemade focaccia is addictive. The fish is fresh and imaginatively presented. The barbecued salmon is a standout, and the trout is perfectly matched with salsa. The kitchen offers a fine apple-wood-grilled steak, but as long as you're on the water, opt for the apple-wood-grilled Dungeness crab. Speaking of water views, you can't reserve a window table. But you can wait for one if you hang out in the bar, which, by the way, has the same amazing view. Lunch and dinner daily. 🛇 (Berkeley Waterfront)

SPENGER'S
1914 Fourth St.
Berkeley
510/845-7771
$-$$

Now in its second century, this beloved and huge (600-seat) seafood restaurant went belly up briefly but was brought back to life by Portland's McCormick and Schmick's. The new owners have retained the woody maze of dining rooms, nautical doodad decorations, and a few menu items familiar to the generations of Cal alumni who made a tra-

dition of eating here. Two favorites: deep-fried shrimp and captain's platter with tartar sauce. Portions are still generous, but the fish is more reliably fresh, especially the locally netted cod, king salmon, and sand dabs. Dessert highlights are the chocolate truffle cake and the three-berry cobbler. Reservations suggested. Lunch and dinner daily. 🛇 (Berkeley Waterfront)

TOWNHOUSE BAR & GRILL
5862 Doyle St.
Emeryville
510/652-6151
$$

Emeryville, before it became a high-tech hit, was a tough, scrappy town. This building was a bootlegger's hangout, and at least on the exterior still looks ramshackle. Inside are funky French antique tables with white tablecloths, and a menu that's quintessential Californian. The garlic fries, the cornmeal-crusted calamari, and the chicken salad with blue cheese and apples literally kick off a meal. Steak with green peppercorn sauce and potatoes with Gorgonzola prove the kitchen isn't holding back on seasonings. The pastas are all outstanding. Live jazz is featured on Thursday nights. Weekends get crowded and reservations are recommended. Lunch and dinner Mon-Sat. (Berkeley Waterfront)

TRADER VIC'S
9 Anchor Dr.
Emeryville
510/653-3400
$$-$$$

Yes, *that* Trader Vic's—the place your grandparents used to go to for bizarre tropical drinks with little umbrellas poking out of them. This one survives and thrives on the rim of the bay. You can still get those drinks with South Sea pirate names such as Scorpion, Black Widow, and Potted Parrot. All of the wooden tiki statues and nautical memorabilia remain in place. The menu is generic Chinese—lots of sweet-and-sour sauces—with a few exceptions. The management seems unable to restrain itself when it names menu items—take, for instance, the name of the oyster and spinach soup: Bongo Bongo. Unfortunately, a marina right in front blocks much of the bridge view. Lunch and dinner daily. & (Berkeley Waterfront)

WEST SIDE BAKERY CAFÉ
2570 Ninth St.
Berkeley
510/845-4852
$
If you don't have the time to wait for brunch at Rick and Ann's or Bette's Ocean View Diner, you'll have better luck finding a table here. You'll still have to wait, at least on Sunday mornings, but not as long. A big winner in their breakfast popularity contest is the Norteno plate—scrambled eggs with black beans and sausage. The oatmeal is their own recipe and is more tempting than plain-old oats when mixed with apple juices, bananas, and oranges. The kitchen also offers an intriguing array of pancakes, including cornmeal-apple and banana-blueberry. They do a lot of interesting things with tofu, too. Lunch consists of mostly hot and cold sandwiches and some pasta dishes. And you can order from the deli to take out. Breakfast and lunch daily. & (Berkeley Waterfront)

XANADU
700 University Ave.
Berkeley
510/548-7880
$$
Think Orson Welles in Shanghai. This restaurant is easily Berkeley's greatest stage set, with silvery, shimmering walls and endless museum-level Chinese furnishings. The clever food is Chinese/Thai/Indian fusion and is dished out with medical advice. The lemongrass pepper chicken is said to "relieve flatulence." The garlic-roasted oysters are "good for the loins." Desserts are particularly inventive. An evening here is like a long, sophisticated, seductive wink. Lunch and dinner daily. & (Berkeley Waterfront)

SOUTH BERKELEY/ NORTH OAKLAND

ASMARA
5020 Telegraph Ave.
Oakland
510/547-5100
$
Berbere sauce, made from chili peppers fermented in olive oil for up to 45 days, is prepared at its seductive best in this Ethiopian/Eritrean restaurant in the cooler-by-the-minute Temescal neighborhood. The beef, chicken, and lamb are outstanding, but vegetarians can find an astonishing variety here, too. Honey is a big draw—traditional honey-wine is available, as well as a small assortment of honey and fruit desserts. The décor is lightly ethnic with handcrafted screens and native textiles. Lunch and dinner daily. & (South Berkeley/North Oakland)

SOUTH BERKELEY/NORTH OAKLAND

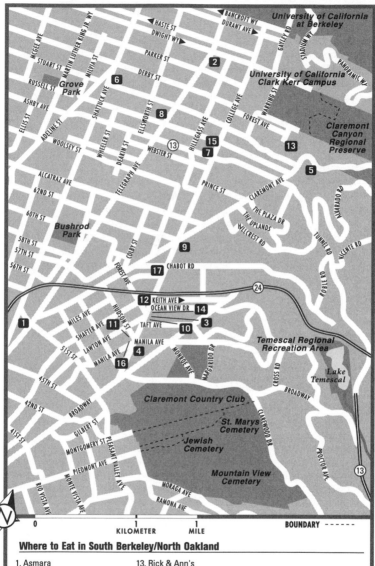

Where to Eat in South Berkeley/North Oakland

1. Asmara
2. Blue Nile
3. Citron
4. Garibaldi's
5. Jordans
6. Kirala
7. La Mediterranee
8. Mazzini
9. Nan Yang
10. Nava
11. Obelisque
12. Oliveto
13. Rick & Ann's
14. Rockridge Café
15. Shen Hua
16. Uzen
17. Zachary's

BLUE NILE
2525 Telegraph Ave.
Berkeley
510/540-6777
$

Forget about forks and spoons. You can enjoy the Ethiopian cuisine in this perennially popular restaurant by scooping everything up with the crisp, unleavened bread called *injera*. The smart way to introduce yourself to this kind of cooking is to order either the meat or vegetarian sampler plates and dip everything into *berbere* sauce. The menu indicates the heat quotient of each dish. Yogurt helps cool down some of the more tongue-curling spices. The setting is quite exotic, with bamboo filtering thin streams of light. Lunch Tue-Sat; dinner Tue-Sun. ঙ (South Berkeley/North Oakland)

CITRON
5484 College Ave.
Oakland
510/653-5484
$$-$$$

Citron prides itself on preparing dishes that are fresh and simply French. The problem in recommending anything is that the restaurant also prides itself on the fact that it rarely, if ever, repeats dishes. In the winter the menu has a distinctly Alsatian feel, with hearty beef stews. In the spring and summer you're more likely to find lamb and seafood with a Provençal touch. It's one of the area's handsomest restaurants, a tailored Parisian boîte humming with soft jazz. Request a table in the back garden when weather permits. Reservations highly recommended. For the budget-conscious, a prix fixe meal is available. Dinner nightly. ঙ (South Berkeley/North Oakland)

DOUG'S BAR-B-Q
3600 San Pablo Ave.
Emeryville
510/655-9048
$

Doug cooked on the rodeo circuit for such folks as Roy Rogers and Gene Autry, using barbecue recipes he grew up on while living near the Louisiana-Texas border. He uses these same recipes at his take-out spot, which he opened 20 years ago. This barbecue is the real stuff: The sauce is sweet and smoky, and you can order it in mild, medium, or incendiary. You can also buy jars to take home. The sauce juices up crusty ribs and great chicken—even a goat if you come in on the right day. Doug's also has special sweet-potato pie, banana pudding, and peach cobbler, all made fresh. Open daily 11-9. ঙ (South Berkeley/North Oakland)

GARIBALDI'S
5356 College Ave.
Oakland
510/595-4000
$$

Historically speaking, this sleek and inviting place made its mark as the restaurant that brought valet parking to the East Bay. It's huge, but it feels intimate, with floor-to-ceiling drapes marking off the eating areas. The lighting may be the most flattering in town. The menu is California and seasonal, but you can always expect to find asparagus with pancetta, rich house-cured olives, a creamy risotto, and crispy chicken roasted in the wood oven. The kitchen experiments with lots of North African, Mexican, and Thai seasonings, modified for local tastes. Few wines cost less than $30, but an eclectic selection is offered. Lunch Mon-Fri; dinner nightly. ♿ (South Berkeley/North Oakland)

JORDAN'S
41 Tunnel Rd.
Oakland
510/843-3000
$$$

The corporation that bought the Claremont Hotel continues to fiddle with the concept of their main restaurant here. What they can't change is the million-dollar view of San Francisco, which glitters outside the windows along the entire west wall. Window seats, however, are never guaranteed. Although it's generally pricey hotel food, the chefs try to meet the standards of the best local restaurants with a menu that is mostly California with some Pacific Rim influences. This resort offers spa-influenced meals without butter or saturated fats. Breakfast, lunch, and dinner daily; brunch Sun. ♿ (South Berkeley/North Oakland)

KIRALA
2100 Ward St.
Berkeley
510/549-3486
$-$$

Berkeley and Oakland are teeming with Japanese restaurants, but this unassuming spot at the southern edge of downtown Berkeley seems to be the people's choice. Customers line up around the corner from the minute it opens. The sushi is remarkably fresh and there are 47 varieties to choose from, a highlight being the tender bonito. Surprisingly, Kirala does just as well with their *robata* grilled items, from steak and scallops to kebabs and tofu. Sit at the counter and watch the kitchen in action. Lunch Tue-Fri; dinner daily. ♿ (South Berkeley/North Oakland)

LA MEDITERRANEE
2936 College Ave.
Berkeley
510/540-7773
$

A little Greek, a little Lebanese, a little Armenian—this restaurant is a venerated Berkeley institution. A few tables are situated on the sidewalk; if the weather's nice, you should wait to get one and check out the intense hobnobbing. Steamed eggs with spicy sausage is about as ethnic as breakfast gets. Lunch and dinner offer mild versions of hummus, tabbouleh, dolmas, and kebabs. The house specialty is phyllo pastry stuffed with chicken, beef, or spinach with feta. Breakfast, lunch, and dinner daily. ♿ (Berkeley)

MAZZINI
2826 Telegraph Ave.

The Gingerbread House

Karena Dacker

Berkeley
510/848-5599
$$

Love of anything authentically Italian, especially light Tuscan cooking, has reached epidemic proportions in Berkeley. Don't even think about trying to get into this eatery without reservations. The menu changes seasonally, but you can always find the lemony *fritto misto* and excellent fish and chicken from the wood-burning oven. If you are looking for heavy pastas drowned in thick tomato sauce, forget about it. All of their housemade ice creams are excellent. The *panna cotta* is even better. A short but stellar wine selection features vintages from many regions of northern Italy. Lunch and dinner daily. & (South Berkeley/North Oakland)

NAN YANG
6048 College Ave.
Berkeley
510/655-3298
$

Burmese food is somewhere between Chinese and Thai and generally pretty mild. A great place to be introduced to it is at Nan Yang, a modern and minimal restaurant decorated with a few small, glittering tapestries. Start off with the delicately balanced and beautifully presented ginger salad. The green papaya salad is also an excellent choice. Other highlights are the chicken coconut noodle soup and the golden curry noodle soup. The five-spice chicken sounds elaborate but tastes quite simple. A velvety tapioca is a wonderful end to the meal. Lunch and dinner Tue-Sun. (South Berkeley/North Oakland)

NAVA
5478 College Ave.
Oakland
510/655-4770
$$

When Nava opened a few years ago, its cuisine was upscale Southwestern and its decor was kind of French Santa Fe. The ambiance is mainly the same now, but the menu has drifted west to California and pan-Asian. You can still get a small tower of crab cakes with chipotle aioli, but you're more likely to find halibut with ginger or chicken breast with sun-dried tomato sauce. Items change frequently. When the weather turns nice, request a table in the trellised terrace out back. Dinner Tue-Sun. & (South Berkeley/North Oakland)

OBELISQUE
5421 College Ave.
Oakland
510/923-9691
$$

Dreams of five-star ratings were in the air when this smartly updated restaurant first opened awhile back. But the menu was half in French, and locals balked at $30 entrées. It's been scaled back, yet the commitment to beautifully prepared food remains. Every five weeks the menu changes; if they are serving the paper-crisp duck confit, don't miss it. The kitchen excels at seafood, especially the calamari salad, and tends to be more generous with sauces than at other California-style restaurants. A short but adventurous wine list is available. Ask about their three-course prix fixe dinner, a bargain at $25. Lunch and dinner daily. & (South Berkeley/North Oakland)

OLIVETO
5655 College Ave.
Oakland
510/547-5356
$$-$$$

Showered with culinary awards, this unpretentious restaurant is another believer in Chez Panisse's gospel of absolute freshness and simplicity. Still, their restraint with seasoning can lead to dishes best described as Quaker Italian. They are certainly ambitious, changing menus weekly, daily, and seasonally, and bringing in celebrated chefs from around the world for special evenings. A good bet is anything from the rotisserie, such as tender arista pork. If you want the experience without the price tag, try the more casual café downstairs, especially crunchy thin-crusted Napolitano pizza. Downstairs is open from seven in the morning every day. Upstairs is dinner only, and it's best to reserve at least a week in advance. & (South Berkeley/North Oakland)

RICK AND ANN'S
2922 Domingo Ave.
Berkeley
510/649-8538
$

Set your alarm and get going early if you want to beat the crowds queuing up for the hearty weekend brunches at this cozy place located just below the Claremont Hotel. They don't take reservations and, after nine, the wait can be up to an hour. Everything is fresh and straightforward, and the specials change daily. The home fries and hash with green onions and sour cream are great. The potato-cheese pancakes taste like they're fresh from a farm kitchen. The lunch and dinners are all-American,

from burgers to macaroni and cheese, but breakfast is king. The restaurant has a take-out deli and bakery next door. Breakfast and lunch daily; dinner Wed-Sun. & (South Berkeley/North Oakland)

ROCKRIDGE CAFÉ
5492 College Ave.
Oakland
510/653-1567
$

College Avenue is going upscale, but this bustling joint is a tasty reminder of simpler days. The prices are sane and a great balance is maintained between all-American fare and some more inventive breakfast dishes, including scrambled eggs with smoked salmon, tomato, and onion, served with Bruce Aidell chicken-and-apple sausages on the side. For lunch, try the 6- to 12-ounce juicy burgers or one of the sandwiches. Dinner specials include artichoke calzone or a thick savory cassoulet. Try a fresh-baked olallieberry pie for dessert. Breakfast, lunch, and dinner daily. & (South Berkeley/North Oakland)

SHEN HUA
2914 College Ave.
Berkeley
510/883-1777
$

Addicts of *mu shu,* those delicate, hand-rolled Chinese pancakes, will have a field day here. Six varieties are available. The whole menu definitely leans toward ginger and a wide selection of spicy dishes, such as a searing Kung Pao beef or steamed fish. Winter melon soup with seafood is pure Chinese comfort food, as is the nori seafood soup. Plenty of options are provided for vegetarians, such as Szechuan-

Trouble Brewing

If you want to gather an angry crowd in Berkeley, just announce that you're putting a Starbucks in their neighborhood. The three current stores were the cause of much late-night haranguing at the City Zoning Adjustment Board. The Claremont neighborhood was the only area that successfully repelled the incursion of corporate coffee. Berkeley has its own home-brewed favorite, Peets, established in 1966 and now boasting 46 outlets itself. In fact, Jerry Baldwin, Peets' owner, was one of the three co-founders of Starbucks. Peets gained national notoriety when Judge Lance Ito drank it during the O. J. Simpson trial.

style tofu served in a clay pot. The restaurant is situated in a startlingly beautiful, wide-open space, pared down with golden sponged walls. Lunch Mon-Sat; dinner daily. ♿ (South Berkeley/North Oakland)

UZEN
5415 College Ave.
Oakland
510/654-7753
$-$$

It's instantly clear why this bright wedge of a sushi restaurant is wildly popular. The high-tech Japanese design and menu with dishes hard to find anywhere else are both intriguing. Entrées are available raw, deep fried, or barbecued. The sashimi salads, such as salmon and scallops with seaweed, are incredibly fresh. Steaming *udon* noodles come with a bowl full of goodies, including a sushi omelet. Try the aromatic steamed egg custard with shrimp, chicken, and shiitake. If you are dining with a party of four or more on the weekend, reservations are definitely recommended. Lunch Mon-Fri; dinner Mon-Sat. ♿ (South Berkeley/North Oakland)

ZACHARY'S
5801 College Ave.
Oakland
510/655-6385
$$

In early evening the entryway here is packed tighter than the 6:15 BART train, and it's easy to see why. Zachary's award-winning Chicago-style pizzas are pizza pies. You can have them with thinner crusts or "stuffed" with a second crust topping. The spinach and mushroom pizza—a big seller in this vegetarian town—is practically a lasagna. And the chicken pizza is moister than most. Bring your appetite and your patience. These pizzas can take 45 minutes to get to your table. Open daily from 11 a.m. A second Zachary's is located at

153 Solano Avenue. ♿ (South Berkeley/North Oakland).

OAKLAND

AUTUMN MOON
3909 Grand Ave.
Oakland
510/595-3200
$$

It only sounds Chinese. Autumn Moon is a quintessential American/ Irish/Jewish neighborhood hangout. This kind of restaurant has special feasts on both St. Patrick's Day and Passover. You can get crisp iceberg lettuce drenched in blue cheese or a not-too-salty matzoh ball soup. The menu ranges from homey favorites, such as the great, juicy hamburger, to the almost exotic, such as the tender red snapper with sweet ginger chutney. A popular brunch is served Saturday and Sunday, but lunch fare is mostly relegated to sandwiches. When the weather is nice, ask for a table on the deck. ♿ (Oakland)

BATTAM BANG
850 Broadway
Oakland
510/839-8815
$-$$

Anyone who hasn't been seduced by the lure of lemongrass, coconut milk, tamarind, and peanuts should stop resisting right now and head directly to this simple but elegant Cambodian restaurant on the edge of Oakland's Chinatown. The sweet dishes, such as the golden chicken soup with a soupçon of pineapple, are the best, whereas creamy meals, such as the curried scallops in coconut milk, are refreshing. The restaurant isn't large but the menu

is, offering more than 100 items, including a whole page of vegetarian choices. Ask the helpful waitstaff for suggestions. Open every day but Sunday. ♿ (Oakland)

BAY WOLF
3853 Piedmont Ave.
Oakland
510/ 655-6004
$$

A more modest Oakland cousin of the celebrated Chez Panisse, Bay Wolf has had its own loyal following for years. Set in a dusky Arts and Crafts-style home, the restaurant transforms the freshest local ingredients into wonderfully subtle and original Italian dishes. The menus change every three weeks to feature cuisine from a different region of Italy, but the signature mainstay ingredient is duck, which makes its way into a velvety flan appetizer or an entrée such as crisp duck with lentils, pecans, and oranges. The wine list is short, international, and surprisingly reasonable. Desserts, such as the silken chocolate malt *pot de crème,* are all standouts. Lunch weekdays. ♿(Oakland)

CAFFE 817
817 Washington St.
Oakland
510/271-7965
$

A small, modish slice of Milan, Caffe 817 is easily the best place for lunch in downtown Oakland. Its selection of salads, sandwiches, and pasta is not extensive, but all choices are impeccably prepared. Even if it's not on the menu, try your luck and ask for the chestnut pasta with chanterelles. If that's a no-go, try any of the terrific sandwiches made with Acme bread, with

DOWNTOWN OAKLAND

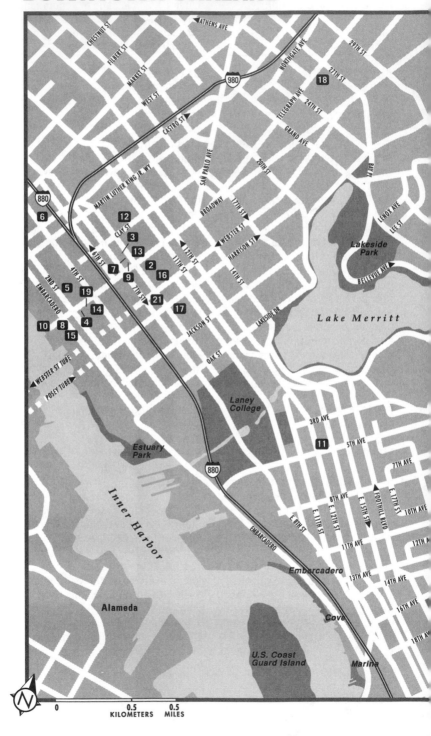

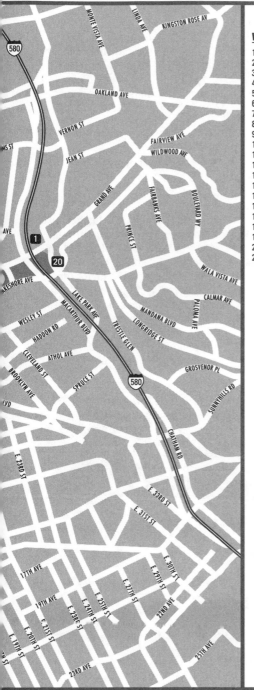

Where to Eat in Downtown Oakland

1. Autumn Moon
2. Battam Bang
3. Caffe 817
4. Everett & Jones BBQ
5. Fat Lady
6. Gingerbread House
7. Gulf Coast Grill & Bar
8. Hahn's Hibachi
9. Jade Villa
10. Kincaid's Bayhouse
11. La Estrellita Café & Bar
12. Le Cheval
13. Oaktown Café
14. Oakland Grill
15. Old Spaghetti Factory
16. Peony
17. Phnom Penh House
18. San Won Kai Bi
19. Soizic
20. Spettro
21. Vi's Vietnamese

BOUNDARY - - - - - -

sweetly marinated olives on the side. The espresso, as you'd expect, is excellent. Have some with a breakfast array of eggs with polenta or chorizo. The short but well-chosen list of Italian wines features a refreshing Trentino. Open Mon-Fri 7:30-5, Sat 9:30-4. ﹠ (Oakland)

EVERETT & JONES BBQ
126 Broadway
Oakland
510/663-2350
$

Neither Cajun nor Creole, the unique kind of Louisiana barbecue featured here comes from recipes inherited from the owner's grandmother. It's a wide, light, jumpin' restaurant that's part loft, part country store. The menus are adorned with praise from Whoopi Goldberg, the Pointer Sisters, and local sportscaster-elder statesman, John Madden. The portions are massive by California standards, and you can choose sauces ranging from mild to incendiary.

Grandma's gook marinade gives the slow-cooled beef a crisp crust but keeps it tender inside. The pork ribs are a standout, and the beef links are made daily in the kitchen. You may want to sit at the bar just to try the bongo stools. Live blues is played on weekend nights. A smaller version is located in Berkeley at 1955 San Pablo Avenue. ﹠ (Oakland)

FAT LADY
201 Washington St.
Oakland
510/645-4996
$$

The lady is not only fat but also naked, and her veiled portrait hangs in the bar of this small, dark, high-testosterone steak, seafood, and pasta restaurant. The décor recalls a cluttered Victorian bordello, but with stained-glass beer ads. The food is straightforward. Go for the juicy, charbroiled 8- to 10-ounce Fat Lady burger. The 16-ounce New York steak is a formidable challenge for

Everett & Jones BBQ serves up Louisiana barbecue

Karena Dacker

carnivores. Occasionally, the kitchen pulls off a fresh idea, such as Pork Porterhouse glazed with calvados and grilled Granny Smith apples. Lunch and dinner are served daily; on Saturday and Sunday they dish out a terrific and unusually elaborate breakfast. (Oakland)

GINGERBREAD HOUSE
741 Fifth St.
Oakland
510/444-7373
$$-$$$

This restaurant, seemingly straight out of a storybook, is located on an unlikely strip between the BART tracks and Interstate 880. The three dining rooms are densely decorated with gingerbread knickknacks—the dream of the obviously obsessed owner, Mrs. Robinson. Fortunately, she is equally obsessed with providing an extraordinary menu, which contains a treasure trove of her family's Cajun-Creole recipes. The smoked-spiced salmon with melon appetizer is a standout. The deeply smoked prime rib is palatably spicy. As you'd expect, the jambalaya and spice-baked catfish are excellent. Dessert is where the gingerbread theme comes alive, especially in the rich ginger cake. The prices are on the high side, but no other East Bay restaurant matches its folkloric theatricality. Enjoy a lovely Sunday breakfast in the glass gazebo. Lunch and dinner Tue-Sat. ♿ (Oakland)

GULF COAST GRILL & BAR
736 Washington St.
Oakland
510/836-3663
$

In the heart of Old Oakland, this unpretentious storefront restaurant is a mecca for fans of Creole and soul food. The staff treats you like family and seems concerned if you're not eating enough, although the portions are generous. The jambalaya has a nice kick. Other specialties hot from the oven include tender Cajun catfish and smoked chicken. Make sure you try the cornbread and the delicious, old-fashioned homemade desserts. Open for lunch every day; dinner Fri-Sun; bountiful buffet on Sun. ♿ (Oakland)

HAHN'S HIBACHI
63 Jack London Square
Oakland
510/628-0717
$

This Korean barbecue is for hipsters. The restaurant sports trendy pale blonde wood and whimsical lighting, and the noise level is shattering. But its strength is in its marinade, the hickory-scented sauce on the large portions of tender barbecued ribs, chops, and chicken. The Korean accent is minimal, although you can order a steaming bowl of *chopchae,* the hearty noodle soup. Several seafood and vegetable tempuras are served as well. Hahn's is one of the few restaurants in Jack London Square that has at least a little outdoor seating. Lunch and dinner Mon-Sat. ♿ (Oakland)

JADE VILLA
800 Broadway
Oakland
510/839-1688
$-$$

If you have a hard time making decisions, this sprawling (400-seat) Cantonese restaurant, which offers 40 kinds of dim sum and 140 items,

GREATER OAKLAND

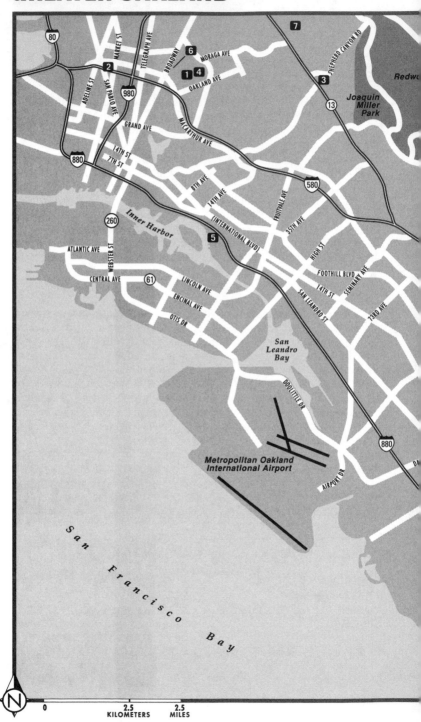

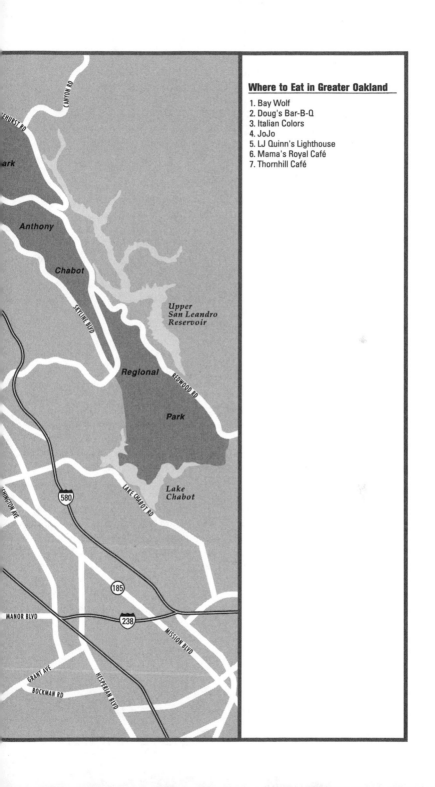

Where to Eat in Greater Oakland

1. Bay Wolf
2. Doug's Bar-B-Q
3. Italian Colors
4. JoJo
5. LJ Quinn's Lighthouse
6. Mama's Royal Café
7. Thornhill Café

may be too much for you. It's hard to go wrong sticking with traditional favorites such as crispy fried prawns, spicy Mongolian beef, sweet lemon chicken, or one of Jade Villa's signature dishes—goat meat in a clay pot. Try the sautéed calamari with chives or mu shu seafood, the Chinese version of wraps. If you're going with the seafood, then you can see for yourself that your fish is fresh: a big tank of live sturgeon, crab, and lobster is kept right in the restaurant. & (Oakland)

JOJO
3859 Piedmont Ave.
Oakland
510/985-3003
$$

Piedmont Avenue is becoming the East Bay's newest restaurant row. This warm, glowing bistro recently moved into the space next door to the venerable Bay Wolf. It boasts an impeccable pedigree, its cooks/owners having previously worked at Chez Panisse and Oliveto's. The food is simple, elegant French that's not too rich or heavy on the cream. The menu changes constantly to take advantage of the Bay Area's freshest produce, meat, and seafood. Portions are not large, but the cooking is quite skillful. Specialties include perfectly braised duck leg with duck sausage, and aromatic sautéed scallops with calvados and apples. Desserts are outstanding. If you're lucky, JoJo may be serving the tangerine ice cream *profiteroles.* Dinner only. (Oakland)

KINCAID'S BAYHOUSE
70 Jack London Square
Oakland
510/835-8600
$$-$$$

If you owned an 80-foot cruiser, this is what your yacht club would look like. The interior wood paneling gleams like brass, and every seat has a serene view of the estuary. Be sure to order the irresistible scallion pan bread. Then start your meal off with an unapologetically old-fashioned blue-cheese salad. Most of the menu is upscale surf 'n' turf, but the kitchen has come up with some fresh twists. Grilled trout with salsa works well, but the chefs went overboard with halibut in raspberry-garlic sauce. The 18-ounce T-bone steak is a good choice for landlubbers. The short beer list offers several international brews, but the wines are mostly from California. Dinner daily. Lunch Sun. & (Oakland)

LA ESTRELLITA CAFÉ & BAR
446 E. 12th Ave.
Oakland
510/465-7188
$

Tequila, anyone? This Mexican restaurant a few blocks east of Lake Merritt has 60 brands of the agave-derived liquor. On the food front, the dishes are fairly familiar, such as quesadillas and burritos, but many choices are offered. The appetizers number at least 18, including the crisp, deep-fried calamari strips. If you feel like venturing farther afield from the Mexican standards, try the sweet chicken mole, in which chicken is sautéed in peanut butter, peppers, and chocolate. Or have your first dish of eggs with cactus. Lunch and dinner daily. & (Oakland)

LE CHEVAL
1007 Clay St.

Oakland
510/763-8957
$-$$
Saigon cuisine, if done right, subtly balances Asian spices with French finesse. And Le Cheval's deft handling of Saigon cuisine draws diners nightly into this warehouse space on the western edge of Old Oakland. You can order five-course shrimp or seven-course beef feasts that provide a combination of the requisite Vietnamese five flavors-plain, salty, bitter, sweet, and sour. Appetizers include roasted quail, shrimp in translucent rolls, and sharply seasoned mussels; the only thing that could be more tempting than these items is the delicious array of dipping sauces that accompany them. The soups are special, particularly the creamy carrot chowder. Ginger abounds, especially in the sweet lemongrass chicken. Even the vegetables, such as perfectly cooked beans in garlic sauce, are outstanding. Dinner nightly. Lunch weekdays. ♿ (Oakland)

LJ QUINN'S LIGHTHOUSE
51 Embarcadero Cove
Oakland
510/536-2050
$$
Of all the boisterous bars and grills on the Oakland Estuary, this former lighthouse seems the most authentic. It has all the required paraphernalia, wooden beams, and beery memorabilia covering every spare inch. The menu is all over the place, ranging from jambalayas to ostrich burgers. Most of it is deep-fried, the way they do it at Fisherman's Wharf on the other side of the bay. But there is a nice choice of pastas, and the prime rib is juicy. Quinn's is at its liveliest Thursday nights,

when the S.O.B.s take the stage and sing sea chanties. Speaking of the sea, you get free mooring when you dock your boat for Saturday or Sunday brunch. ♿ (Oakland)

MAMA'S ROYAL CAFÉ
4012 Broadway
Oakland
510/547-7600
$
The restaurant is old and full of charmingly tacky art, aging wooden booths, and kitschy aprons. The customers are young grad students and professionals who line up down the block for fresh breakfasts and lunches. Eighteen omelets are listed on the menu, but 22 other ingredients are available if you want to customize your dish. Portions are hearty, and the toast, using Acme bread, is great. Some nouveau-California touches are added, such as poached eggs with prosciutto and chicken maple-wood sausage. Breakfast daily; lunch weekdays. ♿ (Oakland)

OAKLAND GRILL
Third & Franklin Sts.
Oakland
510/835-1175
$
Every morning the owner of this old-fashioned café walks outside to pick fruits and vegetables for the day. He has no garden, but he's surrounded by a couple of square blocks of produce warehouses. The streets are jammed with trucks just in from the Central Valley, unloading the season's best. The breakfast menu is nothing fancy, but eggs Benedict are a favorite. You can also try the crepes and 14 kinds of omelets, which use the freshly selected produce. You can even order yours

"*ono yoko*," with egg whites only. Lunches are all-American, such as BLTs and French-dip sandwiches. A special dinner appetizer is beer-battered zucchini. Prices go up slightly for entrées like chicken Marsala, but it's still a good buy. The possible move of the local produce mart means this restaurant may be gone in a few years. Breakfast, lunch, and dinner daily. & (Oakland)

OAKTOWN CAFÉ
499 Ninth St.
Oakland
510/763-4999
$
This glowing, uncluttered, loft-like space in the heart of Old Oakland is basically a lunch place, although it also serves brunch and dinner. The restaurant should be acknowledged for its attempts to come up with some inventive dishes, but it is most successful with pizzas. Highly recommended are the four-onion pizza and the smoky butternut squash, bacon, thyme, and Fontina cheese pie. All of the pizzas are also available as calzones, served with fresh ricotta. If you're hankering for hearty classics, Oaktown has those, too, including meatloaf, roasted chicken, and hamburgers. Lunch daily; dinner Fri; brunch Sat. & (Oakland)

OLD SPAGHETTI FACTORY
62 Jack London Square
Oakland
510/893-0222
$
When you arrive at this wild, over-the-top culinary homage to Victoriana, ask for a table in the cable car, which is set in the middle of the restaurant. The kids will love it, and so will the adults. A stained-glass peacock adorns one whole wall, and the lounges are covered in rich velvets. You'll easily be able to afford to feed a family on such hearty Italian fare as spaghetti with meatballs, baked lasagna, or fettuccine Alfredo. Italian sodas are a fresh alternative to colas. Whatever you choose, make sure you order the buttery garlic-cheese bread. A chocolate mud pie may not be Italian, but it's a perfect dessert. Lunch and dinner daily. & (Oakland)

PEONY
388 Ninth St.
Oakland
510/286-8866
$-$$
Within the Pacific Renaissance Plaza building in Chinatown is a mall called the Oakland Asian Cultural Center, which houses the Peony. This huge, almost elegant, Hong Kong-style restaurant is where local families choose to have big celebrations, and they fill most of the tables. The extensive but not overwhelming menu offers a choice of more than 20 types of dim sum. A full dinner menu is also offered, with a lot of traditional dishes as well as some surprises, such as the catfish casserole. Seven dishes, most of them vegetarian, are served in clay pots. Lunch and dinner daily. & (Oakland)

PHNOM PENH HOUSE
251 Eighth St.
Oakland
510//893-3852
$
A block or two from the mobbed sidewalks of Chinatown, this serene restaurant lets you slow down and savor the essence of Cambodia. Some interesting pieces of folk art

decorate the room, but the highlight, of course, is the cuisine. Phnom Penh has introduced a lot of locals to such special dishes as chicken with banana blooms, beef in creamy peanut sauce, and eggplant stuffed with shrimp and pork. Many of these dishes come with a smooth chile, pineapple, and lemon sauce. Finish your meal with one of the unique desserts, including deep-fried banana in coconut-sesame ice cream. Open daily. ♿ (Oakland)

SAM WON KAI BI
2600 Telegraph Ave.
Oakland
510/834-5727
$-$$

On a forlorn block of Telegraph Avenue—the old Sears building sits abandoned across the street—is one of Oakland's best Korean barbecue restaurants. To experience an authentic meal, ask for a table with its own grill. From there you can enjoy firsthand the aroma of the deep, hickory-scented sauce that wonderfully accompanies the short ribs and chicken. Among the other offerings are several soups and entrées. Try the hearty *croaken.* The traditional buckwheat noodles are available in either cold salads or hot dishes. A side of sharp-tasting *kim chee,* the Korean national coleslaw, is served with every dish. Open daily. ♿ (Oakland)

SOIZIC
300 Broadway
Oakland
510/251-8100
$$

The scruffy Oakland *arrondissement* on lower Broadway is an unlikely place to find a Parisian bistro. But here it is, romantic and elegant, impeccably presenting mostly classic French cuisine. Similar to many East Bay restaurants, though, Soizic's fare is characterized by an Asian accent and many highly inventive touches. The mussels with fennel in saffron cream sauce is a beautifully understated appetizer. Soizic's signature dish is the salmon with soy-sake sauce. Another favorite is the rib-eye steak served with mustard sauce, stilton cheese, and pistachios. If you want to eat a bit more lightly, the kitchen offers large entrée salads, including the elaborate warm duck confit with bacon, red cabbage, and poached pears. You should try their luscious pear tart topped with white-pepper ice cream, if only to say you experienced it. Lunch Tue-Fri, dinner Tue-Sun. ♿ (Oakland)

SPETTRO
3355 Lakeshore Ave.
Oakland
510/465-8320
$$

This will probably be your first experience at a restaurant with an Italian Halloween theme—appropriately enough because *spettro* means "ghost" in Italian. Kids will love it. A skeleton hangs outside the front door, and one of the interior walls is lined with photos from Oakland cemeteries. When you sit down to order, you're in for more, though less frightening, surprises. This home-style restaurant features food marked by California, Italian, Thai, and Mexican influences. The pan-seared coconut-lime mussels or the goat cheese and blueberry salad make sparkling starters. The wildly diverse entrées range from braised tofu and sweet-onion chicken to alligator gumbo and eggplant lasagna.

Eating Out

Pack a picnic for lunch under the shady oaks of Tilden Park. **Genoa Deli** (5095 Telegraph) makes the heftiest sandwiches and the creamiest potato salad. **Made to Order** (1576 Hopkins) has deeply fragrant cold lemon soup. **Le Poulet** (1685 Shattuck) does roast chicken five ways; their best is with chile and garlic. The cold salad cases at the **Pasta Shop** at Market Hall and Fourth Street display exotica such as beets with lemon. Even supermarkets carry the East Bay's Parisian-level bakers like Semifreddi, Grace, Acme, and Arizmendi, whose unusual Italian breads go way beyond baguettes. Haute patisserie desserts can be picked up at **La Farine** (6323 College) and **Masse's** (1469 Shattuck).

They even offer the first peanut-butter pizza in the East Bay. Someone in the kitchen is having a lot of fun. Lunch Tue-Fri. Dinner nightly. & (Oakland)

VI'S VIETNAMESE
724 Webster St.
Oakland
510/835-8357
$

Evenings are quiet here. The local crowds show up for lunch and breakfast. What is a Vietnamese breakfast? The same hearty, pungent noodle soups that are served all day and that have made this plain cafeteria-like restaurant so popular for nearly 20 years. Over the years, the menu has been narrowed down to such customer favorites as braised duck soup, which is heady with star anise, and the mildly exotic five-spice barbecued chicken. The number-one appetizer, shrimp rolls

with peanut sauce, is wonderfully crunchy. Closed Thu. & (Oakland)

THE HILLS

ITALIAN COLORS
2200 Mountain Blvd.
Oakland
510/482-8094
$$

You're high in the lush Oakland Hills in a trendy little strip mall. A fountain splashes next to the tables outside. It's a lively place, bedecked with bright fabrics and wildly splattered with paint. The menu is an Italian hit parade, starting with spicy fried calamari and fresh salads. The pizzas have lighter, more sophisticated seasonings, such as smoked chicken in cilantro pesto and wild mushrooms with fresh thyme and manchego cheese. The Italian burger comes on a zesty focaccia bread. Lunch and dinner daily. Another location is at 101 Broadway in Oakland. ♿ (Hills)

THORNHILL CAFÉ
5761 Thornhill Dr.
Oakland
510/339-0646
$$

You can eat lightly or heartily in this crisp, tearoom-like restaurant located deep in the high, green suburb of Montclair. It's California cooking with a French accent. The onion-soup gratinée is not as crusty as it would be in Paris, but it is satisfying. The Thai chicken salad or the baked goat-cheese salad is also a nice way to start your meal. Classics such as cassoulet are handled lightly, as are the scallops and all the seafood. Or you can try such robust entrées as roast duck in orange sauce and calves-liver Lyonnaise. The Sunday brunch may be the most genteel in town. Dinner daily, lunch daily except Mon. ♿ (Hills)

Marty Forsyth

5

SIGHTS AND ATTRACTIONS

There are fascinating walking tours of Berkeley, Oakland, and the University of California. But there are no tour buses. There are no audio guides. There are no phalanxes of visitors snapping photographs of wacky bumper stickers. It's the kind of place that lets you do something that is becoming more unusual for travelers these days: discover things for yourself.

What will you discover? Well, unless you count Peoples' Park, Berkeley and Oakland have no historic battlefields, but every block in town does have a past. There are great—even landmark—buildings and churches. The University of California is not only an intellectual magnet, but it is also a living textbook of the last 150 years of American architecture. The hills around it are laced with paths that wind by some of the most original homes ever built in the United States. And right at the university's front door is Telegraph Avenue, a 365-day-a-year street fair where the '60s never ended.

In Oakland you'll find a bizarre downtown with block after block of graceful neoclassic and Art Deco "skyscrapers" from the early part of the twentieth century. But most streets—with the exception of the area around city hall—are eerily empty. It's like a day-the-world-ended theme park. Still, downtown is within walking distance of a real Chinatown—not a postcard-and-T-shirt one, like across the bay. And Chinatown is within walking distance of a bustling waterfront that doesn't include the cast of millions that is found at San Francisco's Fisherman's Wharf. The water views are characterized by an ungentrified romance that is purely and stirringly industrial.

BERKELEY

BERKELEY ARCHITECTURAL HERITAGE ASSOCIATION
2318 Durant Ave.
Berkeley
510/841-2242

This association is the single most valuable resource for anyone who gets swept up in the romance of Berkeley's architecture. Throughout the year the association presents a lecture series on the architecture and landscaping traditions so unique to this city. They offer tours of the area and homes to which you otherwise would not have access. They also offer a pamphlet for self-guided tours of historic downtown buildings. Pick one up at the Convention and Visitors Bureau, 2015 Center Street. The schedule varies, so call ahead. (Berkeley)

BUENA VISTA HISTORIC DISTRICT
La Loma, Buena Vista Way,
and Maybeck Twin Dr.
Berkeley

The infamous 1923 Berkeley/Oakland Fire consumed many of the extraordinary homes built by visionary architect Bernard Maybeck. But he and other designers weren't deterred, and in the years following the disaster they rebuilt a conclave of fantastic houses, all of which are now designated historic places. A few examples: **Hume Cloister,** 2900 Buena Vista Way, designed by John Hudson Thomas, is a medieval structure rising up a steep hillside. **Temple of Wings,** 2800 Buena Vista Way, is a colonnaded structure that once served as a studio for students of the dancer Isadora Duncan. The concrete-and-tile **Lawson House,** 1515 La Loma, was designed by Maybeck and is easily the most original home in the area. And the **Annie Maybeck House,** 2780 Buena Vista Way, was Maybeck's most personal creation—the last home he built for himself and his wife. Tours are rarely offered, but contact the Berkeley Historical Society if you are interested. (Berkeley)

CAPTAIN BOUDROW HOUSE
1536 Oxford St.
Berkeley

In 1889 Joseph Hart Boudrow, a sea captain who decided to settle in Berkeley, built this enormous Queen Anne Victorian with an especially high tower to ensure a bay view. It still stands today as a textbook example of residential design of the late nineteenth century. The shingles are patterned like fish scales, the columns supporting the front porch are elaborately ornamental, and there are several fine stained-glass windows. The Berkeley Architectural Heritage Association, 2318 Durant Avenue, 510/841-2242, offers occasional tours. (Berkeley Waterfront)

FIRST CHURCH OF CHRIST SCIENCE
2619 Dwight Way
Berkeley
510/845-7199

Architect Bernard Maybeck warned the parishioners of this church in 1910 that he would build it from unfinished concrete "without shame or hypocrisy." But the result was a masterpiece: a mixture of Gothic, Byzantine, and neo-Classic heavily decorated with Arts and Crafts stenciling existing harmoniously in a building with the serenity of a Japanese temple. If this sounds like the kind of design that

BERKELEY

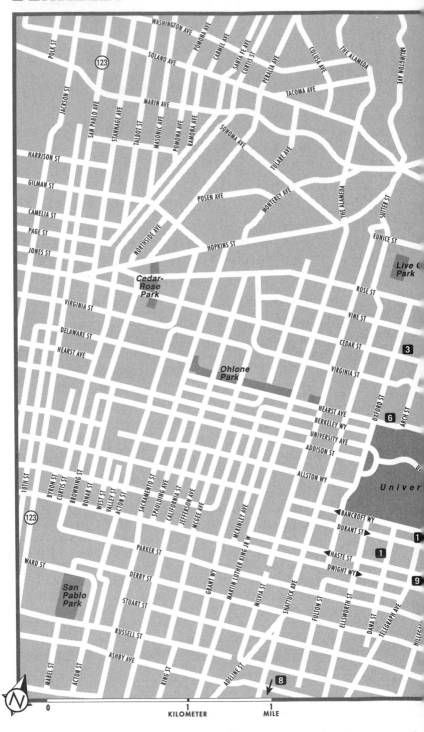

POLK ST
WASHINGTON AVE
SOLANO AVE
POMONA AVE
CARMEL AVE
SANTA FE AVE
CURTIS ST
PERALTA AVE
COLUSA AVE
THE ALAMEDA
WASHINGTON AVE
(123)
JACKSON ST
MARIN AVE
TACOMA AVE
SAN PABLO AVE
STANNAGE AVE
TALBOT ST
MASONIC AVE
POMONA AVE
RAMONA AVE
SONOMA AVE
HARRISON ST
TULARE AVE
GILMAN ST
POSEN AVE
MONTEREY AVE
THE ALAMEDA
SUTTER ST
CAMELIA ST
EUNICE ST
PAGE ST
HOPKINS ST
JONES ST
Live Oak Park
NORTHSIDE AVE
Cedar-Rose Park
ROSE ST
VINE ST
VIRGINIA ST
CEDAR ST
DELAWARE ST
3
HEARST AVE
VIRGINIA ST
Ohlone Park
HEARST AVE
BERKELEY WY
6
UNIVERSITY AVE
OXFORD ST
ARCH ST
ADDISON ST
ALLSTON WY
10TH ST
University
BYRON ST
CURTIS ST
BROWNING ST
BONAR ST
WEST ST
MATHER ST
ACTON ST
SACRAMENTO ST
SPAULDING AVE
CALIFORNIA ST
JEFFERSON AVE
MCGEE AVE
MCKINLEY AVE
BANCROFT WY
DURANT ST
1
(123)
HASTE ST
1
PARKER ST
DWIGHT WY
9
WARD ST
DERBY ST
GRANT WY
MARTIN LUTHER KING JR W
MILVIA ST
SHATTUCK AVE
FULTON ST
ELLSWORTH ST
DANA ST
TELEGRAPH AVE
San Pablo Park
STUART ST
RUSSELL ST
MABEL ST
ACTON ST
ASHBY AVE
KING ST
ADELINE ST
8

N
0   1   1
        KILOMETER   MILE

Sights in Berkeley

1. Berkeley Architectural Heritage Association
2. Buena Vista Historic District
3. Captain Boudrow House
4. First Church of Christ Science
5. Julia Morgan Theater
6. Normandy Village
7. Nyingma Institute
8. Our Own Stuff
9. People's Park
10. Telegraph Avenue
11. Thorsen House
12. University of California at Berkeley (see UC Berkeley map)

BOUNDARY ------

gives eclecticism a bad name, it most definitely is not. Its National Landmark designation is well deserved. You won't see a building quite like this one anywhere else in the world. Spring, when the trellises are draped with purple wisteria, is an especially sublime time to visit. Free tours first Sun of every month at 12:15. &. (Berkeley)

FIRST UNITARIAN CHURCH
2401 Bancroft Way
Berkeley
If you have surmised that there was a "Berkeley school of architecture" around the turn of the century, you get an A. In fact, it was promoted by philosopher Charles Keeler, who believed in turning away from the pernicious effects of industrialism and proposed a more innocent, rustic style of architecture. Today you can see that style clearly in the city's shingled redwood homes and in a few churches, such as this one. The First Unitarian Church may be small, but it's a veritable jewel. Erected in 1898, it has wide porches supported by redwood columns. It also has an enormous round window 12 feet in diameter. Today UC Berkeley uses the building for studio space. Tours are not provided, but you can drop by and try your luck at getting a look inside. (Berkeley)

NORMANDY VILLAGE
1781-1839 Spruce St.
Berkeley
You expect to see Snow White dancing down the winding stairs of this Disney fantasy just north of the UC campus. Instead, however, you'll find only the few very fortunate students and professors who have been clever enough to secure rentals here. Built in 1929, the Normandy Village is the culmination of a World War I veteran's dream to re-create a picturesque village located in Normandy. Today the clutter of gardens, courtyards, cupolas, weathervanes, turrets, and steep, plump roofs all maintain their Grimm Brothers authenticity. This village is private property, not a public park, so look but don't explore. (Berkeley)

NYINGMA INSTITUTE
1815 Highland Pl.
Berkeley
510/843-6812
www.Nyingma.org
The spirits of the football players who used to live in this former fraternity house have been exorcised and replaced with Tibetan Buddhist prayers. The community here not only welcomes visitors who are simply curious about the Nyingma teachings and practices, but it also offers weekend workshops and longer retreats covering instruction in visualization, chanting, and sitting, walking, and movement meditation. Open daily 9-6, free; chanting and lectures Sun 5-7 p.m. (Berkeley)

TRIVIA

UC Berkeley scientists discovered 10 of the elements on the periodic table, including Californium, Berkelium, and Plutonium. Check out the plaque at #303 Gilman Hall, the room where plutonium was discovered.

The Temple of Wings, p. 93

PEOPLE'S PARK
2500 Block of Dwight Way at Haste St.
Berkeley

The teargas-spraying National Guard troops and rock-throwing protesters are long gone. In fact, the park appears rather benign with its small wooded copse, its large lawn, its native plant garden, and its vegetable plots. But the famous 1969 battle over this half-block-sized piece of land still isn't over. The university never shelved its plans for building student dorms here, the tie-dyed Telegraph Avenue population still reveres this land as sacred turf of the counter-culture, and the city considers the park a hotbed of drug dealing and a haven for disturbed runaway teens. Today, designated as a "Monument to Peace" by the Berkeley Landmarks Commission, the park remains a symbol of either pride or embarrassment, depending on which side of the political divide you stand. ♿ (Berkeley)

TELEGRAPH AVENUE
Bancroft to Durant Aves.
Berkeley

The only concessions to corporate America here are a Gap, a Tower Records, and a wall of ATM machines. The remainder of these four blocks is a counter-cultural souk, a proud political throwback to the '60s. Need a tie-dyed T-shirt? How about a rebellious bumper sticker or a new hookah? They're all here, catering to Cal students and to clumps of pale, disaffected youth. The bazaar atmosphere reaches critical mass on the weekends when craftspeople set up booths to sell clothes, candles, and jewelry. In the middle of this carnival are some of the best poster, book, and music stores you'll find anywhere. A dramatic mural on the southeast corner of Dwight recounts the days when Berkeley came close to being a People's Republic. ♿ (Berkeley)

THORSEN HOUSE
2307 Piedmont Ave.

Step Right Up

Many of the 120 footpaths that crisscross the hills of North Berkeley were designed by Bernard Maybeck to give UC professors a shortcut to campus. They give you a close-up view of some of the area's classic residential neighborhoods and exercise worthy of a Stairmaster. The following routes are each two to three miles long:

__Live Oak and Rose Walk:__ Start at Shattuck and Rose and go through Live Oak Park to Spruce Street. Continue to Glen, turn left on Rose, then go right up Scenic to the Hawthorne Steps. At the top, turn left on Hawthorne Terrace and cross Euclid to Rose Walk, which is to the left. Take this charming path up to Greenwood Terrace and turn right. You can make a detour to the left by climbing up Buena Vista to La Loma, which is the heart of Maybeck country. If you're a little winded, turn right after Greenwood and go down Buena Vista to the La Loma steps. It leads to Le Roy. Go left on Le Roy, then take a right on Buena Vista, which leads to Euclid. Go left on Euclid and turn down Vine Lane to Hawthorne Terrace. Straight ahead is Vine Street, which leads back to Shattuck. At Shattuck, turn right. In a few blocks you'll be back at Live Oak Park.

__Creek Walk:__ At the corner of Euclid and Eunice is Cordonices Park.

Berkeley
510/540-9681
Most of the fraternities along Piedmont Avenue occasionally require members to wear togas or demonstrate their ability to throw a luau. Sigma Phi, on the other hand, requires its brothers to assist in the preservation of this astonishing 1909 building designed by the Greene brothers. The Greenes were best known for the Arts and Crafts residences they built in Pasadena, especially the Gamble House. All the elements of this Berkeley landmark are extraordinary. The foundation and stairways are built with rough bricks that look raw yet remarkably elegant. Inside you'll find a variety of wood paneling, Tiffany-glass light fixtures, and fine wrought iron detailing. Call for tour information. (Berkeley)

UNIVERSITY OF CALIFORNIA AT BERKELEY
101 University Hall
2200 University Ave.
Berkeley
510/642-5215
visitorinfo@pa.urel.berkeley.edu
Don't expect UC Berkeley to resemble downtown Tokyo just because it's home to 30,000 students. Sure,

Take the path at the north end and cross Cordonices Creek. Climb up 64 concrete stairs and take a detour on the dirt path to your left. Follow the hillside above the creek to a series of gentle waterfalls. Retrace your steps back to the stairs, take a deep breath, and continue up to Tamalpais Road. Keep going up, turn left on Shasta, then go left on Keith Avenue. Stay on it until you get to the Redwood Terrace Path (after #1140 Keith), which descends to Euclid. Turn left and return to Cordonices Park.

Indian Rock: *The Indian Rock Path begins at the east end of Solano, where Solano meets the Alameda. Stay on the path until you reach Indian Rock (supposedly 9 million years old). Continue to Indian Rock Avenue and go left up to Mortar Rock Park. On the north end move to San Diego Road. Detour through unmarked John Hinkel Park. Get back on San Diego Road and go down Tunbridge Lane. Take a right when you get to the Arlington, then turn left on Thousand Oaks Boulevard. Proceed to San Fernando Avenue via Great Stoneface Park. Take Indian Trail to the Alameda then turn left and go all the way to the Yosemite Steps. Climb the steps to Contra Costa and turn right. Proceed to Indian Rock Path then turn right again.*

the Telegraph Avenue entrance and some of the main campus plazas can get crowded. But the university has 1,232 acres, and many of them—especially those clustered along the banks of Strawberry Creek, which runs through the middle of the campus—are quiet and parklike. Founded in 1868, even today the university retains the verdant feel of a nineteenth-century campus.

By any academic measure, UC Berkeley is one of the most distinguished institutions in the world. The faculty includes 8 Nobel laureates, 198 members of the American Academy of Arts and Sciences, 121 members of the National Academy of Science, and the U.S. Poet Laureate Emeritus. The holdings in its 18 libraries are the fourth largest in North America.

On foot, a self-guided campus tour takes about two hours depending on how many buildings you explore. You can make it slightly less strenuous by avoiding the uphill climb and starting at the Greek Theatre on Gayley Road. It's all downhill from there.

A highlight of the campus is the **Botanical Garden**, Centennial Drive, 510/643-2755. It consists of 34

UC BERKELEY CAMPUS

To Botanical
Garden &
Lawrence
Hall of
Science

PIEDMONT AVE

Law
(Boalt)

Phoebe Hearst
Museum
of Anthropology

U.C. Berkeley Art Museum/
Pacific Film Archive

COLLEGE AVE

Hearst
Greek
Theatre

4

CYCLOTRON RD

GAYLEY RD

Faculty
Club

1

Kroeber

2

Scale Not Available

Hearst
Mining

6

LA LOMA AVE

Bancroft Library

7

5

Hearst
Gymnasium

BOWDITCH ST

LEROY AVE

Evans

Memorial
Glade

Wheeler

Sather Gate

Sproul

BARROW LN

RIDGE RD

HEARST AVE

North Fork of
Strawberry Creek

8

TELEGRAPH AVE

EUCLID AVE

North Gate

Moffitt
Library

Main
Library
(Doe)

Dwinelle

DANA ST

LE CONTE AVE

UNIVERSITY DR

Wellman

Valley Life Sciences Building/
Museum of Paleontology

Eucalyptus
Grove

South Fork of
Strawberry Creek

Zellerbach

3

BANCROFT WY

DURANT AVE

ARCH ST

ENTRANCE

Edwards
Stadium
Goldman
Field

SPRUCE ST

WEST

Visitor
Center

University
Services

Tang Center
(University Health Services)

WALNUT ST

BERKELEY WY

UNIVERSITY AVE

ADDISON ST

CENTER ST

ALLSTON WY

KITTREDGE ST

SHATTUCK AVE

Sights on the UC Berkeley campus

1. Faculty Club
2. Faculty Glade
3. First Unitarian Church
4. Hearst Greek Theatre
5. Hearst Gymnasium
6. Hearst Mining Building
7. Sather Tower
8. Sproul Plaza

Street vendors on Telegraph Avenue

acres spread across Strawberry Canyon and is dedicated to the study and appreciation of more than 13,000 species. Its collection of native plants is outstanding, and the bookstore is a botanist's dream.

Another example of the therapeutic powers of landscape design—the oak-studded **Faculty Glade**—rises from the banks of the gentle Strawberry Creek. It's a great place to bring a picnic or a book and pretend you're studying for finals. Overlooking this bit of Eden is the rustically charming **Faculty Club,** another storybook building by architect Bernard Maybeck.

The **Hearst Gymnasium,** which may be the most perfectly Beaux Arts building on campus, was the 1927 collaborative effort of architects Bernard Maybeck and Julia Morgan. The pedestals and urns along the sides have hints of Maybeck's Palace of Fine Arts in San Francisco.

In 1903 President Theodore Roosevelt gave a commencement address at **Hearst Greek Theatre,** an amphitheater modeled after a Greek theater in Epidaurus. Its 6,000 seats sell out for university activities and rock and jazz concerts during the summer. But during the week it makes a wonderful resting place, set as it is in a eucalyptus grove with a 180-degree view of the bay. Chances are you will have it all to yourself.

Considering that mining was what first made California famous, it's fitting that the **Hearst Mining Building** is dedicated to the study of various ores. The entrance and lobby have the splendor of a Mediterranean villa, and fascinating mineral exhibits are always on display. Shuttle buses depart from in front of the building every 30 minutes and visit several sites of interest east of the campus.

Everyone knows that the 307-foot **Sather Tower** is also called the Campanile and that from the top of this behemoth you can see just about the entire Bay Area. But most people are not aware that two of the building's floors are used to store prehistoric bones. Three times a day and at 2 on Sunday afternoons, the 61 bells in the carillon peal in concert. The tower is open Monday through Friday from 10 to 4 and weekends from 10 to 5. The elevator ride to the observation platform costs one dollar.

Sproul Plaza was ground zero for the Free Speech Movement of the '60s. The cultural carnival has calmed down considerably since then, but political activists of every bent still staff their tables and ask passersby to sign their petitions. Evangelists pray for the souls of the passing sinners. Cadres of musicians play night and day, including a constant contingent of drummers.

BERKELEY WATERFRONT

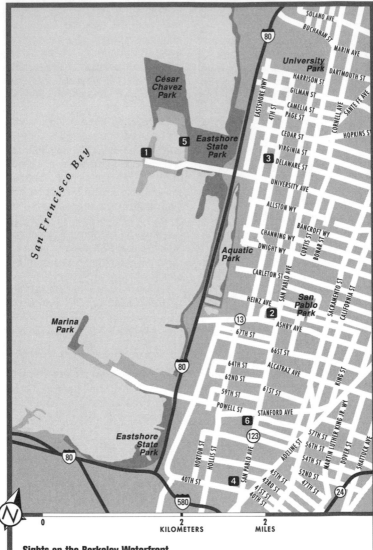

Sights on the Berkeley Waterfront

1. Berkeley Marina
2. Dharma Publishing
3. Delaware Street Historic District
4. Fantasy Junction
5. Hornblower Cruises
6. Siddha Yoga Meditation Ashram

The best time to catch the action is the middle of the day.

Campus parking is at a premium. The only public lots are on Bancroft Way between Telegraph and Dana; on Channing below Telegraph; and in the Sather Gate garage, which has an entrance on Channing and Durant. All three lots fill up fast. Most of the other lots are restricted to evening parking. Street parking allows you only one hour on a meter. A smart alternative is to take BART to the Downtown Berkeley station and then walk. (Berkeley)

BERKELEY WATERFRONT

BERKELEY MARINA
**Foot of University Ave.,
west of I-80
Berkeley
510/644-8623**
The Berkeley Marina, large enough to accommodate nearly 1000 vessels up to 125 feet in length, is also home to a large park where people enjoy water sports, nature study, fishing, play areas, and walking paths. The Berkeley Municipal Pier, built in 1926, originally jutted three and one-half miles out into the bay. Today only the first mile remains, but it's a great place to stroll and watch fishermen hauling in perch, kingfish, striped bass, and the occasional sturgeon. ♿ (Berkeley Waterfront)

DELAWARE STREET HISTORIC DISTRICT
**800 block of Delaware St.
Berkeley**
Everything—the area's first homes, stores, and inn—started here in 1853. They eventually evolved into the town of Ocean View, and later

grew to become the city of Berkeley. Don't expect Victorian curlicues. This is a working-class district, and the restored pioneer homes are small and simple cottagelike structures. Some of the highlights include the **Alphonso House** at 802 Delaware, built in 1878; the gabled **Workman's Cottage** at 1814 Sixth Street; and the **Silva House** at 1824 Fifth Street. ♿ (Berkeley Waterfront)

DHARMA PUBLISHING
**2910 San Pablo Ave.
Emeryville
510/548-5407**
It's hard to believe this structure was once a factory making 57 different Heinz products. Today the

TRIVIA

The following celebrities call or have called the East Bay home:

Jerry Brown
Joan Didion
Allen Ginsberg
Rube Goldberg
Whoopi Goldberg
Tom Hanks
Abbie Hoffman
Timothy Hutton
Dorothea Lange
Timothy Leary
Billy Martin
Robert S. McNamara
Czeslow Milosz
Jessica Mitford
J. Robert Oppenheimer
Gregory Peck
The Pointer Sisters
Alice Walker
Steve Wozniak

building houses, among other things, Dharma Publishing, an extraordinary institution devoted to the preservation and publication of *tankas,* texts sacred to Tibetan Nyingma Buddhism. Stop in and pick up pamphlets and purchase books and posters. See the Nyingma Institute (listed in the Berkeley section of this chapter) for information about their lectures, chanting, and meditation programs. Thu-Sat 12-5. & (Berkeley Waterfront)

FANTASY JUNCTION
1145 Park Ave.
Emeryville
510/653-7555
www.fantasyjunction.com
Have a spare $275,000? Then stop by this showroom and pick up a mint-condition 1954 Europa Ferrari. Short on change? Don't worry. Nobody's going to stop you from looking. Fantasy Junction is home to some of the most glorious automobiles ever produced, from convertibles, vintage racers, and limousines to gleaming 50-year-old Mercedes to Porsches, Thunderbirds, Bugattis, Hudsons, and Asardos. Take it all in—very slowly—and watch your hands. The management is understandably touchy about even the tiniest scratch. Mon-Sat 9:30-5:30. (Berkeley Waterfront)

HORNBLOWER CRUISES
Berkeley Marina
Berkeley
415/788-8866, ext. 7
As the band rocks into your favorite Rod Stewart tune, a swell under the Golden Gate lifts the boat and your partner slips, laughing, into your arms. A three-hour dinner cruise with Hornblower is probably the most romantic way possible to spend a night on the bay. Most of the year they sail from San Francisco's Pier 33, but on special occasions—like Valentine's Day, Mother's Day, Easter, the Fourth of July, and New Year's Eve—they may schedule departures from the Berkeley Marina behind the Marina Hotel or from Jack London Square. Prices, including dinner, start at around $55 a person. Call for reservations at least a week in advance during the summer. & (Berkeley Waterfront)

SIDDHA YOGA MEDITATION ASHRAM
1107 Stanford Ave.
Oakland
510/898-2700
www.oaklandsyda.com
For a few minutes—or, potentially, a lifetime—of peace of mind, you might try visiting this soothing Hindu meditation center located in an un-

Arugula and triple crème Brie are nowhere to be found at Ozzie's, a bona fide old-fashioned soda fountain at 2900 College Avenue. You could be in any small town in the world if it weren't for the conversation, which generally runs to radical politics.

likely industrial area about 10 blocks off Highway 80. You'll find a sunlight temple and meditation breezeway, as well as a large darkened meditation room and a bookstore. If you want something more intensive than their standard classes, call and ask about their continuing workshops. Dress modestly—no tight clothing, miniskirts, or shorts. A cafeteria-like restaurant adjacent to the building serves vegetarian meals. ♿ (Berkeley Waterfront)

SOUTH BERKELEY/ NORTH OAKLAND

CHAPEL OF THE CHIMES
4499 Piedmont Ave.
Oakland
510/654-0123
Really, it's not that depressing. This sprawling columbarium was largely designed by Julia Morgan of San Simeon fame. So expect her usual fantastic mix of Gothic, Romanesque, and Spanish styles. The curlicuing traceries are dazzling, and each one is unique. Richly colorful ceramics include an actual Della Robia plaque. The spaces open into each other and are filled with small gardens, pools, and fountains; all are bathed in a glowing celestial light. The ashes are mostly held in what looks like books, so there is the strange feeling of being in a library of the dead. Daily 9-5. (South Berkeley/North Oakland)

JULIA MORGAN THEATER
2640 College Ave.
Berkeley
510/845-8542
Julia Morgan was way ahead of the French modernists who declared that "less is more." She was the pioneering architect best known for the sprawling Moorish kingdom she designed for William Randolph Hearst at San Simeon. In 1910 the cash-strapped St. John's Presbyterian Church asked her to build as spacious a building as she

Our Own Stuff, p. 106

Karena Dacker

Kristen Loudis

Chapel of the Chimes, p. 105

could on their restricted budget. The result is this romantic, wood-frame structure. Much of the framing is exposed, as are the wall studs and roof trusses. The building today is an active cultural center for the surrounding community and showcases everything from operas to stand-up comics. ♿ (South Berkeley/North Oakland)

MOUNTAIN VIEW CEMETERY
500 Piedmont Ave.
Oakland
510/658-2588
The Victorian way of death was as flamboyant as its way of life. On these 220 acres in the Oakland foothills, California's entrepreneurial pioneers left extravagant memorials to themselves. Pyramids, temples, obelisks, cherubs, and heavenly hosts of angels fill this stately garden graveyard designed by Fredrick Law Olmstead. You can drive through it, but be sure to stop and walk for awhile. The bay view is splendid, and the experience is

more exuberant than ghoulish. Docent tours are provided on the second Saturday of every month at 10 a.m. Gates close at 5. (South Berkeley/North Oakland)

OUR OWN STUFF
3017 Wheeler
Berkeley
510/540-8544
Had enough of those tasteful, historically precise Berkeley landmarks? This house and garden is a wondrous combination of Zap comics and flea-market treasures. The wild garden is layered in a sea of bowling balls. A towering tree blossoms with blue bottles. And everywhere are the brilliant, richly rusted, funky steel cutouts of Mark Bullwinkle (they also decorate the Emery Market in Emeryville). Inside the house is another explosion of creativity, mostly by Marcia Donahue. Every inch consists of one wild, startling, baroque image after another. Some pieces are for sale. It's also possible to have works commissioned. Sun 1-5. (South Berkeley/North Oakland)

OAKLAND

CAMRON STANFORD HOUSE
1418 Lakeside
Oakland
510/444-1876
A century ago the shore of Lake Merritt was a privileged residential area. This proud, slightly worn-out Italianate mansion, built in 1876, is the last vestige of that era. The exterior is all cream-colored Victorian pastry. Inside, it is dark and musty with heavy drapes and sparse but massive furniture. The restoration has been painstaking, and the detail work, especially the hand-

106 C I T Y · S M A R T G U I D E B O O K

stenciled wallpaper, is remarkable. In the basement, a small museum area showcases bits and pieces from California history, which is what saved this stately manse from the wrecking ball. From 1910 to 1967 it served as the Oakland Museum. Open for tours Wed 11-4, Sun 1-5. $4 adults, $2 seniors, children free. ఉ (Oakland)

CHINATOWN
North of Broadway, between 2nd and 12th Sts.
Oakland
This market offers vegetables you have probably never seen in your life and languages you have never heard. Turn the corner on Broadway and you're suddenly halfway around the globe. The sidewalks of this hard-at-work Chinatown are crowded. The energy is nonstop. Locals exchange news, buy their groceries, and come for dinner here.

There are a few jewelry shops, but this is not a tourist bazaar like San Francisco's Grant Avenue. It has more neon than it does pagoda roofs. Chinatown is a bit of a misnomer now. It is the center of an Asian community that includes Vietnamese, Laos, Cambodians, Hmong, and Filipinos, among others. The blandly modern Asian Resource Center, 310 Eighth Street, 510/773-2870, is the political heart of the community. ఉ (Oakland)

COHEN BRAY HOUSE
1440 29th Ave.
Oakland
510/532-0704
The Addams family would be right at home in this dark, mysterious, slightly peeling Victorian just one block away from the multiethnic commercial chaos of International Boulevard. Built in 1884 as a wedding gift, the house's interior is seedy

---

Gospel Churches

Any Sunday morning just come right in, sit down, and catch the infectious, uplifting spirit in dozens of Oakland's gospel churches. The 30-or-more-voice, roof-raising choirs are all amazingly powerful.

- *Allen Temple, 8500 A Street, Oakland, 510/569-9418*
- *Acts Full Gospel, 1034 66th Avenue, Oakland, 510/568-4317*
- *Center of Hope Community Church, 8411 MacArthur Boulevard, Oakland, 510/568-5261*
- *Love Center Church, 10400 International Boulevard, Oakland, 510/729-0680*
- *Olivet Institutional Missionary Baptist Church, 3233 Market Street, Oakland, 510/658-8856*

DOWNTOWN OAKLAND

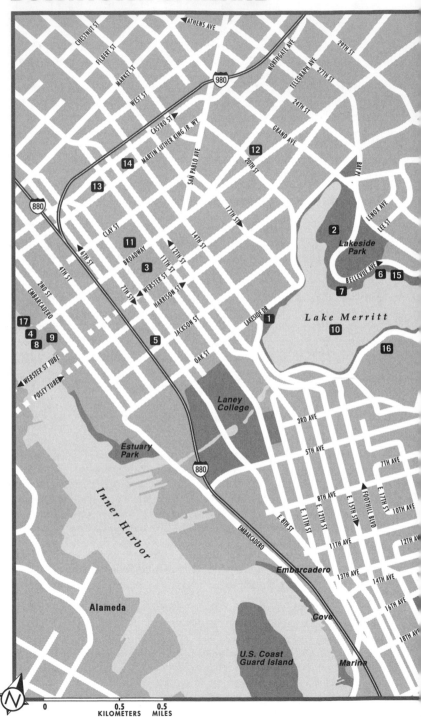

Sights in Downtown Oakland

1. Camron Stanford House
2. Childrens Fairyland
3. Chinatown
4. Oakland Ferry
5. Fortune Cookie Factory
6. Garden Center
7. Gondola Servicio
8. Harbor Tours Ferry
9. Jack London Square
10. Lake Merritt
11. Old Oakland
12. Paramount Theater
13. Pardee Home Museum
14. Preservation Park
15. Rotary Nature Center
16. Tiffany Panels
17. USS Potomac

BOUNDARY - - - - - -

Ratto's

but pretty intact. Downstairs almost every room is magnificently paneled in redwood, including some rare curly grains. The same family has lived here since it was built, and their antiques, china, silver, furniture, photos, and memorabilia are everywhere. Check out the William Morris wallpapers in the upstairs bedroom and the Japanese-influenced ones downstairs. Open every fourth Sunday at 2. $5. Reservations suggested. (Oakland)

FORTUNE COOKIE FACTORY
221 Seventh St.
Oakland
510/832-5520
You will enjoy good health, good luck, and peace of mind—or anything else you'd like when you order your fortune cookies at this little storefront factory on the edge of Chinatown. They'll custom-make your fortune for you. Or you can order from their selection of sassy, X-rated, or biblical quotes. They sell so many different cookies—from wildly colored ones to

giant ones to chocolate ones— that you may have trouble deciding how you want your fortune packaged. Open for tours Mon-Sat 10-3. & (Oakland)

JACK LONDON SQUARE
Embarcadero West at Clay St.
Oakland
510/208-5126
It is fair to say that Jack London, the passionately socialist author of *Call of the Wild,* would not be caught dead here. These six blocks along the Oakland Estuary are unabashedly tourist-oriented. But even though London might have avoided the cavernous Barnes and Noble, and a cheerful chain restaurant like El Torito, he would have appreciated the "workingman's view" of gigantic cranes loading and unloading at the docks. The square hosts a large farmers' market every Sunday from 10 to 2 and transforms into a large antique and collectibles fair on the first Sunday of every month. You can keep busy or you can just drink in the view of sailboats and kayakers

(rent from the California Canoe and Kayak shop here) and rowers gliding up and down the waterway.

Some architect decided that the original square should look like a small town in colonial Massachusetts. So, in contrast to the newer areas to the north, Jack London Village is all weathered and shingled. It's also jammed with gift shops and restaurants. But you should definitely visit the little Jack London Museum for a closer look at the writer's adventurous life. ᕫ (Oakland)

LAKE MERRITT
**Between W. Grand, Lakeshore, Lakeside, and Harrison Sts.
Oakland**
The East Bay environmental movement goes back more than one hundred years to when this 122-acre saltwater lake became the state's first wildlife refuge. Lake Merritt's three-and-one-half-mile perimeter is flat and, as such, attracts a steady stream of walkers, joggers, bicyclists and in-line skaters. Still, it never feels crowded. Other people boat, windsurf, canoe, and row on the water, or enjoy free Sunday concerts by the Oakland Civic band at the bandstand, on the northwest tip of the lake. This urban jewel of a lake (which is still a wildlife refuge) becomes a real one at night when the Florentine lamps around it are lit to create the "Necklace of Lights."

The **Garden Center,** 510/238-3187, on the north side of the lake includes a few unusual displays, such as a fragrance garden. Admission is free.

In the early years, wealthy families built estates along the shore. Today only one remains: the **Camron Stanford House** (see listing in this section).

Lake Merritt is a popular stopover for migrating birds. Eighty species return to this spot every winter. You can learn more about them at the **Rotary Nature Center,** 552 Bellevue, 510/238-3739. The center's exhibit hall has mounted ducks, gulls, geese, grebes, herons, and more, allowing you to easily identify the flocks along the shoreline. September through February you'll see cormorants, terns, and egrets. Goslings and ducklings hatch March through July (be warned that your kids could see a western gull swoop down and swallow a baby). The wheelchair-accessible center is open daily all year long and admission is free.

A trip with **Gondola Servicio,**

Harbor Tours

How do those towering cranes loading and unloading thousands of containers in the Oakland Harbor work? What kinds of ships dock here? Where do they come from? What sorts of products are being handled? To find out, take a free sailing tour. Call 510/272-1188 for details.

Brewery Trail

What better way to see Berkeley than while simultaneously sampling its fine local brews? Here's a brief rundown on the city's eight breweries: First, try the **Golden Pacific Brewery** *(1404 Fourth Street, 510/558-1919). Then have a sake chaser at nearby* **Takara Sake USA** *(708 Addison, 510/540-8250). From there, stock up on home-brewing gear at* **Oak Barrel** *(1442 San Pablo, 510/849-0400). Then, if you can't wait to brew your own, head over to* **Berkeley Brew Haus** *(1615 University, 510/841-3527), where they'll do it for you in only two hours. Finally, for a great meal (and music) with your beer, stop at* **Pyramid** *(901 Gilman, 510/528-9880),* **Jupiter** *(2181 Shattuck, 510/558-1919),* **Triple Rock** *(1920 Shattuck, 510/843-BREW), or* **Bison** *(2598 Telegraph, 510/841-7734). For a brewery trail guide, call the Berkeley Convention and Visitors Bureau at 800/847-4823.*

568 Bellevue Avenue, 510/663-6603, is a great way to tour the lake. The authentic, made-in-Venice, over-the-top romantic gondola is guaranteed to give you a fresh perspective on the lake and all its intricacies. It also might stir up a little romance: The gondolier was trained in Venice and provides romantic vocalizing at no extra cost. $45 per couple. Reservations are required. (Oakland)

MILLS COLLEGE
5000 MacArthur Blvd.
Oakland
510/430-2255

A sweet menthol fragrance from groves of eucalyptus trees perfumes this small, quiet, bucolic 136-acre campus in the Oakland hills. The landscape, with its rolling lawns, redwood glades, gentle streams, and mix of Victorian and Spanish Colonial architecture, is pretty. The art gallery's glass ceiling is stunning. The music building auditorium has fantastically carved and brilliantly painted beams. Julia Morgan designed three buildings here, including a sturdy bell tower. Take half an hour and walk the Pine Trail, which circles the campus and passes Lake Alviso. All buildings are open daily. ♧ (Oakland)

OAKLAND/ALAMEDA FERRIES
Clay and Embarcadero
Oakland
510/522-3300

It's like the opening shot of a movie: First, the camera sweeps across the white-capped bay, then it rises to follow the silver steel arc of the Bay Bridge and zooms up into the towers perched on the hills of San Francisco. Twelve times a day and

Fourteen creeks flow through Berkeley, but most of them were turned into culverts and paved over long ago. Strawberry Creek, which meanders across the UC campus, was named for the wild strawberries that used to grow along its banks.

five times on weekends, Oakland/ Alameda Ferries give visitors this privileged view on trips that never take more than 30 minutes. You can depart from either Jack London Square or Alameda, which is just across the estuary. The ferries stop at San Francisco's Embarcadero and at Pier 39. From there it's possible to connect to boats to Alcatraz and Angel Island. One-way tickets to San Francisco are $4.50 each for adults and children. Drinks and snacks are available. & (Oakland)

OAKLAND WALKING TOURS
Downtown Oakland
510/238-3243
Who built that extraordinary jade-tile frieze covering the face of the **I. Magnin** building at Broadway and 20th Street? Why does the **Fox Theater,** at Telegraph Avenue and 19th Street, look like a set from Phantom of the Opera? Where did nineteenth-century arrivals on the Union Pacific step off the train? The closer you get to the details of

downtown Oakland, the more you want to know. On these one-and-a-half-hour walking tours, you learn everything about these buildings and others, including splendid structures like the Flatiron and the Rotunda. Seven tours are available, including trips through Chinatown, Jack London Square, and Old Oakland. May-Oct Wed and Sun at 10. Free. (Oakland)

OLD OAKLAND
Bounded by 8th, 10th, Washington, and Broadway
Oakland
Can the heart of Oakland be resuscitated? Dramatic efforts are currently underway to revive what was once the commercial core of the city—the pristine brownstones of the 1870s. Today block after handsome block is slowly filling with offices, restaurants, and shops. The façades are wonderfully nostalgic, the brickwork is full of artful detail, and the ceramic tiling is colorful and distinctive. But not all the

Straighten your life out. For a couple hundred dollars, the Feng Shui Shop at 301 13th Street in Oakland will come to your home and consult with you on how to align your furniture so that your life is in harmony.

tenants are newcomers. Ratto's worldly deli, for instance, at 820 Washington Street, has been here for years, as has Housewives Market in the newly restored Swans Market. ⅊ (Oakland)

PARAMOUNT THEATER
2025 Broadway
Oakland
510/893-2300, 510/465-6400 (tours)
The Paramount Theater is Oakland's answer to Radio City Music Hall. This theater, a vast 1931 Art Deco movie palace that has been impeccably and lavishly restored, is well beyond fabulous. Facing Broadway is an intricate 80-foot tile tableau. The sleek silver metal and black marble interior stirs fantasies of Astaire-Rogers musicals and proves to be a perfect setting for the classic Hollywood films that are shown here many times each year. A full schedule of live performances by well-respected companies includes the Oakland Ballet and the Oakland East Bay Symphony. Individual artists as varied as Tom Waits and Al Green are also known to stop by to perform. Tours are given on the first and third Saturday of each month. $1. ⅊ (Oakland)

PARDEE HOME MUSEUM
672 11th St.
Oakland
510/444-2187

Obsession was accepted as normal behavior by the Victorians. This immaculately restored 1868 three-story Italianate villa just off Highway 880 proves it. The acquisitive wife of George Pardee, governor of California during the 1906 earthquake, collected more than 60,000 objects. The collection includes fascinating Alaskan folk art, elegant and refined altarpieces from China, and Philippine tobacco pipes. On the walls are many fine examples of the creamy landscapes of California from the turn of the century. This home is on the National Register of Historic Places. Guided one-and-a-half-hour tours are offered Fridays and Saturdays at noon. Adults $5, children under 12 free. Reservations recommended. (Oakland)

PRESERVATION PARK
13th St. at Martin Luther King Way
Oakland
510/874-7580
This delightful gardenlike block of Victoriana could be considered a hero's monument to East Bay preservationists. The first street plans for Oakland were plotted here in 1853. Twenty-three homes in seven distinct architectural styles (1870 to 1919) were on their way to demolition (mainly because of the construction of Highway 880 one block away) when they were rescued and transplanted here. Today

Lost? One of the largest map collections in the United States can be found at the map room at Giannini Hall on the UC Berkeley campus. It's open from 10 to 5 weekdays and from 1 to 5 on Saturday.

they are all poised around a small fountain, which is a great place to sit and have a picnic. The buildings now house community enterprises and nonprofit organizations, but every home has a story, and a wonderful self-guided tour is a great way to hear them. Partially wheelchair accessible. (Oakland)

TIFFANY PANELS
Lake Merritt United Methodist Church
1330 Lakeshore Dr.
Oakland
510/465-4793
Built in 1923 for a church in Los Angeles, these three Tiffany panels weighing one ton each were shipped to this nondescript church on Lake Merritt in 1990. The center panel, *Te Deum Laudamus,* shows Christ surrounded by angels, martyrs, and saints, all in a silvery white light. The left panel is a procession of worshipers, and the right panel depicts John reading from the Bible. This is not Tiffany stained glass. Rather, it's Tiffany mosaic—more than two million iridescent pieces of glass. Particularly glorious are the lamps and torches and the three shimmering crucifixes. Open daily. ♿ (Oakland)

USS *HORNET* AIRCRAFT CARRIER MUSEUM
Old Alameda Naval Air Station
Pier 3
Alameda
510/521-8448
This 41,000-ton war veteran has a distinguished battle record that you can explore from deck to deck, from bow to stern. She saw heavy action during World War II and was attacked 59 times during her stay in the Pacific. From her flight decks,

Karena Dacker

The historic Paramount theater

U.S. planes destroyed 1,210 enemy aircraft and 1,250,000 tons of enemy shipping. The first strikes to liberate the Philippines and attack Tokyo were launched here. In 1969 the *Hornet* recovered the *Apollo 11* space capsule and the first men who walked on the moon. On deck you can check out a vintage torpedo bomber and an F-8U Crusader and watch videos of the *Apollo* recovery. Daily 10-5. $9 adults, $5 children 5-18, $7 seniors and military. (Oakland)

USS *POTOMAC*
540 Water St.
Oakland
510/839-8256
usspotomac@aol.com
Economic strategies to end the Depression and top-secret plans to stop the Nazis during World War II were discussed here when FDR sailed down the Potomac on this ship, his 165-foot "floating White House." After 12 years and $5 million, it has been restored to its original state and is now a National Historic Landmark. Wed and Fri

GREATER OAKLAND

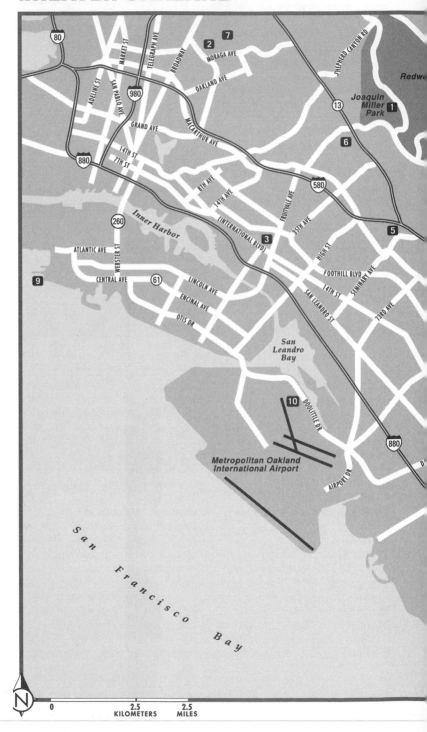

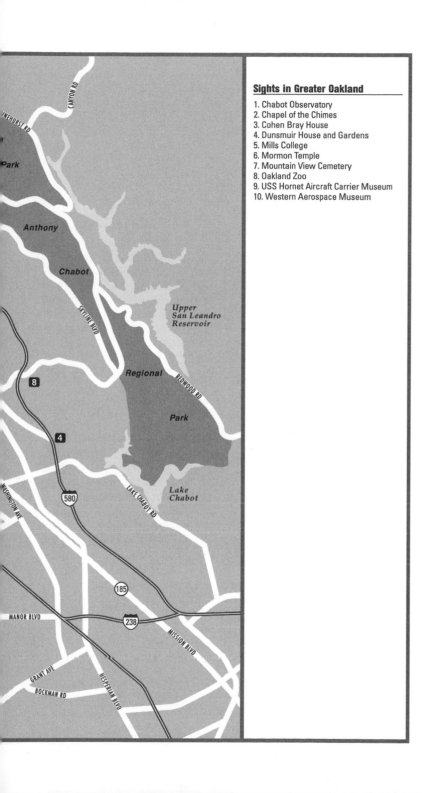

Sights in Greater Oakland

1. Chabot Observatory
2. Chapel of the Chimes
3. Cohen Bray House
4. Dunsmuir House and Gardens
5. Mills College
6. Mormon Temple
7. Mountain View Cemetery
8. Oakland Zoo
9. USS Hornet Aircraft Carrier Museum
10. Western Aerospace Museum

10-1:15, Sun noon-3:15. $3 adults, $2 seniors, $1 students 6-17, children under 6 free, family rate $5. Two-hour history cruises across the bay mid-Mar-mid-Nov. $30 adults, $27 seniors, $15 students 6-17, children under 6 free. & (Oakland)

WESTERN AEROSPACE MUSEUM
Oakland Airport
North Field
Oakland
510/638-7100
The last, fateful flight of Amelia Earhart in 1937 started here a few miles from Oakland's current international airport. A craft nearly identical to hers is exhibited, as are a 4-14 Tomcat and one dozen or so other historic planes. The museum's prize is the 90-foot, four-engine *Flying Boat,* built in 1946. It served as one of the first luxury passenger planes and was owned by the legendary Howard Hughes. Video clips of the plane in action are featured in the movie *Indiana Jones and the Raiders of the Lost Ark.* The museum's other exhibits include a fully operative World War II Link instrument trainer and a collection of important engines. Wed-Sun 10-4. $6 adults, children under 12 free. & (Oakland)

THE HILLS

CHABOT OBSERVATORY

10902 Skyline Blvd.
Oakland
510/530-3499
www.cosc.org
This new, state-of-the-art astronomy facility in Joaquin Miller Park boasts an enormous 36-inch reflector telescope and an IMAX-like screen designed to carry its viewers off on electronic fieldtrips to the South Pole, orbiting space stations, and other far-out places. The geodesic planetarium's special-effects projectors simulate eclipses and supernovae, and its "Music under the Stars" concert series is out of this world. A permanent exhibit entitled *Our Place in the Universe* uses 3-D effects and holograms to take onlookers on a tour through the heavens. The Challenger Center has space station and mission-control simulators. Call for hours and entry fees. & (Hills)

DUNSMUIR HOUSE AND GARDENS
2960 Peralta Oaks Court
Oakland
510/615-5555
What wedding gift would you give your bride if she had just divorced her husband to marry you? In 1899 Alexander Dunsmuir built his betrothed this 37-room colonial-revival mansion. It sits in sylvan splendor on 40 acres just off Highway 13. Much of the home is in

Slow down as you drive away from the Berkeley Marina. The road starts to ripple radically because of the remnants of the old pier buried underneath it.

pristine historical condition. The arcadian gardens are being restored to their original design. The meadow and the bamboo shore of the pond make ideal picnic spots. Even the pool, empty and crumbling, maintains a ruined sense of glamour. Grounds open Tue-Fri 10-4. Free. The mansion has docent tours only, Apr-Sept, Wed 11 and 12. $5. (Hills)

MORMON TEMPLE
4770 Lincoln Ave.
Oakland
510/531-1475
Take a wonderful walk through the lovely gardens and fountain-covered terraces of this dramatic religious edifice. The temple, a windowless building with a central white-granite tower shooting 170 feet into the sky, is somewhat reminiscent of a mid-century World's Fair structure. The four other towers are covered in blue-glass mosaic and gold leaf. Inside, the walls are made of golden-hued wood and marble, the central

columns are layered with onyx, and the font is pure gold leaf. Guided tours 9-9. Free. ♿ (Hills)

OAKLAND ZOO
Golf Links Rd. (off Hwy. 580)
Oakland
510/632-9525
This cage-free zoo focuses on endangered species. Nearly 300 animals, both imported from foreign lands and native to the area, roam in approximations of their natural habitats. Highlights include a rainforest with gibbons, chimpanzees, and sun bears; an African savanna with lions, giraffes, and elephants; a miniature Australia with wallaroos, wallabies, emus, and kangaroos; and a 17-acre hillside inhabited by bison and elk. The Skyride tram offers a great bird's-eye view of everything, and the surrounding Knowland Park is a good place for a picnic. Daily 10-4. $6 adults, $3 seniors and children 2-14, children under 2 free. Parking is $3. ♿ (Hills)

Marty Forsyth

6

MUSEUMS AND GALLERIES

The nineteenth century set the tone for the Bay Area's appetite for culture and knowledge. From the outset, the area's natural beauty, as well as a local tolerance for a wide spectrum of human behavior, has drawn artists to the East Bay. Add to this atmosphere the stimulation and high standards of one of the world's great universities, and the result is a rich visual, scientific, and historic opportunity for visitors. Museums are sized so that in an afternoon you can relive the Gold Rush, explore a couple hundred million years of prehistory, dig deep into the folklore of a south sea island, or absorb a world-caliber traveling exhibition.

Local art has a long lineage, from the anti-industrial early bohemians to mid-century explorations like Diebenkorn's abstract landscapes. Today Oakland officials claim that more artists live here than in any city this side of the Hudson River. Yet the gallery scene is surprisingly limited. You are more likely to find local crafts than local arts. And you're more likely to see them in coffeehouses and restaurants than in galleries.

ART MUSEUMS

OAKLAND MUSEUM
1000 Oak St.
Oakland
510/238-2200
Artfully concealing its treasures under four acres of lush garden terraces, this museum is large but

not overwhelming. The ambitious aim of the Oakland Museum is to cover the art, history, and environment of California. The bottom level is dedicated to ecology and showcases nine separate habitats. The second floor re-creates the Golden State's history and includes an amazing collection of Gold Rush memorabilia. California art, from wistful early landscapes to recent and radical local works, is the focus of the top floor. The Great Hall offers important special exhibitions. If you have time for only one museum, this is the place to go. Wed-Sun. $6 adults, $4 seniors and students, children 5 and under free. ♿ (Oakland)

UC ART MUSEUM
2625 Bancroft Way
Berkeley
510/642-0808
www.bamfa.berkeley.edu
A striking work of art itself, the UC Art Museum has seven cantilevered galleries that appear to be airborne. Its permanent collection—small but well edited with major Western and Asian artists represented—is remarkable for a university. One entire room, for example, is devoted to the explosive abstractions of Hans Hoffman. The changing exhibits tend to be provocative and often include displays by artists from hot New York galleries. The museum also happens to be the home of the Pacific Film Archives, which shows a regular schedule of classic American and foreign cinema. Museum open Wed-Sun. $6 adults, $4 students and seniors. ♿ (Berkeley)

SCIENCE AND HISTORY MUSEUMS

BANCROFT LIBRARY
UC Berkeley
Berkeley
510/642-3781
Sure, the massive Bancroft Library does hold millions of volumes of books, but it's also home to many permanent exhibits. For one, there's the first gold nugget mined in California. There's also a brass plaque left behind by Sir Francis Drake when he landed on the California coast in the 1570s. Ask at the reference desk to look at the library's papyrus fragments, medieval manuscripts, Renaissance works by Luther, Shakespeare folios, and Mark Twain's original diaries. Mon-Sat. Free. ♿ (Berkeley)

BERKELEY HISTORICAL MUSEUM
1931 Center St.
Berkeley
510/848-0181
Nearly 50 videos are available for viewing here. Among the better ones, you'll find a chilling record of the 1991 Firestorm and an interesting recollection of "Life on the Hill" by the daughter of visionary Berkeley architect Bernard

Presidents aren't the only ones who get their own museums. Today, even rice wine can lay claim to such an honor. The Takara Sake Tasting Room and Museum in Berkeley is open daily from noon to six. Stop by and sample the six local sakes and check out the collection of authentic pails, tubs, and other implements. The adjacent tasting room is as serene as a teahouse.

Maybeck. This facility, located in the Civic Center across from Berkeley High, is small but well stocked with memorabilia dating back to the mid-nineteenth century. Exhibits change two or three times a year and cover everything from transportation to art. Thu-Sat. Free. &
(Berkeley)

LAWRENCE HALL OF SCIENCE
Centennial Dr.
Berkeley
510/642-5132
The Lawrence Hall of Science is purported to be a children's museum, but the exhibits and hands-on activities cover everything from astronomy to computers to biology, and they are fascinating no matter how old you are. The building is a concrete lump, but the terrace offers a smashing view of the bay. Museum open daily. $6 adults; $4 seniors, students, and children 7-18; $2 children 3-6. Planetarium ($2) open weekends only. & (Berkeley)

MUSEUM OF PALEONTOLOGY
Valley Life Sciences Building
Near Oxford and University
Berkeley
510/642-1821
You're bound to feel younger after a stroll around this compact gallery. A complete Tyrannosaurus Rex skeleton rises to its full height in the three-story atrium. Hovering over it is a pterosaur. The collection is quite extensive, covering both vertebrate and invertebrate species with an emphasis on California dinosaurs. It includes the world's largest-known Triceratops skull, as well as skulls from duck-billed dinosaurs. The second floor houses a skeleton of an archaeopteryx, the earliest known bird. Mon-Fri 8-4. Free. & (Berkeley)

OAKLAND LIBRARY
Oakland History Room
125 14th St.
Oakland
510/238-3222
Daily life in Oakland for the past century and a half is recorded in minute detail here, but you don't need to be interested in local history to be mesmerized. The photos, postcards, diaries, street plans, newspapers, theater programs, and memorabilia should fascinate anyone interested in witnessing the rise of a great city.

Making friends at the
Lawrence Hall of Science

Lawrence Hall of Science

Street Murals

The city of Oakland has been especially accommodating to outdoor artists. You can see their work all over town. A few of the best are Giraffe Mural, where 580 crosses over Harrison; Grand Performance, at Grand Avenue and the 580 underpass; Street Tattoo, at San Pablo and Grand; and Mitzvah, at Franklin and 14th Street.

A fairly recent exhibit featured photos of a radical sculpture on the Emeryville mudflats from only a decade ago. This library is also a rich resource for material on local literary figures such as Jack London and Joaquin Miller. Open daily. Free. & (Oakland)

PHOEBE HEARST MUSEUM OF ANTHROPOLOGY
103 Kroeber Hall
Bancroft Way at College
Berkeley
510/643-7648
This museum is another drab midcentury building with a jewel inside. The Phoebe Hearst Museum of Anthropology maintains an enormous collection, small samples of which are shown in rotation. You won't find the standard selection of museum trinkets here. But you will find a wonderful collection of pieces from around the world, ranging from beautifully preserved California Indian baskets to pre-Columbian pottery to Alaskan carvings to sub-Saharan textiles. A prominent part of the collection is artifacts from the life of Ishi, the last Yahi Indian in northern California. Wed-Sun. $2 adults, $1 seniors, 50¢ children. & (Berkeley)

OTHER MUSEUMS

EBONY MUSEUM OF ART
30 Jack London Square
Oakland
510/763-0745
The Ebony Museum of Art, tucked away amid the old New England-style shops of Jack London Village, is easily one of the most original exhibit spaces in the East Bay. It's not exactly large, but it does have a wealth of African and African American art. The West African log and gourd drums are unusual. Fabrics include beadwork that is so sophisticated it's hard to call it folk art. The museum even displays examples of "derogatory" commercial art, such as Aunt Jemima figurines and Darkee toothpaste. And one of the most appealing features is that nearly everything in this museum is for sale. A larger version of this collection is located at 1034 14th Street, but it's shown only by appointment. Tues-Sun 12-6. Free admission. (Oakland)

JUDAH MAGNES MUSEUM
2911 Russell
Berkeley
510/ 849-2710
www.jfed.org.magnes

TRIVIA

In a long-overdue attempt to provide public art, Berkeley hired local bard Robert Haas to oversee the implanting of poetry on the sidewalks of Addison Street near Shattuck Avenue. The poems are interspersed with inlaid ceramic and bronze pieces by local artists.

The archives in this rambling Elmwood-district home are rich with diaries, photos, and letters tracing the history of Jews in the western United States. They also include a fascinating collection of Judaica from around the world and going back hundreds of years. You'll find a wide range of materials from rare books to ceremonial ornaments. Exhibits by contemporary artists such as Andy Warhol and Ben Shahn are among the recent highlights of this scholarly but accessible museum. Sun-Thu; closed for Jewish holidays. Suggested donation $5. Call for wheelchair assistance. (South Berkeley/North Oakland)

GALLERIES

ANDERSON GALLERY
2243 Fifth St.
Berkeley
510/848-3822
The Anderson Gallery is located in a framing shop tucked away in a little courtyard amidst industrial-style offices and gardens. It offers a small but intriguing collection of works, most of which were created by local artists. Styles vary, but everything is decorative and colorful. One specialty is antiquarian prints, including eighteenth-century maps. A few pieces of locally crafted jewelry are usually on display as well. Prices range from about $20 to $1,000. Tue-Sat. ♿ (Berkeley Waterfront)

BERKELEY ART CENTER
1725 Walnut St.
Berkeley
510/644-6893
First prize for Most Serene Setting goes to this small but avant-garde civic gallery in what looks like a treehouse perched over a creek in beautiful Live Oak Park. The Berkeley Art Center's shows usually feature established local artists. And although it features a multicultural bent, the center is not as openly political as similar Oakland galleries. Standards are quite high and installations are polished and professional. Recent shows include artists' interpretations of the art of bookmaking and a craft-oriented display of Japanese influence in American culture. Wed-Sun. Free. ♿ (Berkeley)

BERKELEY POTTERS' GUILD
731 Jones St.
Berkeley
510/524-7031
On weekends the streets in this post-industrial neighborhood are dotted with signs inviting anyone driving past into the local pottery studios. One of the major venues is this group of 19 artisans. Adjacent to their workspace is an exhibit and sales area for their high- and low-fire works as well as *raku.* You'll find everything from the wildly

whimsical to the simple and sincere, from teacups to earrings to bowls to candlesticks. Weekends only. Major sales events in the spring and during the holidays. ♿ (Berkeley Waterfront)

CECILE MOOCHNEK GALLERY
1809 D Fourth St.
Berkeley
510/549-1018

Take a break from Fourth Street's hopping shopping scene at this light-filled atelier. It's as spare as a Zen meditation space—small but soothing, all blond wood and lyrical contemporary works. The emphasis is on emerging artists from the Bay Area and the owner's former home in New Mexico. Because of the size of the space, the works tend to be small, but whether they are collages or photographs or paintings or watercolors, they are invariably sophisticated and accessible. Occasionally shows include African American or African art. Prices start around $200. Wed-Sun. (Berkeley Waterfront)

GALLERY OVISSI
1425 Park
Emeryville
510/601-6874

The third floor of this galvanized-steel loft space is devoted to the works of Nasser Ovissi, a celebrated Iranian artist whose work has the colorful charm of Chagall. The lower two floors offer rotating shows of mostly contemporary Iranian artists. There is nothing naive about the work here. The experimentation, especially in the photography, is quite surprising, and the level of sophistication is high. A political subtext is present, but it never takes away from this truly original display of

Top 10 Offbeat Favorites

By Mal and Sandra Sharpe, local columnists and authors of *Weird Rooms*

1. Visionary and Jail Art Store in Oakland
2. Berkeley Ice Skating Rink
3. Marsha Donahue's Exotic Berkeley Garden
4. Bonnie Grossman's Outside Art Gallery on Cedar Street
5. The Ivy Room on San Pablo, a combination bar and bomb shelter
6. DDB Brown records on Claremont Avenue and its collectible LPs
7. The Jazz School on Shattuck above La Note restaurant
8. Colin Smith's unique furniture gallery on 10th Street near Gilman
9. Kayaking at the Jack London Marina
10. The produce district in Oakland at seven in the morning

> The ratio of artists to galleries here is about 500 to 1. The best spots for viewing work being done right now in the East Bay are restaurants and coffeehouses. Two of the better options are Café Temescal on Telegraph and the Third Street Grind in downtown Oakland.

pure talent. Shows change every six weeks. Open weekends. (Berkeley Waterfront)

KALA ART INSTITUTE
1060 Heinz Ave.
Berkeley
510/549-2977
It's well worth walking up three flights of stairs to see the master prints on display in this industrial building. But it's also worth the effort to see the master printers in action because you must first pass through the workshop area of the artists-in-residence when you enter the gallery. The caliber of the work here is high, and it's a great opportunity to see some of the East Bay's best artists. You'll find Roy de Forest, Squeak Carnwath, and Peter Voulkos, among others. Their experimentation, especially with color, is

brilliant. Prices range from about $100 to $1,500. Tue-Fri. (Berkeley Waterfront)

MILLS COLLEGE ART MUSEUM
5000 MacArthur Blvd.
Oakland
510/430-2164
This art space is easily the most beautiful in the East Bay and, arguably, the entire Bay Area. Designed by Walter Ratcliff in the '20s, the Spanish colonial-style building includes a ceiling of gold-coffered glass and a single large room bathed in shimmering sunlight. Although the permanent collection is international, with a strong selection of Asian textiles and ceramics, prints, and drawings, most shows are by contemporary American and European artists. When you're finished, walk outside through the cloisterlike studio areas to the rolling lawn. It's so beautiful that it's nearly possible to forget that Highway 580 is just a few hundred yards away. Tue-Sun. (Oakland)

MOUNTAIN LIGHT GALLERY
1466 66th St.
Emeryville
510/601-9000
This gallery is a one-man operation. All of the photographs here are by the celebrated wilderness and wildlife photographer Galen Rowell.

You may have seen his work in the 15 or so books he's completed for organizations such as the Sierra Club and UC Press. But you won't be prepared for the real thing—the sharp, glasslike clarity of his high-end digital color prints. In addition to his well-known photographs of the western United States, many of his shots were taken in the Himalayas and elsewhere in the world of mountaineering. Prices range from $150 to $1,800. Matting and framing is available. Mon-Sat. Free. ♿ (Berkeley Waterfront)

NEW LEAF
1286 Gilman St.
Berkeley
510/525-7621
A garden of earthly and unearthly delights in a quiet Northside Berkeley residential area, this gallery showcases fountains and sculptures from the soulful to the playful. The works range in size from small to monumental and include a familiar variety of styles: Henry Moore-ish nudes; Noguchi-like slabs; and wiry, wildly colored pieces that move in the wind. The pieces are all one-of-a-kind works executed by artists from across the country. There are a few offbeat pieces of outdoor furniture as well. Prices range from about $500 to $80,000. Shows change about six times a year. Wed-Sun. ♿ (Berkeley)

OLIVER ART CENTER
5212 Broadway
Oakland
510/594-3650
Emerging U.S. and international artists direct from hot debuts in New York City display their works at this small but striking glass and gray-stucco gallery on the East Bay

campus of the California College of Arts and Crafts. Everything is quirky and cutting edge. While you're here, be sure to check out the three galleries in the administration building to the west. They display quality student work, from performance videos to jewelry. Call ahead in the summer to make sure they are open. ♿ (South Berkeley/North Oakland)

PACIFIC BRIDGE GALLERY
95 Linden St. #6
Oakland
510/451-8840
When most people picture Southeast Asian art, they think of religious or folk art, like Balinese puppets. This Soho-like gallery in an old warehouse next to the railroad tracks in downtown Oakland has set out to remedy that situation. The Pacific Bridge Gallery is the only gallery in the country to showcase the talents of modern-day artists from the Philippines, Vietnam, Laos, Cambodia, and other Southeast Asian countries. Their

Judah Magnes Museum, p. 123

Jennifer Suttlemyre

That unsightly lump at the tip of the Berkeley marina is a 14-foot repli-ca of a seventh-century Chinese sculpture. The artist, Fred Fierstein, is a Berkeley electrician who offered it to the city but, frustrated by their delays, moved it to its present site one dark night in 1985.

artist-in-residence program en-hances cross-cultural creativity. The works displayed here are var-ied, but they're often vivid, colorful, and politically charged. Tue-Sat. (Oakland)

PRO ARTS
461 Ninth St.
Oakland
510/763-4361
No place in the Oakland area works harder to promote the work of living local artists. When you stop in at this storefront gallery in the reno-vated section of Old Oakland, you're likely to see a wide and proud range of ethnically diverse photographs, paintings, prints, sculpture, and crafts. In fact, if the selection has one drawback, it's that quality sometimes suffers in the name of inclusiveness. Two main juried shows are held annu-ally in the spring, and it's possible to preview the works of the nearly 400 artists who participate in the Open Studios tour. Call ahead because the gallery can be closed for up to two weeks between shows. Wed-Sat. Free. & (Oakland)

SHAMWARI
4176 Piedmont Ave.
Oakland
510/923-1111
Every year owner Lillian White trav-els to Africa and returns with a gallery's worth of sculptures, paint-

ings, and pottery. She specializes in carvings from Zimbabwe that are so sophisticated it doesn't seem right to call them primitive. Human figures carved by the hands of con-temporary African artists writhe nobly out of lustrous serpentine and verdite stone. White also carries unusual artifacts such as enormous wooden combs from Ghana. The framing here is some of the most unusual in the Bay Area. Prices start at around $200. Tues-Sun, 10-6. & (Oakland)

TRAX
1306 Third St.
Berkeley
510/526-0279
Park carefully when visiting this studio and ceramics gallery be-cause it is about 10 feet away from the Amtrak rail lines. The pottery is mostly the work of a group of artists from Minnesota and is done in a deceptively simple homespun style of clean, functional lines and soft earth tones. Ask to see the studio operation downstairs where the legendary Peter Voulkos once worked. If the gods are smiling on you, the staff might show you the studio's living quarters, in which is housed an impossible-to-believe collection of works by the Bay Area's greatest clay sculptors of the last 50 years. Prices range from $5 to $5,000. Open weekends. (Berkeley Waterfront)

TRAYWICK
1316 10th St.
Berkeley
510/527-1214

A long and narrow storefront in the same shopping area as Smith and Hawken, this gallery is one of Berkeley's newest. It is probably as close to a cutting-edge San Francisco-style space as you will find in the East Bay. The exhibits here are focused and contemporary and are usually by a single artist from anywhere in the country. They show a variety of media—painting, drawing, and sculpture—and feature print works from the highly regarded Paulsen Press in Emeryville. Tue-Sun. ⅜ (Berkeley Waterfront)

PUBLIC ART

LAKE MERRITT ESTUARY SCULPTURE PARK
East 10th St.

(south of Laney College)
Oakland

This canal links Lake Merritt to the Oakland Estuary and is bordered by a lawn studded with one dozen or so major sculptures. Most of the works are of the raw-slab and monumental-kids'-blocks variety. You'll share the breezy space with egrets, ducks, and studying students from adjacent Laney College. (Oakland)

OAKLAND MUSEUM SCULPTURE COURT
1111 Broadway
Oakland

You'll find sculpture in front of, behind, and inside this downtown office building. On the Broadway side are dramatic erect and fallen stone slabs. In the back are Richard Deutsch's Stella-like propeller pieces adjacent to a small, rocky waterfall. The lobby displays works by wildly colorful sculptors such as Joseph Slutsky. (Oakland)

Susan Smythe

7

KIDS' STUFF

Just gawking at the wild denizens of Telegraph Avenue can be eye-popping fun for kids, but Berkeley and Oakland have considerably more to offer than a freak show. Geared just for children—even small ones—are art spaces, zoos, museums, science labs, nature centers, toy stores, soda fountains, and even a multicultural storybook park. On a small scale, puppet shows and children's theater are produced by local talents. Major venues offer ice shows and circuses and visits by celebrated troupes like Mummenshanz. Even sometimes-tough-to-please older children can have a great time at stores that sell baseball cards or vintage comic books.

For fun far from the pavement, there's an estuary, a beach, and even a playground right on San Francisco Bay. There are parks all over both towns and most include well-equipped playgrounds. But for real freedom, definitely make sure you get to the wide-open spaces up in the Berkeley and Oakland hills. Here a kid can swim in a mountain lake, hike through fields of wildflowers, and ride a miniature train, a real pony, or a bright pink merry-go-round.

And if the strains of togetherness start to show—as they do in even the best of families—never fear. Berkeley and Oakland have their share of quick getaways. One of the best options is to take a ferry from Jack London Square to Alcatraz or Angel Island. Or, if your kids are suffering from theme-park deprivation, jump in the car and head for the waterslides. Great America and Six Flags/Marine World are less than one hour away.

ANIMALS AND THE GREAT OUTDOORS

CAL ADVENTURES
5 Haas Clubhouse
Berkeley
510/642-4000
If you're planning to stay in the East Bay in the summer with kids for at least one week, you can enroll them in some great outdoor adventures. This organization is full of avid, capable UC Berkeley students who will teach your children the fundamentals of sailing, windsurfing, and sea kayaking at their headquarters on the Berkeley Marina. They also offer rock-climbing classes on the UC climbing wall and in the Berkeley Hills. Classes last for half a day Monday through Friday and cost about $125 per child. Limited to kids ages 8-17. (Berkeley)

CESAR CHAVEZ PARK
Berkeley Marina
Berkeley
510/235-5483
Bay winds sweep across these 95 wide-open acres of rolling lawns at the tip of the Berkeley Marina, making it one of the world's great kite-flying sites. Most afternoons you can buy a kite in a kiosk near the parking lot for less than $10. There are also some beautiful—and much more expensive—silk and bamboo kites imported from China. The last weekend in July, the park hosts a kite-flying festival that includes individual and team competitions. Kids and adults alike are guaranteed to love it. (Berkeley Waterfront)

LAKE ANZA
Lake Anza Rd.
Tilden Park
Berkeley
510/562-PARK
Get here early on hot summer weekends. The parking lot and the strip of sandy beach fill up fast. Despite the lake's nine acres, swimming is allowed only in a small, roped-off area. Facilities include a snack bar, a changing room, and a large lawn perfect for picnicking, Frisbee, and volleyball. Swimming permitted May-October; lifeguards on duty 11 a.m.-6 p.m. $2.50 adults, $1.50 seniors and children ages 1-15, children under 1 free. (Hills)

OAKLAND ZOO
977 Golf Links Rd.
Oakland
510/ 632-9523
Three hundred exotic creatures roaming 433 acres can be too much of a good thing for small legs, so the Oakland Zoo has made special arrangements for its younger visitors. A children's-zoo area includes an array of animals from otters to iguanas and allows kids to hold or pet pygmy goats and sheep. Special rides, including a "sky ride," an old-fashioned merry-go-round, and a

Theater Piccoli's tiny troupe performs lively musical folk tales and requires lots of audience participation. Most of their monthly shows are at area libraries. Track them down at 510/650-0967.

Camels at the Oakland Zoo

miniature train (a two-thirds replica of an old-fashioned locomotive), are designed to keep kids off their feet as much as possible while offering great views of the zoo and all its inhabitants. Open daily 10-4. $3 per car. Adults $6.50. Children 2-14 and seniors $3.50. Children under 2 free. (Hills)

SHOREBIRD NATURE CENTER AND ADVENTURE PLAYGROUND
160 University Ave.
Berkeley
510/644-8623

The facilities are primitive, but the location is prime. Steps from the water, the **Shorebird Nature Center** teaches children about the bay's many species of sharks and rays. On a fieldtrip out on the water, they catch (and release) fish and study tidal patterns and bird life. Onshore, a 100-gallon chilled saltwater aquarium is usually home to crabs, perch, and flatfish. Admission to the nature center is free.

Nearby **Adventure Playground** puts the fun in funky. Dozens of weather-beaten climbing structures are scattered across the grounds here with zip lines that kids can ride between the structures and rowboats marooned in sandboxes. Kids are even given the materials and tools to build, paint, and decorate their own forts. Children can be left here for up to three hours for a five-dollar babysitting fee. Nature Center open Tue-Sat. Adventure Playground open daily in summer, Sat-Sun in winter. No admission charge. (Berkeley Waterfront)

STEAM TRAIN
Lomas Contatas and Grizzly Peak Blvd.
Tilden Park
Berkeley
510/548-6100

TIP

All the big-time national circuses and ice shows make stops at the Oakland Coliseum (now officially known as Network Associates Coliseum). More esoteric children's shows like Mummenshanz and Chinese acrobats show up regularly at UC's Zellerbach Theater, on the UC campus off the main Telegraph Avenue entrance.

It's only a little more than one mile long, but this 15-inch-gauge steam railroad packs a lot into 12 minutes. It winds through redwood groves, into tunnels, and over trestles and offers a terrific view of the North Bay. It's tiny, but parents can usually squeeze in next to their kids. Single ticket $1.50, five rides $6; children under 2 free. Open 11-5 daily. (Hills)

TILDEN CAROUSEL
Central Park Dr.
Tilden Park
Berkeley
510/524-6773
Built in 1911 for Los Angeles' Griffith Park, and relocated to its present location in the middle of the Berkeley woods, this carousel is the real thing. In fact, it's listed on the National Register of Historic Places. Spin in circles on this big baroque merry-go-round with a wooden menagerie of 57 real and mythic animals and charming old-fashioned panels. A soda fountain next door sells snacks and little toys. Out in front is a big lawn perfect for sprawling and picnicking. $1 per ride, 13 rides for $10. Open weekends. (Hills)

TILDEN NATURE CENTER AND LITTLE FARM
Central Park Dr.
Tilden Park
Berkeley
510/525-2233
The well-equipped **Tilden Nature Center** is a great source for information on the rich natural world of Tilden Park. Kids can walk through a cavelike re-creation of the Walnut Creek watershed, with layers of volcanic rock and displays of the region's small birds and animals. Very simple microscopes let them examine the smallest creatures of the undersea world. At the entrance they can measure the weight and volume of water in their own bodies. The bookstore is small but well stocked with nature games, books, and toys. Nature trails wind all around this area, and instructive walks are geared for kids.

Tilden Carousel

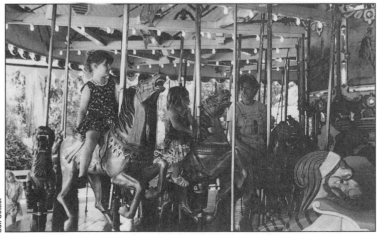

Gail Gettler

Steam Train in Tilden Regional Park

Just south of the nature center is the **Little Farm.** Kids are encouraged to feed and—in some cases—pet the tame donkeys, cows, rabbits, ducks, chicken, and geese. Tilden Nature Center and Little Farm both open daily 10-5 except Mon; call ahead for a schedule. Free. (Hills)

TILDEN PARK PONY RIDES
Central Park Dr.
Tilden Park
Berkeley
510/527-0421
The arena, restricted to kids age five and up, is a great place for a child to experience his or her first real pony ride. But that doesn't mean the smaller children in your crew will be disappointed. Those age two and up can ride the "merry-go-round" ponies in a slow circle. The docile ponies in both areas guarantee kids the gentlest of equine experiences. $2.50 per ride, 10 rides $23. Open 11-5 on weekends. During the summer open every day except Monday. (Hills)

MUSEUMS AND LIBRARIES

HABITOT CHILDREN'S MUSEUM
2065 Kittredge St.
Berkeley
510/647-1111
Every inch of this cozy downtown space is bursting with supervised activities for children age 7 and under. There's a face-painting station, an art room with nonstop creative projects, a mock grocery store, a toddler "garden" of soft mats, and a water area with plenty of room for splashing. Kids should wear old clothes and bring backups to change into at the end of the day. There's even a quiet area where parents can take a well-deserved break. Daily except Sun during summer. $4 adults, $6 first child, $3 each additional child; parent and one infant $8. ♿ (Berkeley)

HALL OF HEALTH
2230 Shattuck Ave.
Berkeley
510/549-1564
Kids love to play doctor, and this

series of interactive exhibits in the lower level of a former department store in downtown Berkeley allows them to do just that. Children age 3 and up can use stethoscopes to hear their own heartbeats and can even count calories as they're burned. Computers are set up to allow kids to explore the human body. Puppet shows on a variety of medical subjects are performed every third Saturday. There's even a clear and entertaining exhibit that shows kids what not to do, specifically drugs, tobacco, and alcohol. Open Tue-Sat. Free. ᘒ (Berkeley)

JUNIOR CENTER OF ART AND SCIENCE
558 Bellevue
Oakland
510/839-5777
This place is in perpetual motion. A constant series of hands-on workshops designed for children ages 5 to 16 keeps even those tykes with short attention spans on the move. Children can choose from pottery, carpentry, drawing, and puppet workshops for just $5 per hour plus materials. The center's science classes examine the squawking geese that live just outside in the Lake Merritt Wildlife Refuge. Inside, the so-called Discovery Row includes a collection of small crea-

tures such as geckos and stick bugs. Exhibits such as *California Native Americans* and *African American Inventors* are attuned to the local kids who visit. Open Tue-Sat. Free. ᘒ (Oakland)

LAWRENCE HALL OF SCIENCE
Centennial Dr.
Berkeley
510/642-5132
www.lhs.berkeley.edu
Kids love this place. On weekdays the Lawrence Hall of Science is a great place for hands-on exploration of everything from lasers to earthquakes. It's also fun to scramble around on its climbing structures, play with its science toys, and experiment with its computer games. On the weekends and during summer months, extra workshops are thrown into the melange. In the biology lab, instructors let kids hold gentle animals. And the Holt Planetarium allows children to both watch and conduct interesting experiments. Open daily. $6 adults; $4 seniors, students, and children 7-18; $2 children 3-6. Planetarium open weekends only; $2 additional. ᘒ (Berkeley)

MUSEUM OF CHILDREN'S ART
Ninth and Washington Sts.
Oakland
510/465-8770

Children really get a bang out of the drumming classes held every Saturday morning at the Alice Arts Center, 1428 Alice St., Oakland, 510/238-7222. No appointments are necessary—just drop in and pay eight dollars.

"Museum" probably isn't the right word for this place. MOCHA includes open studios and daily freeform projects—using paint, paper, feathers, tires, salt, seeds, and more—designed to keep kids occupied all afternoon. Four- and five-day workshops teach kids drawing techniques, sculpting skills, the art of the airbrush, and how to create commedia dell'arte masks. You'll also find one of the area's best children's stores around with, not surprisingly, a terrific selection of art supplies. Tues-Sat 10-5, Sun noon-5. Free. & (Oakland)

PUPPETS AND THEATER

EAST BAY CHILDREN'S THEATER FESTIVAL
2900 College Ave.
Berkeley
510/84-JULIA
A rapid-fire repertory of constantly changing musicals, puppets, circuses, and magicians fills this landmark Julia Morgan–designed building and one-time church. The Theater Festival, which targets kids ages 3 to 12, has an ambitious year-round Sunday afternoon schedule. *The Nutcracker* is performed at Christmas and a puppet show is fea-

tured over Halloween. Otherwise, anything goes and you can usually drop by and find tickets available one hour before the show. On Fridays, swing and ballroom drop-in dance sessions are offered for teens. Call for schedule. Kids' tickets generally run in the $5 range, adults up to $25. & (South Berkeley/North Oakland)

STORES KIDS LOVE

BRUSHSTROKES
745 Page St.
Berkeley
510/528-1350
Kids and parents can drop in here and make their own pottery. Well, the pottery is actually already made for you, in a wild variety of shapes, such as bud vases, heart boxes, goblets, cow pitchers, and some simple dog and cat dishes. But you can choose from more than 35 colors and get instruction on all kinds of glazing and decorating techniques. The store does the firing, and finished pieces can be picked up in five days. The whimsical design of the studio and the adjoining garden is inspirational. Wed-Mon. $5.50 per hour. & (Berkeley Waterfront)

If your kids can't imagine a vacation that doesn't include a theme park, Six Flags Marine World is just 25 minutes north of Berkeley in Vallejo. The park is home to more than 3,000 animals. Its main attractions are its water shows, in which dolphins and killer whales take center stage. And tots just love the Bugs Bunny at the Looney Tunes Seaport. There are plenty of wild rides, too, including two wicked roller coasters.

Games of Berkeley, 2151 Shattuck Ave., Berkeley, 510/540-7822, sells the UC Berkeley version of Monopoly, called Calopoly, for about $30.

COMIC RELIEF
2138 University Ave.
Berkeley
510/540-1731
www.comicrelief.net

Intense teenagers from nearby Berkeley High and comic book fans of all ages congregate at this cluttered shop at the top of University Avenue. Although the store does offer reprints of old classics—like bound "graphic novels" of the first 10 issues of *Superman,* for example—their concentration is not on superheroes. Rather, most of what you'll find leans toward unusual French comics and Japanese action figures and animé. Open daily. Another good comics store is Comics and Comics, 2502 Telegraph Avenue. ও (Berkeley)

DAVE'S DUGOUT
863B San Pablo Ave.
Albany
510/527-7120

This is the place to come if you want to buy a hero. Dave's Dugout offers what is probably the best inventory of sports cards in the Bay Area. A constant stream of kids of all ages (and plenty of adults, too) pours through the store's doors to check out the selection, which includes football, baseball, basketball, and hockey players; racecar drivers; and even the stars of women's basketball. Other items in stock include posters, old photos of Joe DiMaggio, and collectors' cards (a $1,500 1909 Walter John-

son, for example). There's also a small comic book section and a decent selection of baseball caps. Open daily. ও (Berkeley Waterfront)

FENTONS CREAMERY
4226 Piedmont Ave.
Oakland
510/658-7000

This neighborhood institution has been an Oakland mainstay since 1889. It's big and plain, but the chills are thrilling. The ice cream is made three times a week right on the premises. The flavors are rich, especially the toasted almond and Swiss milk chocolate, and the sundaes are gargantuan. Try to grab a seat on a red-leatherette banquette, but don't be surprised if you have to wait 10 or 15 minutes. On the weekends this place is jammed. Open daily. ও (Oakland)

KIMONO MY HOUSE
1464 62nd St.
Emeryville
510/654-4627

Anyone who is into the bizarre and colorful world of Japanese animé sci-fi will find a visit to this rooftop shop well worth the three-story climb. The owners claim they have the largest selection of esoteric games, videos, model kits, T-shirts, stuffed animals, toilet-seat covers, dolls, and action figures in the United States. Many of the pieces from the '50s and '60s, such as some original Godzilla merchandise, are rare. Be prepared for

Children's Fairyland

prices as steep as the stairway. Thu-Sat 11-6, Sun 12-5. (Berkeley Waterfront)

MR. MOPPS
1405 Martin Luther King
Berkeley
519/525-9633
This long-time children's store began in 1962 with a book catalog. Today Mr. Mopps still has one of the area's largest selections of history, science, and storybooks for kids, plus two large rooms filled with endless entertainment, from games to costumes to crafts to model cars. They specialize in low-tech, old-fashioned toys such as Etch-A-Sketch, as well as small games

perfect for traveling. You'll also find classic porcelain dolls, a nice lineup of ethnic dolls, and all the latest Barbies. A collection of Piñatas parades along the front wall. This lively place is a welcome antidote to mall superstores. Tue-Sat. &. (Berkeley)

SWEET DREAMS
2901 College Ave.
Berkeley
510/549-1211
Fifteen kinds of licorice, 28 types of jellybeans, and gumballs two inches in diameter make this store no place for dentists. Sweet Dreams is devoted to the kind of unsophisticated sweets kids love. You'll also find toys, tchotchkes, and cards galore, and, in the back room, clothing and jewelry. This is a great place to find unusual treats. Open daily. &. (South Berkeley/North Oakland)

VIVARIUM
1827 Fifth St.
Berkeley
510/841-1400
Kids who love creepy, crawling creatures will have to be pried out of this, the largest retail reptile store in the U.S. There are lizards and snakes from around the world, ranging in length from a few inches to 14 feet. The savvy staff can sell you an albino Burmese python for around $250 or a red-legged Mexican tarantula. They have an enormous selection of tanks

Who needs babysitters to go out and see Hollywood's latest? Every Monday night at 6 at Oakland's Parkway Theater, 1834 Park Blvd., 510/814-2400, infants are admitted for free, as long as they can't walk or talk. Getting the kids through the entrance can be more fun than watching the flicks.

Tilden Park's 2,065 open acres cap the hills above Berkeley and are crisscrossed with hiking and biking trails and several entertainment and educational facilities for kids.

and other supplies and plenty of mice, rats, crickets, earthworms, and maggots to feed your pets. Yummy. Open daily. ♿ (Berkeley Waterfront)

THEME PARKS

CHILDREN'S FAIRYLAND
Grand and Bellevue Aves.
Oakland
510/238-6876
Older, jaded, Disney-sated kids might find this seven-acre playground a little old-fashioned, but younger children love it. Everything from a small carousel to a tiny lake used for boat rides is scaled down for the little ones. The 30 or so attractions range from classic *Mother Goose* and *Alice in Wonderland* sites to more multicultural ones such as Ananse, an African Spider-man. Using a plastic key, kids can turn on little music boxes that explain each attraction. Farm animals are available for petting and, during the summer, there's a full schedule of musicians, magicians, storytellers, and kids' theater. Daily. $5 children age 1 and up. ♿ (Oakland)

RECREATION

ICELAND
2727 Milvia St.

Berkeley
510/647-1600
Tara Lipinski and Brian Boitano have practiced in this 1938 Art Deco rink, which, at 2,000 square feet in size, is still the largest ice-skating facility in California. It is starting to show its age, and the snowy alpine scenes painted across the back wall seem a little corny, but it's still family-friendly. On Friday nights the fun picks up when disco lights flash. Open daily year-round; call for schedule. $6 adults, $5 children 16 and under. (Berkeley)

OAKLAND ICE CENTER
519 18th St.
Oakland
510/268-9000
The neighborhood is old and eerily empty, but rising from the middle of the block is this massive modern arena. Especially on weekends, this place swarms with activity. There are two rinks—the NHL, which is used primarily for hockey games; and the Olympic, which is used by individual skaters. Older kids are fairly likely to find a pick-up hockey game. There is also a weight room and a snack bar. The crowd is pure Oakland—a noisy, laughing cross-section of every racial group. Open daily. $5 adults over 55 and children 12 and under; $6 ages 13-54. (Oakland)

Todd Jokl

8

PARKS, GARDENS, AND RECREATION AREAS

Few urban areas are greener than Berkeley or Oakland. In fact, throughout the two cities, you're rarely more than 10 minutes away from some kind of open space. There are more than 50 miles of accessible waterfront, and wildlife, marine or otherwise, is abundant. The bay is chock-full of fish, including 14 species of sharks (all harmless). Loons, snowy egrets, and swans live along the shore and on Lake Merritt, the nation's first wildlife refuge.

Thousands of acres of open land span the ridgelines of both cities, and the voluptuous hills are covered with grasses as green as Ireland after the winter rains. Trees are abundant, too, which is how Oakland got its name. Clusters of hardy, twisted oaks with umbrellalike branches share the hills with aromatic bay laurels and eucalyptus. A few dense redwood groves remain from the much larger stands that were cut down for lumber a century ago. And although the hills may not be as alive as they once were, on almost any hike you're bound to see deer, rabbits, or opossum. And if you look up, there's a good chance you'll see hawks and bald eagles circling in the sky.

All of this open space doesn't include the 147 public parks, the specialized botanical gardens, and the hundreds of square miles of private gardens. The truth is, vast amounts of land in the area have yet to see development or have otherwise retained their natural character. People get passionate about the environment here. Oakland was the first city in the country to elect a state representative from the Green Party.

ANTHONY CHABOT REGIONAL PARK
Main access points off Redwood Rd., Skyline Blvd., and Lake Chabot Rd.

Stretching for almost 5,000 acres along the Oakland ridgeline, Chabot is the biggest—although not the most scenic—park in the East Bay Regional Parks District. It's also the only park with campgrounds, a 315-acre lake big enough for boating, and a firing range. There are fewer trails than you might expect for such a vast area. The easiest is the bicycle path that circles Chabot Lake in a 14.5-mile loop. For a less populated and more serene route, take the Grass Valley Loop. It begins at the Bort Staging Area and crosses the rolling meadows on the valley floor. Guided horseback rides are available through the Equestrian Center (510/638-0610), and camping is permitted in designated areas above the lake. To reserve a campsite, call at least two weeks in advance (510/636-1684). The nightly fee is $15. (Hills)

BERKELEY MARINA
Foot of University Ave., west of I-80
Berkeley
510/644-8623

You never know how fast the wind will be blowing here at the tip of Berkeley, so bring a windbreaker. Don't be fooled by the landscape; this is not a natural coastline, but landfill. (The bay fills easily because most of it is less than 18 feet deep.) Despite the presence of a marina, a hotel, and several restaurants, you can take an hour-long walk around the entire area and get a good dose of aerial and aquatic wildlife. There is an even shorter walk at nearby

Docks at Lake Chabot in Anthony Chabot Regional Park

Aquatic Park (Heinz and Seventh Street). (Berkeley Waterfront)

BERKELEY ROSE GARDEN
Euclid Ave. and Eunice St.
Berkeley
510/644-6530

Watch the sun go down in flames behind the Golden Gate from a bench perched on this garden amphitheater. Around you, tier after tier of roses—more than 190 varieties and 1,900 bushes in all—rise in perfect half circles. Built as a WPA project in 1933, the garden is crowned with a redwood pergola. The display of color in spring and summer is downright dazzling. Unfortunately, the gardeners have had difficulties preventing deer from eating the buds, so they've had to erect a wire fence around it. Open dawn to dusk. (Berkeley)

CLAREMONT CANYON REGIONAL PRESERVE
Off Stonewall Rd. or the east end of Dwight Way

Your calf muscles will certainly be

BERKELEY/OAKLAND

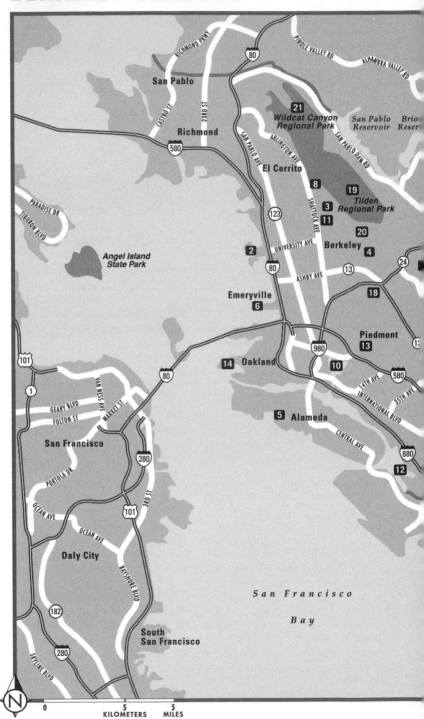

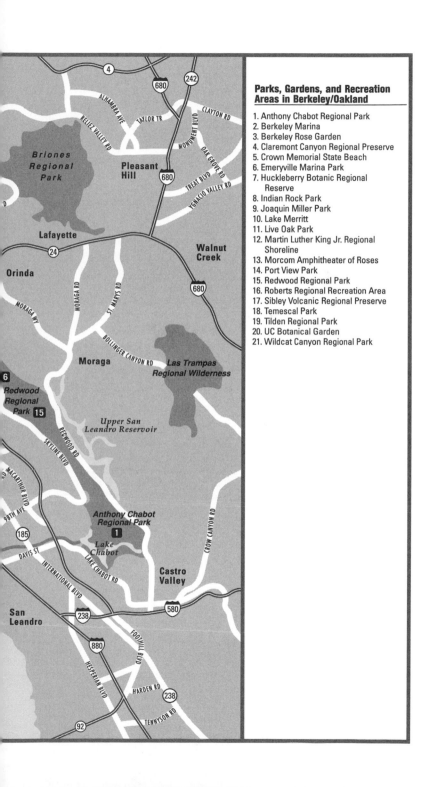

Parks, Gardens, and Recreation Areas in Berkeley/Oakland

1. Anthony Chabot Regional Park
2. Berkeley Marina
3. Berkeley Rose Garden
4. Claremont Canyon Regional Preserve
5. Crown Memorial State Beach
6. Emeryville Marina Park
7. Huckleberry Botanic Regional Reserve
8. Indian Rock Park
9. Joaquin Miller Park
10. Lake Merritt
11. Live Oak Park
12. Martin Luther King Jr. Regional Shoreline
13. Morcom Amphitheater of Roses
14. Port View Park
15. Redwood Regional Park
16. Roberts Regional Recreation Area
17. Sibley Volcanic Regional Preserve
18. Temescal Park
19. Tilden Regional Park
20. UC Botanical Garden
21. Wildcat Canyon Regional Park

tested on the radically steep trail that goes up, around, and down the 200 acres of Claremont Canyon. Why should you do it? Because it's a wide-open, wildflower-filled grassland with a great view of the Golden Gate Bridge. The spring show of golden poppies and blue lupines are supposedly the source for UC Berkeley's school colors. In the summer, when the cool fog rolls in, the hike is a bit less torturous. Nevertheless, frequent stops are recommended. The four-mile walk ends at the steam trains on Grizzly Peak. (Hills)

CROWN MEMORIAL STATE BEACH
Shoreline Dr.
Alameda
510/636-1684
Once upon a time, Alameda was a beach resort—a big, splashy, Victorian playground with boardwalks, hotels, a roller coaster, and a sunny view of San Francisco. Now, all that's left is the sand and the view. This 2.5-mile strip of beach has picnic tables but no lifeguards, and the water can be extremely cold, even in the summer. But the tidal life is intriguing, and you can study it at the Crab Cove Visitor Center (510/521-6887). Call them for information about their annual Sand Sculpture contest, held in June. (Oakland)

EAST BAY REGIONAL PARK DISTRICT
2950 Peralta Oaks Court
Oakland
510/562-7275
www.ebparks.com
The East Bay Regional Park District maintains and preserves 55 parks on more than 91,000 acres, from the shores of the bay to the slopes of Mount Diablo in Contra Costa. The district offers educational programs at every level in every location almost all year long. All parks are open from 10 to 5 unless otherwise posted. Detailed brochures, which outline the generous variety of trails, including ones for biking and horseback riding, are available at each park. Many parks are accessible via bus through AC Transit (510/817-1717). (Hills)

EMERYVILLE MARINA PARK
Frontage Rd. off Powell St.
Emeryville
Before Highway 880 was widened to 12 lanes, the tidelands here were an open-air sculpture gallery. Using driftwood and other debris, local artists created funny, political, sometimes traffic-stopping works. Today, a tidy little park and trellised pier pay homage to that muddy art movement. A few hardy timbers, each

Dogs rule in the East Bay, especially at canine-friendly Cesar Chavez Park in the Berkeley Marina and, even more so, at Point Isabel in Richmond. Great ideas on where to walk your dog, what to feed your dog, and just about everything else you ever wanted to know about dogs is available in *Bark*, an elegant magazine published in Berkeley. Go to www.thebark.com to see the magazine online.

capped with a sculpture, poke out of the water. Dress warmly because the winds blow straight in from the Golden Gate Bridge. (Berkeley Waterfront)

HUCKLEBERRY BOTANIC REGIONAL RESERVE
Off Skyline Blvd., south of Sibley Park
Oakland

Few areas in the East Bay hills are as rich in plant life as these very green 235 acres. As you enter the park to begin the one-and-a-half-mile loop, pick up a brochure designed to help you identify the plants you'll find along the way. The left fork zigzags down into the canyon and is densely vegetated. The upper fork is level and wider. At the spot marked #8, there is a particularly stunning view. The roundtrip should take only two hours. Bring water with you because none is available on the trail. (Hills)

INDIAN ROCK PARK
Shattuck Ave. and Indian Rock Rd.

Berkeley
Looking up from the road at this volcanic outcropping, you see what seems to be a craggy profile of an Indian chief. You can walk up on stairs cut into the rock or you can try climbing on the face if you know what you are doing. At the top is another one of those heart-stopping bay views from San Jose to Mount Tamalpais. Mortar Rock, farther up the hill, has holes like Swiss cheese where the Ohlone Indians once ground acorn meal. This park is located in a residential district just five minutes from University Avenue. (Berkeley)

JOAQUIN MILLER PARK
Off Hwy. 13 on Joaquin Miller Rd. (bordered by Skyline Blvd.)
Oakland
510/238-3481

Poet and Pony Express rider Joaquin Miller settled on this high Oakland hillside in 1870 when it held nothing but redwood tree stumps. It was his failed attempt to start an artist's

Berkeley Marina, p. 141

Susan Smythe

The Garden District

*The East Bay was into gardening long before it became America's favorite hobby. The rare and unusual are not rare and unusual in these nurseries. Far and away the largest selection of old and new roses is at **Berkeley Horticulture** (510/526-4704). **Magic Gardens'** (510/644-1992) forte is unusual perennials, especially salvias and camellias. **Yabusakai** (510/845-6261) has nearly 200 bonsai. After the scary drought years of the '70s, gardeners in the East Bay have learned to appreciate less-thirsty plants like you'll find at **The Dry Garden** (510/547-3564).*

commune. Today a few traces of Miller's presence remain, but if he were to return he might be startled to see *The Music Man* playing down the road in the Woodminster Amphitheater. On its 425 mostly wooded acres, you'll find plenty of easy walking trails, especially the Sequoia Bayview and the Chinquapin. Ask at park headquarters for a guide to the plant life. Open daily. (Hills)

LAKE MERRITT
Oakland
510/238-7275
The trail around this saltwater lake in the heart of the city may be only three and one-half miles long, but it takes you traveling through time and fantasies. Lining it are sites such as the turn-of-the-nineteenth-century Camron Stanford house and Children's Fairyland. The trail is dotted with fountains and sculptures. The lake was the first wildlife preserve in the United States. It's almost impossible to make this a solitary journey because families, joggers, and walkers circle the lake all day, beginning early in the morning. The best way to

get away on your own is to rent a sailboat or kayak and hit the water. (Oakland)

LAKESIDE PARK GARDEN CENTER
666 Bellevue Ave.
Oakland
510/238-3187
If you're as interested in learning about gardens as you are in looking at them, then make a point of stopping here on your visit to Lake Merritt. Although it does have some beautiful bedding areas, including roses and a remarkable collection of old bonsai, the garden's strength is in its capacity to educate. Several demonstration gardens are featured in the center, and a wealth of information is available on everything from mulching and composting to dealing with horticultural ailments. The center's specialization is community gardens. Open daily. (Oakland)

LIVE OAK PARK
1301 Shattuck
Berkeley
510/644-8153

What was Berkeley like when redwood-lined creeks meandered through it? This deeply shaded five-and-one-half-acre park on the city's north side is one of the last reminders of that greener time. Although the heavily used park includes basketball courts, playgrounds, a recreation center, and an art gallery, it's possible to achieve instant serenity by traversing Cordonices Creek, which flows through its center. Crisscrossed by bridges, it's easily accessible and includes several picnic areas along its banks. On summer afternoons the warm perfume of bay laurel trees and the gentle splashing of the dark creek are as soothing as a full-body massage. (Berkeley)

MARTIN LUTHER KING JR. REGIONAL SHORELINE
Entry points off Hegenberger Rd.
Oakland

Only 10 percent of the intertidal salt marshes that once ringed San Francisco Bay still remain. And that's what makes these 1,220 windswept acres so precious, especially considering that they are bordered by the heavy traffic of Highway 880 and Oakland International Airport. The bird life here, including blue herons, egrets, avocets, ducks, and grebes, is prolific. A good place to bird-watch is from the raised structure at Arrowhead Marsh. Bring a pair of binoculars. Trails traverse most of the marsh, which includes a fishing pier, picnic areas, and a boat launch. (Oakland)

MORCOM AMPHITHEATER OF ROSES
Jean St. above Grand
Oakland
510/658-0731

This park is so dedicated to mothers that the roses are nurtured to bloom all at once in early May, right around Mother's Day. More than 1,000 varieties grow in this seven-and-one-half-acre sloping hollow. The gardens are modeled after fifteenth-century Italian ones and include a watery cascade on the west side, a large reflecting pool in the center, and a dramatic allée of pink floribunda trimmed like small trees. At the upper end of the hollow are older noisettes and tea roses. Benches circle the area so you can stop and—you guessed it—smell the roses. Open daily dawn to dusk. (Oakland)

PORT VIEW PARK
Western tip of Seventh St.
Oakland

The screams of huge semis' air-brakes drown out the calls of the seagulls at this surprisingly pristine little park at the far end of the Port of Oakland. Surrounded by cranes and shipping containers and often wind-

Joaquin Miller Park, p. 145

Gail Gettler

PARKS, GARDENS, AND RECREATION AREAS **147**

whipped, the park has lawns to loll on, a colorful play structure for small kids, a nice fishing pier, and a snack bar. It's a great place to watch tugboats as they set off to work, but the best view is that of the Bay Bridge. Open dawn to dusk. (Oakland)

REDWOOD REGIONAL PARK
Redwood Rd., off Skyline Blvd.
Oakland
510/636-1684

Legend has it that the twisting Rainbow creek running through the center of 1,836-acre Redwood Park is where rainbow trout were first named. The creek and a few trout remain in this densely forested park, but they're not as well off as they once were. Today an effort is being made to bring the stream back to its natural state. Needless to say, fishing is not allowed, nor is walking in the stream or on its banks. Still, there's plenty left to see. For a good hike, take the Stream Trail and cross at the French Trail to West Ridge Trail. It's a breathtaking 1,000-foot climb, but the reward is a heavenly view of the bay. (Hills)

REGIONAL PARKS
BOTANIC GARDEN
Tilden Park
Berkeley
510/841-8732

The entire state of California has been squeezed into this magnificent 10-acre garden. More than 300 varieties of plants native to the Golden State are displayed in 10 distinct zones, including a redwood zone, a sea bluff zone, and a Pacific rainforest zone. The trails are ideal for an easy, ambling walk. Signs describe each plant in the garden, which includes a large collection of manzanitas and endangered flora. The visitors center offers more information and lectures every Saturday November through February. Many plants go on sale in the spring; call for dates. Open 8:30-5:00 daily. (Hills)

ROBERTS REGIONAL
RECREATION AREA
Skyline Blvd.,
off Joaquin Miller Rd.
Oakland
510/636-0138

On weekends and all week long during the summer you'll find kids all over this 82-acre recreational area. You'll also find a 25-yard pool, a baseball field, an archery range, volleyball courts, and playgrounds with climbing equipment. Day camps operate here during the summer, so it's best to get in early if you want to secure a picnic table. If you don't beat the rush, however, the day is not over. Just park your car and set off on the

TIP

If you happen to see a mountain lion while you're out and about in one of the area's parks, keep the following in mind: Lions are antisocial and avoid people. The more singing, whistling, and talking you do the better. Never run from a lion. Face it, wave your arms slowly, and speak in a loud voice. Then, very carefully, back away.

hiking and biking trails that lead into the adjacent Redwood Park. (Hills)

SIBLEY VOLCANIC REGIONAL PRESERVE
Off Skyline Blvd., one-quarter mile south of Grizzly Peak Blvd.
Ten million years ago, Sibley was a volcano. Today, at the Sibley Park headquarters, an exhibit explains what happened then and shows what remains, including lava flows, cinder piles, and caldera walls. The 387-acre park includes an easy half-hour trail that circles Round Top, a 1,761-foot-high rounded peak. Take the trail for fantastic views of the rolling hills and valleys of western Contra Costa. In 1913 this was the center of Frank Haven's misbegotten eucalyptus empire. He had no idea that the thousands of trees he had planted could not be milled. (Hills)

SKYLINE NATIONAL TRAIL
Seven designated entrances from Wildcat Canyon to Proctor Gate
This 31-mile trail loops through all the parks that top the ridgeline of the Berkeley/Oakland hills. It actually starts well south of Oakland and ends north of Berkeley in Richmond. It's possible to hike the entire length in two or three days, but no campsites are available. Nor are there many places to find drinking water. In places the trail rises and falls pre-

cipitously—up 600 feet, down 300 feet, up 900 feet, down 200 feet, up . . . you get the picture. Bicycles and horses are permitted on about 65 percent of the trail. (Hills)

TEMESCAL REGIONAL RECREATION AREA
Intersection of Hwys. 13 and 24 Oakland
This park is the most accessible (and crowded) in the area. Both ends of the 48-acre park include lawns and picnic tables, and a fairly flat trail circles 13-acre Lake Temescal, which is popular with anglers and swimmers alike. The lake is well stocked with largemouth bass, trout, and catfish. A state fishing license is required for all anglers over the age of 15. Beach fee: $1.50 age 15 and under, $2.50 age 16 and older. (Hills)

TILDEN REGIONAL PARK
South entrance off Claremont Blvd.; north entrance off Spruce St. Berkeley
510/562-7275
Fortunately, immense popularity has not yet spoiled 2,077-acre Tilden Regional Park. Berkeley's green backdrop includes a 19-hole golf course, a merry-go-round, a beautiful botanical garden, pony rides, a nature-study center, and Lake Anza, where half of Berkeley seems to be swimming on any

given summer weekend. A paved trail, which at times can be as busy as a city street, leads to the appropriately named Inspiration Point. Four or five other main trails are more isolated and quiet. (Hills)

UC BOTANICAL GARDEN
200 Centennial Dr.
Berkeley
510/642-3343
Come here and wind your way through a world of wild plants. All told, more than 13,000 species flourish on 34 gently hilly acres of Strawberry Canyon. The 12 distinct sections include everything from a rhododendron-filled Japanese glade to a succulent-laced desert. The basic loop around the spectacular garden takes about 30 minutes, but if you want to savor the experience, plan on staying at least an hour or two. Call ahead for a schedule of special events and plant sales. Limited parking is available, but find-

---

TOP TEN

Top 10 Ways to Get in Touch with Nature
by Priscilla Wrubel, founder of The Nature Company

1. Go to **Tilden Park** when the fogs spills through the Golden Gate like a giant tidal wave coming to claim the bay.

2. Visit **Blake Gardens** in Kensington for a peaceful weekday lunch.

3. See the **Rose Garden** in spring when it's in full bloom.

4. Take your dog to the **Berkeley Marina Dog Park,** where you'll find great views of the bay and San Francisco.

5. Visit the **UC Botanical Gardens** in late spring and watch hummingbirds as they feed on the cactus blossoms.

6. Drive down **Hopkins Street** in the fall as the plane trees drop their brown leaves.

7. Shop at **Monterey Market,** where heaping cases of fruits and vegetables alert you to the seasonal changes: mushrooms and asparagus in the spring; melons, tomatoes, and corn in the summer; pumpkins in the fall; and citrus, broccoli, and kale in the winter.

8. Listen to the high-pitched call of the **cedar waxwings** as they pass through on their spring and fall migrations.

9. Go to **Oxford Street near Rose** to witness the February flowering of the huge tulip tree with its big, showy, white blooms.

10. Visit **Aquatic Park** in the fall and welcome the shorebirds as they arrive for the winter.

---

ing spots can be difficult on spring weekends. Open daily 9-4:45. $3 adults, $2 seniors, $1 children ages 3-18; Thursdays are free. (Berkeley)

WILDCAT CANYON REGIONAL PARK
Tilden Park
Berkeley
510/236-1262
This place is surprisingly wild for an area with such a long history of human settlement. The Spanish soldier Pedro Fages first passed through here in 1772, stopping at an Indian village near the mouth of Wildcat Creek. Later the area was severely overgrazed and, in the early 1900s, became a heavily used park. Now thick stands of oaks, laurels, and maples serve as habitat for foxes, squirrels, deer, and gopher and king snakes. The park's 2,428 acres include some moderately steep trails and a lush one along Wildcat Creek. (Hills)

Lisa Lefkowitz

9

SHOPPING

Still happily out of step with the rest of America, Berkeley and Oakland have mostly resisted the lure of malls. But if you're looking for a satisfying shopping fix, you can, with a little digging, find small, one-of-a-kind shops with the newest fashions as well as the oldest, vintage ones. From faraway places come crafts, Indonesian jewelry, Mexican armoires, Indian saris, Middle Eastern carpets, French garden furniture, and troves of stuff from the American Southwest. More than 65 chain and independent stores specialize in rare books, used books, spiritual books, feminist books, ethnic books, and architecture books. As befitting one of America's recycling capitals, the area is home to a tempting array of flea markets, whole neighborhoods of antique shops, and half a dozen stores specializing in urban salvage. The most indigenous items can be found weekends on the sidewalks of Telegraph Avenue and its four blocks of counter-cultural wares, including jewelry, tie-dyes, buttons, and bumper stickers that would get you run off the road just about anywhere else in the United States. But perhaps the best thing about shopping in Berkeley and Oakland is the fact that you don't have to drive all over the place to find what you need. You could spend a whole afternoon just exploring the shops in one neighborhood.

SHOPPING DISTRICTS

Telegraph Avenue
The '60s never died on these four carnival-like blocks off the main entrance to the University of California.

Grunge and punk weren't passing fads. In stores and on sidewalk card tables, you'll find merchandise and crafts from a more bizarre time. And the density of great bookstores is unmatched. For the full time-travel *effect, go on the weekends when it's busiest.*

AMOEBA MUSIC
2455 Telegraph Ave.
Berkeley
510/549-1125

The "Avenue" has half a dozen music stores, but this one is the least chainlike and the most Berkeley. Half of Amoeba's 250,000 titles are used. They stock a lot of local hip-hop and underground deejay mixes. Their classical section consists primarily of twentieth-century music. Definitely check out their bargain bins—you won't believe the deals. (Berkeley)

MARS MERCANTILE
2398 Telegraph Ave.
Berkeley
510/843-6711

There are several vintage clothing stores in the city, but this one covers the most ground. You'll find just about everything you could possibly need here, from Victoriana to slinky '30s gowns to the fashions of the synthetic '70s. Some things—such as vinyl see-through handbags, hotly colored dynel wigs, and fake furs—are absolutely wild. Everything is in cherry condition, from the aloha shirts to the sexy black cocktail dresses to the quilted housecoats. (Berkeley)

REPRINT MINT
2484 Telegraph Ave.
Berkeley
510/841-9423

Students with a $20 budget to decorate their dorm rooms flock here. This landmark store claims to be the largest print retailer in North America, with more than 7,000 designs that range from old masters to old movie posters, Art Deco European ads, botanicals, historical photos of the Berkeley area, and a rich selection of Ansel Adams photos. (Berkeley)

WICKED
2431 Telegraph Ave.
Berkeley
510/883-1055

This store tries hard to be bad, but it's fairly innocuous for punky Telegraph Avenue. The bottom floor has (mostly black) Gen X men's and women's clothing. The back is the place to go for tattoos and body piercings, and upstairs is a huge collection of water pipes. Don't know what a water pipe is? Then you're in the wrong store. (Berkeley)

Fourth Street

Someone's been reading your mind. The developers of these five blocks of contemporary stores in a former warehouse district have the ideal mix of modern shopping down perfectly. You'll find absolutely original merchandise, high fashion, European housewares, tasteful outlet stores, restaurants, coffeehouses, bookshops—everything for the sophisticated shopper, except enough parking.

ERICA TANOV
1827 Fourth St.
Berkeley
510/849-3331

A local girl makes very, very good. New York City's Barney's carries a few pieces of these rich bohemian clothes designed by a young Berkeley native, but if you want to see the whole collection in all its delicate glory, stop in here. Expect a lot of handkerchief linen and silk organza with delicately layered pale, sheer colors. The children's clothes and bed linens are just as sophisticated. (Berkeley Waterfront)

THE GARDENER
1836 Fourth St.
Berkeley
510/548-4545
Very few of the extraordinary furnishings you'll find here are intended for the garden. But whether it's a glass bowl of Zen simplicity, a table inlaid with delicately broken crockery, or wildly French salad servers, you can be sure you've never seen it anywhere else. When it comes to style, this unique, ever-changing store is always slightly ahead of the curve. (Berkeley Waterfront)

HEAR MUSIC
1809 Fourth St.
Berkeley
510/204-9595
Hear Music is a world away from the superstores. The stock here is small, as if it's the private collection of a very selective music lover. You'll find a little bit of everything but mainly jazz, blues, and folk. This place was a pioneer in the movement to bring back listening stations, which allow shoppers to hear almost any CD in the store before they purchase it. And if that's not enough, the staff is tremendously knowledgable. (Berkeley Waterfront)

MARGARET O'LEARY
1832 Fourth St.
Berkeley
510/540/8241
This young Bay Area designer definitely hails from Ireland. The colors of her hand-knit, hand-loomed sweaters are as soft as a Killarney morning. She uses all natural cashmere, cotton, and linen yarns for her sophisticated yet relaxed dresses and separates. There's also a high-end selection of bags, shoes, scarves, and jewelry with prices to match. (Berkeley Waterfront)

Gilman and 10th St.
Shoppers are in for some genuine

Erica Tanov

Susan Smythe

surprises in this slowly gentrifying, though still somewhat industrial neighborhood.

ETHNIC ARTS
1314 10th St.
Berkeley
510/527-5270

This large, spare space and an even larger back room may be the best example of local fascination with Third-World crafts. Here you'll find stone Buddhas, African ceremonial masks, charming metal cutouts made in Haiti from oil-drum lids, a softly colored collection of batik and Kuba textiles, and cabinets full of exotic jewelry. Prices range wildly, from a $7 sarong to a $6,000 African house post. (Berkeley Waterfront)

REAL GOODS
1324 10th St.
Berkeley
510/558-0700

This is guilt-free materialism—a store with nothing but what's good for the environment. You'll find solar-powered radios and flashlights, clothing made from all-natural fibers that were never sprayed with pesticides, composting gear, and lots of bright science toys and games. And if you like your environmentally friendly products at bargain prices, you can just head across the parking lot to the store's close-out outlet. (Berkeley Waterfront)

SALSA
1328 10th St.
Berkeley
510/526-8590

Although the oversized Santa Fe-style furniture here is new, it looks as if it's been around for a while. A lot of the wood has been recycled, and many of the finishes have a macho Southwest rusticity. Check

TO MARKET

Grocery shopping approaches an art around here. **Monterey Market** *(1550 Hopkins, Berkeley, 510/525-5600) is like the world's greatest roadside stand, with oddities such as purple beans, pixie tangerines, and taxicab-yellow canary melons. They don't treat fruits and vegetables like they belong in a Tiffany jewel case like* **Andronico's** *(1550 Shattuck, 1850 Solano, 2655 Telegraph, 1414 University, all in Berkeley) does. For sheer stupendous selection, try to find a parking space at the club store-like* **Berkeley Bowl** *(2020 Oregon, Berkeley, 510/843-6929). In Oakland,* **Ratto's** *(827 Washington, Oakland, 510/832-6503), which has been around since 1897 and looks it, has an endless variety of Indian curries, German mustards, and Swiss chocolates, plus 10 kinds of risotto.*

out the terrific accessories like Zapotec rugs, copper-lathed outdoor furniture, and intricately carved leather bags. (Berkeley Waterfront)

ZIA HOUSEWORKS
1310 10th St.
Berkeley
510/528-2377
Have you ever wondered what happened to that mania for wildly painted Southwest furniture? It's been refined and updated in this sophisticated country store. The cabinets, tables, chairs, and bedsteads have leaner lines and simpler painted decorations. A recent addition is an urbane interpretation of Maine cottage furnishings. The handsomely minimal pottery and glassware is especially enticing. (Berkeley Waterfront)

Ashby and Adeline
This sentimental little neighborhood has survived shifting tastes and, more threateningly, the construction of a massive BART parking lot across the street. You'll find a good cross-section of French, Victorian, Arts and Crafts, and Early American antiques (primarily of the elegant, grandmotherly variety). Some of the stores have been around for more than 25 years, which, around here, is a lifetime.

ANTIQUES BY TONY
3017 Adeline
Berkeley
510/649-9016
Be careful. Be extremely careful. This froufrou china shop is full of exquisite—and highly breakable—porcelain, such as Sevres urns and Meissen shepherdesses, delicate cameos, finely cut crystal, and magnificent gilded bronze clocks. The

small collection is mostly eighteenth-century French and the prices are serious. An 11-piece dinner service, for example, runs about $4,000. (South Berkeley/North Oakland)

JACK'S
3021 Adeline
Berkeley
510/845-6221
It's as if you wandered into an antiques store on a Connecticut back road. You'll find classic Early American pieces—some plain and some quite fancy—in pine, cherry, walnut, teak, and mahogany. There are even a few Chinese tables and Japanese *tonsus*. Specialties include handsome coverlets from the 1830s, antique duck decoys, and early silver. Don't miss the back room's enormous selection of chairs and bedsteads. (South Berkeley/North Oakland)

LACIS
2982 Adeline
Berkeley
510/843-7290
Lace and nothing but lace is the story here. This store is full of yards and yards of delicate, antique, imported, colored, simple, ornate, and extraordinarily beautiful lace. It also has a small but unique selection of wedding dresses and Victorian shawls. And if you've ever wanted to impress your friends with your ability to make lace, this is the place to learn how (and buy the requisite equipment). (South Berkeley/North Oakland)

The Elmwood
College Avenue, the main artery in this charming old neighborhood, stretches from UC Berkeley to Oakland. The main shopping areas are

clustered near Ashby Avenue and Claremont Avenue. You'll find more of the unique Berkeley mix of hip clothing, imports, books, and antiques. And should your energy flag, a coffeehouse is located on almost every block.

CRAFTSMAN HOME
3048 Claremont Ave.
Berkeley
510/655-6503
You've been admiring the handsome Arts and Crafts-style homes of Berkeley. Now you can take a little of that style home. This store carries original furnishings as well as reproductions by local craftspeople. The tables and chairs are dark oaks and cherry, many in the starkly beautiful Mission style. The copper and verdigris lamps are wonderfully romantic, and there are some great milky glazed tiles. (South Berkeley/North Oakland)

DISH
2981 College Ave.
Berkeley
510/540-4784
Berkeley isn't all Birkenstocks and tie-dyes. This sliver of a store carries some of the hippest young designers in the United States—ones that don't show up in department stores, like Darryl K. It also carries a nice selection from up-and-coming local talent. Look for bright, modern, minimal designs in separates, jewelry, shoes, and handbags. You'll find equally trendy menswear on the second level. (South Berkeley/North Oakland)

FIORI SECCHI
2911 Claremont Ave.
Berkeley
510/649-8432

At first you might think a bomb has gone off and sent sheaves of dry wheat, armfuls of roses, yards of satin ribbon, and antique birdcages flying in a mad jumble across this floral-design store. But you'd be wrong. In fact, the clutter is just the whimsically overdone style of the owner, who specializes in dry flowers but also carries candles, tassels, and even stuffed roosters. (South Berkeley/North Oakland)

TAIL OF THE YAK
2632 Ashby Ave.
Berkeley
510/841-9891
Worldly shoppers who think they've seen everything are in for a pleasant surprise at this beautifully idiosyncratic store. Most of what's here is antique jewelry scoured from European sources, but there's also a unique selection of candles, paper goods, ribbons, Mexican silver, and anything that strikes the store owner's particular fancy. If you have time to shop at only one store, make this your choice. (South Berkeley/North Oakland)

NOTABLE BOOKSTORES AND NEWSSTANDS

BLACK OAK BOOKS
1491 Shattuck Ave.
Berkeley
510/486-0698
blackoakbks@earthlink.net
The exotic collection at this Northside institution leans toward contemporary fiction with a large helping of poetry. While they once sold mostly used books, today they favor new ones. Rare first editions include books by Dickens, Nabokov, and Toni Morrison. If you've been

Top 10 Favorite Unadvertised Things About Living in Oakland

By Jeff Goodby, creative director of Goodby, Silverstein & Partners, San Francisco

1. Walking the wholesale **vegetable markets** around Third and Franklin Streets on a weekday morning, then having breakfast at the **Oakland Grill**.

2. The **Black Panther Party Tour** of Oakland, which leaves from the West Oakland Branch of the Oakland Public Library.

3. The **Morcom Amphitheater of Roses** at 600 Jean Street.

4. The **Davie Tennis Stadium** at 198 Oak Road.

5. Walking the dozen or more **stairway "paths"**—with names like Verona, Chaumont, and Belalp—off Golden Gate, Buena Vista, and Contra Costa on a summer's night.

6. Enjoying a margarita on the rocks at the **Fifth Amendment**, 3255 Lake Shore Avenue.

7. The fly-casting pools at **George F. McCrea Memorial Park** on Carson Street.

8. Peach cobbler at **Doug's Barbecue**, 3600 San Pablo Avenue. (Doug's is officially in Emeryville, but the place is Oakland all the way.)

9. The **Christmas house light show** at Temescal Shopping Center.

10. The much touted but rarely witnessed springtime **steelhead run** at Redwood Regional Park.

---

searching for a particular old title, visit their Web site. More than 20 readings are held here every month. (Berkeley)

BUILDERS BOOK SOURCE
1817 Fourth St.
Berkeley
510/845-6874
If architecture and landscape books strike your fancy, or if you've ever even considered remodeling your home, then don't miss this place. You'll find volumes on historic local

stars Bernard Maybeck and Julia Morgan as well as the world's top cutting-edge designers. The 4,200 titles include some on practical subjects like graphic design, old roses, sprinkler systems, and plumbing codes. (Berkeley Waterfront)

CODY'S
2454 Telegraph Ave.
Berkeley
510/845-7852
Independent Cody's has been a fierce David to all the chainstore

Goliaths for more than 40 years. Still, Cody's isn't exactly small, though. They have more than a quarter-million titles—not necessarily bestsellers, but important books and literary works. The material here is a little heavier than that you'll find at the "lite" version of Cody's at 1730 Fourth Street (Berkeley Waterfront). (Berkeley)

DARK CARNIVAL
3086 Claremont Ave.
Berkeley
510/654-7323
An enormous silver coffin straddled by a giant spider sets the tone for this small but well-stocked sci-fi/fantasy/mystery bookstore. It's Halloween all year here with lots of little toys like baby gargoyles and loose plastic eyeballs. Dark Carnival carries mostly paperbacks, classics, and contemporary works by writers such as H. P. Lovecraft and Neal Stephenson. (South Berkeley/North Oakland)

DAVE'S INTERNATIONAL NEWS
2444 Durant Ave.
Berkeley
510/883-0325
This underground store caters to academics and the Telegraph Avenue community. And the selection is awesome. You'll find hundreds of magazines (like one catering to heavy-metal tattoo artists), arcane philology journals, and yesterday's editions of a dozen or so newspapers from Europe, Asia, and South America. (Berkeley)

DELAUER SUPER NEWSSTAND
1310 Broadway
Oakland
510/451-6157
It's three in the morning and you can't go to sleep without the latest issue of *People.* Thanks to this place, you're in luck. This huge store is open 24 hours a day, and it's doubtful that there's any publication they don't have. Delauer Super Newsstand has shelves of out-of-town papers, your favorite old *Superman* and *Archie* comics, a vast section of craft publications, and the best selection of maps in town. (Oakland)

GAIA
Shattuck and Rose
Berkeley
510/548-4172
Have you been trying to find a book on Sufi medicine or nutritional healing? Then you've come to the right store. Gaia's shelves are filled with New Age and feminist titles, from spiritual texts to fiction, plus gifts,

The western end of University Avenue is slowly becoming an Indian bazaar. In addition to sari, jewelry, and music stores, it's also home to several terrific Indian markets. Viks, at 726 Allston Way, has a huge selection of spices and curries. Next door, at the Chaat Corner, they serve what must be the least expensive meal in town. Entrées run from $2.75 to $4.

cards, and CDs. If you want to know what's happening in Berkeley's alternative world, you'll find it posted here. (Berkeley)

JUICY NEWS
1778 Fourth St.
Berkeley
510/558-8415
No one bothers you if you just like to stand and read any of the hundreds of publications here, from teen rock magazines to a rich selection of literary reviews. They also offer a whole section of European publications and those $10-a-copy French gardening extravaganzas. (South Berkeley/North Oakland)

MARCUS BOOKS
3900 Martin Luther King Way
Oakland
510/652-2344
The pride shows in this definitive, 40-year-old black bookstore. A literary oasis in a rough-edged neighborhood, it carries 18,000 titles, including classics, children's books, audiotapes, cookbooks, posters, puzzles, cards, and signed first editions by some of the luminaries who read there frequently, such as Toni Morrison and Terri McMillan. This place is especially strong in current fiction and music. (Oakland)

MOE'S
2476 Telegraph Ave.
Berkeley
510/849-2087
Don't look for bestsellers in this five-story literary emporium. Although new books are carried here, they take a back seat to the largest collection of high-quality used books in Northern California. Is classic hardcover fiction selection is extensive, and there's a full range

of art and antiquarian books. Pick up a 25¢ paperback or a $10,000 volume of rare seventeenth-century drawings. (Berkeley)

REVOLUTION BOOKS
2425 Channing
Berkeley
510/848-1196
Chairman Mao still presides in this last bastion of die-hard Marxism. Appropriately located underground in a retail complex, it has a few thousand titles on workers' struggles around the world, plus magazines and newspapers from the U.S. Communist Party. Even if your politics are somewhere to the right of this store, you could still pick up a T-shirt emblazoned with the words, "Wage Slave." (Berkeley)

SHAKESPEARE AND COMPANY
2499 Telegraph Ave.
Berkeley
510/841-8916
Like one of those musty bookstores off London's Strand, this longtime Berkeley institution is rich in tradition. They have about 70,000 used books with considerable depth in classic and contemporary fiction, California history, metaphysics, and, surprisingly, children's books. The Ph.D.-laden staff is extremely knowledgable. Prices are quite reasonable—eight dollars, on average, for hardcover books in remarkably good condition. (Berkeley)

UNIVERSITY PRESS BOOKS
2430 Bancroft Ave.
Berkeley
510/548-0585
What are professors thinking about these days? This is the place to find out. University Press Books has more than 20,000 titles that cover an

Cody's Books, p. 158

Grand Lake Theater on the corner. (Oakland)

OTHER NOTABLE STORES

ADDISON ENDPAPERS
2003 Hopkins St.
Berkeley
510/524-7852
You might want to get married just so you'll have an excuse to buy the whimsically French stationery and invitations at this simple and romantic paper shop. Everything here is made on hundred-year-old letterpresses. They use eighteenth- and nineteenth-century designs with pale Parisian stripes. Small boxes start at $12; photo albums start at $45. If you know someone who appreciates sweet sophistication, this is the place to buy them a gift. (South Berkeley/North Oakland)

AFIKOMEN
30421 Claremont Ave.
Berkeley
510/655-1977
You could start your own synagogue from Afikomen's vast inventory of Jewish art and books. The collection runs the gamut from serious to funny. You'll find a lot of Jewish history and biblical commentary, as well as 130 different Passover Haggadahs and a rich selection of prayer shawls and kiddush cups. You'll also find an entertaining selection of Hebrew baseball caps, Israeli bubblegum, and bagel-shaped refrigerator magnets. (South Berkeley/North Oakland)

BERKELEY MILLS
2830 Seventh St.
Berkeley
510/549-2845
This furniture showroom is full

amazing amount of academic ground. You'll find selections from the top 100 U.S. university presses, as well as works from Oxford, Cambridge, and some Canadian institutions. UC Press is well represented, too, with several books on regional subjects such as Sierra wildflowers. Lighter material such as jazz guides and hip-hop studies is also available, and constant sales make bargain hunting a treat. (Berkeley)

WALDEN POND BOOKS
3316 Grand Ave.
Oakland
510/832-4438
The owners gave up on their fight with amazon.com, so don't look for Danielle Steele in this medium-sized, politically progressive store. Half of the books are new and half are used. The well-edited collection includes a particularly in-depth selection of used hardcover fiction and mystery classics. It's a perfect place for browsing before or after catching a movie at the Art Deco

of modern designs. The Mission- and Frank Lloyd Wright–influenced pieces are made with unstained woods (all from "certifiably sustainable harvests") and have a lighter, richer glow than most of the furniture you'll find elsewhere in town. It's all custom-made and it's all pricey. (Berkeley Waterfront)

THE BONE ROOM
1569 Solano
Berkeley
510/526-5252
Give the person who has everything a mounted Malayan dung beetle. There are some beautiful things in this store, such as butterflies under glass, but most of the 700 or so items require a specialized taste in skulls, skeletons, and animal remnants. And if you're not ready for the real thing, you may find what you're looking for among the rubber snakes and plastic roaches. (Berkeley)

CAMPS AND COTTAGES
2109 Virginia
Berkeley
510/548-2267
This outpost of Americana on the city's Northside is a tiny, rustic shop filled to the rafters with original vintage furniture and knickknacks. This is the kind of store where the owners scour items from the Ozarks, not from gift-show conventions. They have a terrific assortment of Beacon, Pendleton, and Hudson Bay blankets. Their specialty is items made from recycled materials, whether it's wooden trays or metal birdcages. Check out their lush back garden with its butterfly habitat. (Berkeley)

EMMET EILAND'S ORIENTAL RUG COMPANY
1326 Ninth St.
Berkeley
510/526-1087
This place is well worth a visit, not just because it's the largest in Berkeley or the oldest in Northern California, but because the selection of new homespun oriental rugs with natural dyes offers so many unusual designs. It's hard to imagine a wider selection of Tibetan carpets or hard-to-find, light-toned rugs. (Berkeley Waterfront)

GILMAN SALVAGE
Sixth and Gilman
Berkeley
510/524-5500
The art of scavenging hits its apex here. There appears to be a little of everything in this store, from antique

---

Spare Change?

Panhandling is not as prevalent as it used to be here. Court decisions have defined it as a form of free speech, but local ordinances forbid aggressive panhandling. You're more likely to be asked to buy a newspaper than for a handout on Telegraph Avenue or Shattuck Avenue.

Twice a year the Gardener (510/548-4545), consistently the most original shop on Fourth Street, puts merchandise (mostly furniture) on sale for up to 40 percent off retail. Dates vary, so call ahead.

vacuum cleaners and Schwinn bicycles to restaurant "silver," high-tech shelving, '50s leatherette sofas, and cocktail stools. It's impossible to know what you'll find. One thing you definitely *won't* find, however, is price tags. Everything is negotiable. (Berkeley Waterfront)

IGUANA AMEREMEX
301 Jefferson
Oakland
510/834-5848
Here's all the great Mexican furniture you could never find in Puerto Vallarta—more than 50,000 square feet of pine and mesquite tables, dressers, bedstands, and chairs. Take your choice of plain or painted. If you don't want to cart home an armoire, they have charming paper calla lilies, colorful papier-mâché fruit, and an unmatched selection of garden pots. (Oakland)

KERMIT LYNCH
1605 San Pablo Ave.
Berkeley
510/524-1524
The lack of pretentiousness in this cool, brick wine shop is shocking, considering the caliber of French vintages they offer. The peripatetic Mr. Lynch makes constant forays to all the important French winemaking regions and brings back his discoveries for his loyal customers, who order out of his chatty catalog from across the country. You'll actually

find great bottles here for less than $15. (Berkeley)

THE MAGAZINE
1823 Eastshore Highway
Berkeley
510/549-2796
Furniture that makes you smile is what this very L.A. store is about. They carry the old masters like LeCorbusier and the new ones like Phillippe Starck. Wild, whimsical, brightly colored chairs, sofas, and tables from Milan, Paris, and Amsterdam fill the two airy floors. Plus, there are shelves full of witty accessories. You could easily fit one of their droll ice cube trays into your luggage. (Berkeley Waterfront)

MIKI'S PAPER
1801 Fourth St.
Berkeley
510/845-9530
As much a gallery as a store, this is a showcase for Japanese papers handmade from mulberry trees and printed in a variety of elegant colors. You'll also find a variety of striking silkscreen prints, often imbedded with leaves and blossoms. Use them as hangings or have them made into covers for photo albums. Considering the artistry, the prices are quite reasonable. (Berkeley Waterfront)

MOLLY B
1811 Fourth St.

Berkeley
510/548-3103
Berkeley women who like their clothes long, loose, and a bit theatrical do their shopping at this overcrowded Left Bank store. You'll find rich, voluptuous fabrics in the winter, assorted linens in the summer, and offbeat hats, lacy jewelry, and inventive purses all year long. Things are a little more restrained in their 2112 Vine Street shop. Both stores are generally expensive, but if you choose carefully, the prices can be manageable. (Berkeley Waterfront)

MUSICAL OFFERING
2430 Bancroft Way
Berkeley
510/849-0211
The offering here includes a carefully chosen collection of 14,000 classical CDs with an emphasis on medieval music and the early Renaissance. For Baroque aficionados, this store is already well known. They even have their own label, Wildboar, which focuses on early harpsichord music. In the front is a sweet café, a relaxing place to enjoy dinner (reservations required) before a concert across the street at Zellerbach Hall. (Berkeley)

OMEGA TOO
2204 San Pablo Ave.
Berkeley
510/843-3636
Whatever happened to all the beautiful old lighting fixtures from Berkeley's classic Arts and Crafts-style homes? A lot of them, along with sinks, mirrors, finials, and hat hooks, seem to have ended up here. Although only half the items are antiques, the reproductions are authentic. Up the street at 2400 and 2407 San Pablo, the same family

offers high-quality architectural salvage. (Berkeley Waterfront)

SARI PALACE
1000 University Ave.
Berkeley
510/841-7274
For sheer dazzle, nothing in Berkeley matches the glittering, extensive inventory of this Indian sari store. Even nonpatterned fabrics come in jewel-like dyes. The intricate embroidery is extraordinarily skillful. And this is nothing compared to the wedding attire on the second floor. The beadwork on the tissue silk is breathtaking. (Berkeley Waterfront)

SOLANO CELLARS
1580 Albany Ave.
Albany
510/525-5560
Save yourself a trip to the best wine country vineyards by stopping here instead. This neighborhood wine shop carries more than 700 of the smaller, more interesting Napa, Sonoma, and Central Coast labels.

The Bone Room, p. 162

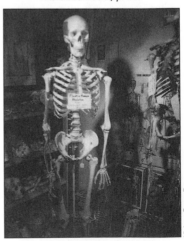

Viviana Rennella

A surprising number of bottles sell for less than $10. And there are tastings, too—more than 20 different bottles every week. Bistro dinners are offered Wed-Sun. (Berkeley)

STRAW INTO GOLD
3006 San Pablo Ave.
Berkeley
510/548-5243
Does your local yarn shop carry cotton chenille from Belgium in 64 colors? That's just a sampling of the huge selection in this 6,000-square-foot, faintly musty textile store. They specialize in natural fibers from alpaca to silk, but they stock everything you need from spinning wheels to a staggering library of magazines and pattern books. There store is where George Lucas found the fur for the original Chewbacca. (Berkeley Waterfront)

TROUT FARM
2179 Bancroft
Berkeley
510/843-3565
If you can see past the chaos and the clutter, you'll find some twentieth-century treasures in this eccentric little store. Modern-style furniture from the '40s and '50s in plastic, metal, and Naugahyde is available at prices that might make you feel like going home to take an inventory of all that stuff you have stored in your garage. There's also a terrific collection of old *Life*

magazines and advertising signage. (Berkeley)

WOODEN DUCK
2919 Seventh St.
Berkeley
510/848-3575
A Shaker-style bench made from high school bleachers. A Craftsman-style dining room table built with English floorboards. This is recycling as fine design—more than 15,000 square feet of unique furniture created right in the factory behind the store. They do amazing things with recycled materials from Asia, such as make bowls carved out of Sumatran coconut trees. Even more startling are the surprisingly reasonable prices. (Berkeley Waterfront)

SHOPPING MALLS

Berkeley and Oakland have not yet succumbed to suburban America's infatuation with malls, but Emeryville (Berkeley Waterfront) is a different matter. Turn west off San Pablo Avenue at 45th Street, and you'll find all-American favorites such as Kmart, Home Depot, PetClub, and Toys R Us. The area is called the East Bay Bridge. More impressive than the shopping are the metal sculptures studding the vast parking lots and some rakishly beautiful new apartment buildings. Continue on 45th Street and you'll come to a massive IKEA, the only northern California outpost of the famous Swedish furnishing store. Keep on driving and you'll hit Powell Street Plaza, which has stores such as Old Navy, Trader Joe's (a discount gourmet emporium), Pier One Imports, and Tower Records. If you cross Powell Street and keep heading north, you'll come to the Emery Market, which is mostly foodstands but does have a large Borders bookstore.

FACTORY OUTLET CENTERS

ANY MOUNTAIN
2990 Seventh St.
Berkeley
510/704-9440
Come here for 20,000 square feet of outdoor gear. Tents, backpacks, sleeping bags, boots, and camping equipment, as well as great prices, entice Bay Area adventurers to this warehouse just off the freeway. Most items are at least 20 percent off. The main focus here is on heavy-duty winter wear, but they do carry in-line skates and a few other year-round items. (Berkeley Waterfront)

AW POTTERY
2908 Adeline
Berkeley
510/549-3900
If you're looking for a pot, you'll find every size and shape imaginable in this huge lot. AW Pottery offers more than 100,000 of them in plain, fancy, or Italian palazzo styles. They also offer unglazed and elegantly colored Chinese vases, as well as stock fountains and figurines, tea sets, and bamboo chests. And everything is priced at 20 to 50 percent off retail. Another AW Pottery outlet is at 601

50th Street in Oakland. (South Berkeley/North Oakland)

CRATE AND BARREL
1785 Fourth St.
Berkeley
510/528-5500
It's a small store, but the discounts are huge at this national home-accessories retailer's only Northern California outlet. Crate and Barrel is known for its clean, colorful designs, especially its dishes and glassware. Most things never go out of season, and everything is in great condition. (Berkeley Waterfront)

DANSK
1760 Fourth St.
Berkeley
510/528-9226
Their classic stoneware is all here. So are most of their bright, clean, and colorful Danish-designed housewares—cutlery, glassware, wooden bowls, table linens, and cookware. But lucky for you, they are priced at up to 60 percent off retail. It's not last season's merchandise, either. They're items your local department store is selling right now for twice the price. (Berkeley Waterfront)

NOLO PRESS
950 Parker St.
Berkeley
510/704-2248
Fire your lawyer. Who needs her when you can do it yourself with the help of this store's hundreds of books and software items? Divorces, driving tickets, home sales, wills, bankruptcy, copyrights, cyberlaw—you name it, this place has all the legal details. And you won't just save on lawyers' fees. Much of the material is offered at

20 to 50 percent off retail. (Berkeley Waterfront)

SMITH AND HAWKEN
1330 10th St.
Berkeley
510/527-1076
Local taste-makers eye the shipments that show up every two weeks at this store, which is one of the few outlets in the country for this English-style garden store. The superb teak outdoor furniture and market umbrellas are the first things to go. Discounts run 30 to 60 percent, sometimes more if items have flaws. You'll find some great deals in their off-season items and their stylish but comfortable clothing. (Berkeley Waterfront)

SWEET POTATOES
1716 Fourth St.
Berkeley
510/527-5852
Check out the back of this cheerful children's store because that's where the discounts are. You'll find savings from 30 to 50 percent on everything from newborn to size 7 for boys and size 14 for girls. Most of the best prices are on items that are one season old, but there are a lot of dresses and T-shirts you can use anytime. (Berkeley Waterfront)

THE NORTH FACE OUTLET
1238 Fifth St.

Berkeley
510/526-3530
People who take their outdoor adventuring seriously respect the outstanding techno-textiles of this major manufacturer. In their large, décor-free warehouse, you can save up to 30 percent on their parkas, thermal shirts, hiking shoes, and tents, as well as their more conventional sports clothes. Regular delivery of new merchandise guarantees a good selection of sizes. (Berkeley Waterfront)

TOM TOM
1716 Fourth St.
Berkeley
510/559-7033
These are the kinds of comfy dresses, skirts, tops, and pants that actually look good wrinkled. They're made of all-natural fabrics, mostly in a soothing palate of colors. Even more soothing are the prices. For starters, they're 50 percent off retail. A whole rack of "seconds" with minor flaws is even less. And twice a year they take an additional 50 percent off everything. (Berkeley Waterfront)

FLEA MARKETS

ALAMEDA ANTIQUE FAIR
Alameda Naval Air Station
Since the Navy shipped out, this

T I P

Cyclamen sells its pricey, summer-colored dishware at places like Saks Fifth Avenue. But twice a year it's available at their Emeryville factory for up to 35 percent off. Call 510/597-3640 for exact dates.

**T
I
P**

CP Shades (177 Fourth St., 510/843-0681), the store famous for slouchy women's apparel, has an annual New Year's Sale where everything is the same price as the year. So, in 2001, everything will be $20.01.

bay-view airfield has become home to multimedia studios and, on the first Sunday of every month, a 500-booth collectibles fair. The gates open at six in the morning, and the quality varies wildly. Admission starts at $10 but drops to $3 by the middle of the day. *Antiques Road Show*-style appraisers mingle with shoppers to help decipher the trash from the treasures. (Oakland)

BERKELEY FLEA MARKET
1937 Ashby Ave.
Berkeley
510/644-0744
Just when you're about to give up on finding anything worth keeping here, you'll come across something amazing like a Tibetan carving or a Kenyan drum. That's because a lot of African, Asian, and Middle Eastern immigrants trade here. Recently, if you had moved quickly, you could have picked up an Afghani rug with a Soviet land-mines design. Sat-Sun. (South Berkeley/North Oakland)

COLISEUM SWAP MEET
66th St. exit off Hwy. 880
Oakland
510/534-0325
Mercado is a more apt description than "swap meet." Sprawling across a former drive-in theater, this massive display of mostly new merchandise draws a largely Spanish-speaking clientele. Anyone with a taste for kitsch can find Jesus beach towels, nylon tiger-striped rugs, and plastic everything, from brilliantly colored flowers to jewelry to dishware. There are also tons of Mexican CDs. Wed-Sun 6:30-4. Admission $1 on weekends. (Oakland)

NORCAL SWAP MEET
Seventh and Fallon
Oakland
510/769-7266
You have to really love yard sales to have the patience it takes to sift through the acres of dreck here. There are miles of glittery barrettes and table after table of rusting old tools. But the deals are great, and occasionally you'll come across some little gems, like hand-painted Chinese tin plates, jars of dried orange blossoms, and amazingly intricate little jade-green plastic dragons. Weekends only. Admission $1. (Oakland)

John Elk III

10

The East Bay is incurably sports-crazed. Oakland is the only city in California with three professional sports teams. The fans are die-hards. Legend has it that this is where "the wave" began. The A's, the Raiders, and the Golden State Warriors all have their share of national trophies, but like Oakland itself, have been scrappy underdogs lately. Still, the grateful city has given the teams an up-to-the-minute, state-of-the-art sports complex and, even better for fans, their own BART station.

There is a monumental new venue at the University of California, too. The Haas Pavilion hosts NCAA teams, mostly from the Western Conference. It joins the other historic facility at the University of California, the vast Memorial Stadium. If you want to see some of the most fervent alumni this side of Nebraska, come here when the Big Game is played against arch-rival Stanford. The Cal Bear's 37 teams have a long, long history of championships. You can drop by anytime and see an ESPN-like range of sports activities, from men's tennis to women's crew.

If you like to play sports more than you enjoy watching them, then you're in luck. Head to the bay and rent a wetsuit and a windsurf board. Hire a boat and go deep-sea fishing outside the Golden Gate. Head to the hills with your nine-iron or, if golf's not your thing, just your T-shirt, shorts, and running shoes. Break out your bike for some of the best road riding in the country. Or jump in the car. Only one hour away you could be surfing the tubes off the California coast; three hours away are ski slopes on par with some of the best resorts in the world.

SPORTS ARENAS

- ***Oakland (Network Associates) Coliseum**, 7000 Coliseum Way, Oakland, 510/569-2121, www.stadianet.com/oaklandcoliseum. Something's always going on at this massive sports complex, either in the 19,200-seat arena or the 63,000-seat stadium. Although it's a venue for circuses, wrestling, monster-truck rallies, ice shows, and rock concerts, the main attraction is sports and Oakland's three professional teams. The coliseum is right off Highway 80 near the airport; there are two exits and 11,000 parking places. But it's always smarter to take BART directly to the coliseum station. Tickets can be purchased at the Coliseum Box Office on the day of the game, but tickets are also sold at BASS outlets in Berkeley, at Tower Records at 2518 Durant Avenue, and at 1221 Broadway in Oakland. You can also buy tickets by phone (510/762-2277). Food prices are steep, so bring your own picnic. Just leave your beverages at home.*
- ***Memorial Stadium**, Gayley Road, Berkeley. Size isn't everything. This 75,000-seat stadium, built in 1923, makes up in location for what it lacks in capacity. Resting in the green embrace of Strawberry Canyon, it's a beauty, and from the top seats on the east side you get full sun and a panoramic slice of bay view. Thrill seekers just need to*

PROFESSIONAL SPORTS

GOLDEN GATE FIELDS
Gilman St. (off Hwy. 80)
Albany
510/559-7300
www.ggfields.com
Purses can run as high as $300,000 at this track perched on the edge of the bay. The two seasons gallop from March to June and from November to January, but daily simulcasts from tracks across the country are shown year-round. You can view them from 700 monitors throughout the facility. General admission is $2, parking is $3. Take the #304 bus from the North Berkeley BART. (Berkeley Waterfront)

GOLDEN STATE WARRIORS
Network Associates Coliseum
510/986-2222
This recently rebuilt arena rises like the world's largest snare drum from Highway 80. The Warriors now play on a brighter court, one that's considerably lower than it used to be. So the seats at the top—in the nosebleed section—feel even farther away. Warrior's fans are among the most laidback in sports, which means it's not too

remind themselves that the Hayward Fault runs diagonally down the length of the field. There is no parking (welcome to ecotopia), but lots are open on campus and at fraternities and sororities for $5 to $10, depending on the demand.

- **Haas Pavilion**, corner of Bancroft Way and Dana Street, Berkeley. An expansion and renovation of the former Harmon Gym now allows the UC Bears to play NCAA basketball games right on their own campus. And with 12,000 seats below the concourse line, it means more spectators are closer to the action. The Deco décor of the old building has been beautifully restored. To get there, take BART to the downtown Berkeley station and walk four blocks. Tickets go for $18 to $20.

- **Spieker Pool**, Bancroft and Dana Sts., 510/643-7470. Olympic star Matt Biondi did laps for the UC Bears, and the team still regularly makes it into the top 10 nationally. Meets usually take place on Saturday afternoons in the winter. Men's water polo matches are held in the fall, whereas women's games take place in the spring. Both teams have been major trophy winners over the past few seasons. There is a minimal admission charge and seating is limited.

difficult to find a good seat. Expect to shell out from $18 to $220 for tickets. (Oakland)

OAKLAND ATHLETICS
Network Associates Coliseum
510/638-0500

Fans keep hoping for a return to the A's glory days of Reggie Jackson and their three World Series titles. But that's not likely to happen anytime soon. Still, newly renamed Network Associates Coliseum is a great place to see talent working its way up (Mark McGwire was here a few seasons back). Most of the time this field is a fog-free zone, although night games can be chilly. Plenty of good seats are available. Prices run from around $22 for reserved seats in a good section to 99¢ for special promotions in the bleachers. (Oakland)

OAKLAND RAIDERS
Network Associates Coliseum
510/864-5000
www.raiders.com

You won't see Hell's Angels at the games anymore, but the team's "outsider" reputation still lingers, and so does the feisty atmosphere. The players have taken the best seats for themselves, but good seats are often available on the day of the game on the corner end zone of the second deck and on the third deck (with bay views). With a mere 60,000 seats, this stadium is one of the smallest in professional football, so even up in the top tier you won't feel too far away. Tickets cost $40-$80. (Oakland)

AMATEUR SPORTS

UC BASEBALL
Evans Diamond
800/GO-BEARS
www.calbears.com
A steady blast of hits and runs keeps these games moving and the scores rising. Cal is part of the PAC-10, possibly the leading conference in the country, and has been running a respectable .500 average for years. They play about 25 home games every spring on Fridays and weekend afternoons. Tickets cost $3-$5. (Berkeley)

UC BASKETBALL
Haas Pavilion
800/GO-BEARS
www.calbears.com
Definite contenders over the past decade, this team has gone to a lot of NCAA playoffs and even won the 1999 National Invitational Tournament. It's also spawned NBA stars such as Jason Kidd and Kevin Johnson. The annual Christmas Tournament here brings in power teams such as North Carolina and Temple. After Christmas, they play home games every other week on Thursday and Saturday. Seats are tough to come by, but you can usually pick up tickets from scalpers outside. (Berkeley)

Oakland A's Ben Grieve

UC FOOTBALL
Memorial Stadium
800/GO-BEARS
www.calbears.com
Local senior citizens can recall the days when the Bears made regularly scheduled appearances at the Rose Bowl. As recently as the early '90s, they placed in the top 10 in the United States. Lately, though, they've suffered from a revolving door of coaches, but their wide-open offense with plenty of air play is always entertaining. Besides West Coast PAC-10 teams, they occasionally take on bruisers such as Michigan and Nebraska. Getting tickets on game day is not a problem. (Berkeley)

UC SOFTBALL
Levine-Fricke Field
Berkeley
800/GO-BEARS
www.calbears.com
Pitching duels are common when this women's team takes to the field on spring weekend afternoons. Their

recent record has shot them into some major championships, and just a few years ago they tied for third in the College World Series. Tickets cost $3-$5. (Berkeley)

UC TENNIS
Hellman Tennis Stadium
Berkeley
800/GO-BEARS
www.calbears.com
Both genders consistently make their way to the top of the national rankings—the men in the top 15 and the women often in the top 5. Matches are played on Friday and Saturday afternoons between January and May, and usually consist of six singles and three doubles matches. Tickets are free. (Berkeley)

RECREATION

Biking
EAST BAY REGIONAL PARKS
510/562-7275
A combination of gentle grades and long, flat stretches makes the roads in the Berkeley and Oakland hills ideal for bicycling. Getting up to them, though, can be hairy, especially when you're sharing the narrow road with internal-combustion vehicles. Once at the crest you have a choice of routes, some of which go as far as 75 miles into Contra Costa. Two of the most popular routes less than 25 miles in length are the **Pinehurst Loop,** which takes Skyline Boulevard to Redwood Road to Pinehurst; and the slightly steeper **Three Bears Loop,** which goes from the San Pablo Dam Road to Don Castro Ranch Road, right to Alhambra Valley Road, and, finally, to Bear Valley Road. For more information on these

and other great routes, contact a local biking club such as the **Grizzly Peak Cyclists,** 510/843-1931. Ask them about races and whether the proposed Bay Trail is any closer to becoming a reality. Bike rentals are available at several locations, including **Start to Finish Bicycles,** 510/704-1000; and **Round the World Bikes,** 510/835-8763.

Although most trails in the hills are closed to mountain bikers, every Regional Park does provide a few routes that are clearly designated for them. One of the shorter and more pleasant ones is the **Seaview Trail** in Tilden. It runs from the Steam Train to the Pony Rides and is basically a fire trail that's wide enough to allow bikers and hikers plenty of space. You can also take it to Inspiration Point, where it connects with the **Wildcat Canyon Creek Trail.** For a longer ride of an hour or two, try the East Ridge and West Ridge loop in Redwood Park. (Hills)

Bowling
ALBANY BOWL
540 San Pablo Ave.
Albany
510/526-8818
You expect to see the entire cast of *Happy Days* tossing balls down the 36 lanes of this retro bowling alley. They have automatic scoring and, to keep the action going, 7 pool tables, 11 video games, a soft dart board, and a Chinese-American restaurant. Open daily until 2 a.m. Adults $2.75 a game; seniors and kids $2.25; $1.50 Tue nights. (Berkeley Waterfront)

Cards
OAKS CLUB ROOM
4097 San Pablo Ave.

Emeryville
510/653-4456
This is definitely not Vegas. This big card den has less glitz than a dentist's office, but it's open 24 hours and has no distractions for avid practitioners of Seven Card Stud, Omaha, or Texas Hold 'Em. The pit supervisor will be happy to introduce you to some of the variations on Asian games played here, like Pai Gow. There's a pretty large crowd, but players come and go and you should never have to wait more than 20 minutes for a table. (Berkeley Waterfront)

Chess

LAIR OF THE BEAR
Zellerbach Plaza
Berkeley
If you're polite, you call the chess hustlers who hang out at the picnic tables behind this place "coffeehouse players." But you'd be lying to yourself. They're here every day from one o'clock until dusk and will play for money, beer, or even a cup of coffee. A lot of professors and street people step up to the

challenge and play them in timed or regular matches. Up the street you'll find even more action and better skills at the **International House** (Bancroft and Piedmont Avenue). They claim that chess masters show up there from time to time. (Berkeley)

Climbing

BERKELEY IRONWORKS
800 Potter St.
Berkeley
510/981-9900
If you don't have time to get to the mountains on this trip, let the mountains come to you. The lead wall here is 48 feet high. With 14,000 square feet of climbing terrain and 40 top and lead ropes, you won't be bumping into anyone. There's also an even more demanding boulder section. Get in early for beginners' classes, then enjoy an entire day of climbing for $25. Time your visit right and you might be able to sign up for one of their outdoor climbs. Weight room and aerobics classes are offered, too. (Berkeley Waterfront)

View Points

Recent renovations have boosted the seating capacities of the Oakland Coliseum (now Network Associates) stadium and arena. Not all the fans are happy with the now steeply banked basketball stands in the arena, where a distant seat can require binoculars to see the action. And the stadium, home to the Oakland Athletics, has been reconfigured so it works better for football—at the expense of baseball. A wall in front of the bleachers now blocks the sight lines to the outfield.

Fishing

BERKELEY MARINA SPORT CENTER
225 University Ave.
Berkeley
510/849-2727

The Berkeley Marina Sport Center offers deep-sea-fishing excursions to as far away as the Farallon Islands, 25 miles outside the Golden Gate. Boats troll in search of salmon, halibut, striped bass, crab, rock cod, tuna, sturgeon, and shark. Fishing licenses are required, but you can pick one up for the day at their tackle shop, which also stocks the provisions you need for a sea-going picnic. Dress warmly no matter what the season. $55 per person, plus $8 per rod. (Berkeley Waterfront)

BERKELEY PIER
Far western end of University Ave.

Because bass like to feed close to shore, fishing along the East Bay waterfront can be very rewarding. This pier is particularly popular because it comes with its own cleaning stations and because the nearby **Marina Sports Shop** (510/849-2727) stocks bait and other supplies. Halibut and bass reeled in here can run up to 40 inches. Perch can weigh 2 pounds and stingrays up to 80 pounds. Fishermen also line up along the waterfront's Frontage Road. (Berkeley Waterfront)

Fitness

CLUB ONE AT CITY CENTER
1200 Clay St.
Oakland
510/835-2000

Before you leave home, make sure your gym is affiliated with the Inter-

A climber at the Berkeley Ironworks, p. 174

Todd Jokl

national Health, Racquet, and Sports Club Association (IHRSA). If it is, you'll enjoy guest privileges at facilities like this one. You'll find 65,000 square feet of gleaming, beautifully maintained facilities, including an indoor track; a lap pool; squash, racquetball, and basketball courts; and a weight room. And if that's not enough, you can enroll in an aerobics class. Once you've worked yourself to your peak, unwind with a massage or a sauna. Childcare is offered and there is a women-only section. Open daily. (Oakland)

RECREATIONAL SPORTS FACILITY
2301 Bancroft Way
Berkeley
510/642-7796

If you're unfazed by the proximity of young, strong, undergraduate athletes, this Olympic-size facility offers large helpings of every kind of exercise. For a $10 visitor's fee you have access to their pool; exercise rooms; weight centers; cardiovascular studios; and basketball, squash,

racquetball, handball, and bad-
minton courts. If you need equipment, you can rent it in the Pro Shop.
In case you overdo yourself, they
even have a massage center. High-
tech and deeply carpeted, it looks
like an exercise facility fit for the
world's largest, most expensive
hotel. (Berkeley)

Frisbee

AQUATIC PARK
Berkeley
If you're strolling on the east side of
this lushly landscaped lagoon next
to Highway 80, you may wonder
about the chain-metal baskets
posted every few hundred feet.
They're the 18 "holes" in a rolling,
tree-studded disc golf course. The
discs are about half the size of regular Frisbees and, yes, there are
putters and drivers. Every hole is a
par three, and because of the
winds off the bay, it's considered a
challenging course. Discs are available at **Berkeley Sports,** 2254 Bancroft Way, 510/848-3669. (Berkeley
Waterfront)

Golf Courses

CHUCK CORICA GOLF COMPLEX
1 Clubhouse Memorial Dr.
Alameda
510/522-4321
Among the more interesting haz-
ards here are the flocks of Canadian geese that call these two
18-hole, par-71 courses home. Right
near the bay, the courses are almost pancake-flat and can get
pretty windy. The north course, with
more water and trees, is the bigger
challenge. A nine-hole executive
course, driving range, and full
restaurant are also available. Fees

range from $24-$27. Schedule a tee
time at least one week in advance.
(Oakland)

GALBRAITH DRIVING RANGE
10505 Doolittle Dr.
Oakland
510/569-7337
Located on the windswept landfill
near the Oakland Airport, Galbraith
generally requires warm clothing.
There are 40 spots, so unless it's a
summer weekend afternoon, you
probably won't have to wait for
long. There are no lights, so it's only
open from about 7:30 a.m.-dusk.
Large buckets are $7. (Oakland)

LAKE CHABOT MUNICIPAL
GOLF COURSE
End of Golf Links Rd.
Oakland
510/351-5812
This course's 18th hole, at 668 yards,
is the only par six in northern California. The 16th hole is impressive, too,
consisting of a lengthy stretch
across a deep ravine. You can get a
great workout by walking this city-
owned course or its companion
nine-hole course. Call for reservations at least six days in advance if
you plan to play during the summer.
Fees are $8-$22. (Hills)

MONTCLAIR GOLF COURSE
2477 Monterey Blvd.
Oakland
510/482-0422
They're promising a remodeling job
on this temporary-looking, raffish
"Tin Cup" facility. The nine-hole,
pitch-and-putt course winds up in
an arroyo, and the longest hole is 80
yards. Tee times are available on a
first-come, first-served basis. Fees
are $3-$4. There's also a 40-slot driving range, which stays open until

11 p.m. A big bucket of golf balls goes for $5. (Oakland)

TILDEN
Grizzly Peak and Shasta Rd.
Berkeley
510/848-7373
This par-70, 6,300-yard course— cradled in a redwood and pine valley above the UC campus—is a true beauty. Watch the trees, though, because they can be tricky. Lately, Tilden has been a victim of its own popularity, with heavy crowds slowing down the play. A game can take up to five hours. It also has a nine-hole course and a three-tier driving range that's open until 10 p.m. in the summer. Green fees range from $20 to $40. Book tee times at least a couple of days in advance. (Hills)

at individual park headquarters. RoundTop at Sibley Park takes about 45 minutes and has dramatic east-facing views of Contra Costa. Lake Chabot Road at the southern tip of Anthony Chabot Park is also accessible and popular. The Skyline National Recreation Trail is the route that links all of the parks together. The north-end entrance is Richmond's McBryde Avenue. The southern entrance is at the Proctor Gate Staging Area on Redwood Road. In between are 31 miles of gorgeous northern California topography, from rolling, bosomy hills to bosky redwood forests. You'll often find yourself suddenly at an open hilltop with yet another take-your-breath-away view of the Bay Area. (Hills)

Hiking

EAST BAY REGIONAL PARKS
510/562-7275
Every park in the East Bay hills has its own network of well-maintained trails. You can find maps of them

Horseback Riding

ANTHONY CHABOT
EQUESTRIAN CENTER
14600 Skyline Blvd.
Oakland
510/569-4428

A biker contemplates the view from Inspiration Point

Gail Gettler

The hilly terrain up here is home to wide paths that go on for miles. You could ride for days if you had your own horse. In the event that you don't, however, sign up for a one- or two-hour guided tour with the Anthony Chabot Equestrian Center. Beginners—even children—should have no trouble on these gentle trails. Reserve one of their 12 horses at least one day in advance. If you plan to go on one of their breakfast or barbecue rides, contact them even earlier. Rates are around $25 per hour. (Hills)

Ice Skating

ICELAND
2727 Milvia St.
Berkeley
510/647-1600
The University of California's ice hockey team practices here during off hours. That leaves you plenty of time and 2,000 square feet of space to practice your double axels. Built in 1938, Iceland is still the largest rink in California, although time is beginning to take its toll on the facilities. Fridays, when disco music rocks the house, things get pretty lively. Open daily during the summer; otherwise, call for a schedule. Adults $6, children 16 and under $5. (Berkeley)

OAKLAND ICE CENTER
519 18th St.
Oakland
510/268-9000
Located right in the middle of downtown Oakland, the Oakland Ice Center is a fairly new, big, brash, and high-tech facility. One rink is for individual skaters; the other is for ice hockey games. Chances are pretty good that you can find a pick-up game to join on the weekends. There

is also a weight room and a snack bar. Open daily. $5 adults over 55 and children 12 and under; $6 ages 13-54. (Oakland)

Lawn Bowling

LAKESIDE PARK
Oakland
510/832-9236
Up for a sports activity that's a little more genteel? This club has been around for a century and now plays year-round at three well-clipped greens near Lake Merritt. Tuesday and Thursday mornings you can join a pick-up game, take a lesson, or sign up for a "draw" in the afternoon. If you've brought your whites with you, then wear them, but they're not required. Lawn bowling is also available in Berkeley at 2270 Acton Street. (Oakland)

Marksmanship

CHABOT MARKSMANSHIP RANGE
Marciel Gate off Redwood Rd.
Oakland
510/569-0213
National Rifle Association members find camaraderie in this almost-hidden range in a small canyon on the western slopes of giant Chabot Park. Bring your own arms. They have trap, rifle, and pistol ranges up to 100 yards in length. Non-members pay $10, juniors $3. This fee entitles you to practice as long as you want. Open Mon-Fri. (Hills)

Pool

THALASSA
2367 Shattuck Ave.
Berkeley
510/848-1766

You might shudder at the thought of a New Age pool hall, but once you get past the Aquarian theme, the fishing nets that drape the windows, and the high-tech porthole decorations, it's easy to have a great time. The 21 tables get busy with 20-something locals and students after 10 p.m. Generally, however, you won't have to stand around waiting for a table. And if you must, the jumping bar scene will keep you distracted. Daily until 2 a.m. $5 per hour, $10 per hour Wed-Sat after 9 p.m. (Berkeley)

Racquetball

OAKLAND ATHLETIC CLUB
1418 Webster Ave.
Oakland
510/893-3421
Don't let the big "private club" sign scare you away. A $15 fee will get you access to their six well-maintained racquetball and handball courts. Pick-up games are almost always available, but local players are pretty hardcore. You had best know what you're doing. The entrance fee also allows access to all the fitness equipment in this three-story facility, from weight rooms and cardio studios to a lap pool and wet and dry saunas. (Oakland)

Roller Hockey

DRY ICE ROLLER HOCKEY ARENA
210 Hegenberger Loop
Oakland
510/562-9499
Watching the slam-bang action is free in this 180-by-80-foot rink located in an industrial park on the way to the Oakland Airport. If you've never seen hockey played on in-line skates, then you should stop by for some entertainment. If you have your own gear, pick-up games take place Monday and Wednesday nights. For players over the age of 30, games are Saturday nights from 9:30 to 11. The pick-up fee is $10. Open daily from 4 p.m., weekends from 8 a.m. (Oakland)

Running

INSPIRATION POINT
Tilden Park
Berkeley
If the elevation doesn't affect your breathing, then the views certainly will. This auto-free paved road snakes for four miles along the ridgeline, so a roundtrip run of eight miles is possible. To the east are the Contra Costa hills. To the west is a continuing series of jaw-dropping bay views. For a more secluded, less-public run, turn left onto the unpaved Nimitz Way (which is part of the Skyline Trail) and run as far as you like. (Hills)

Skateboarding

CITYVIEW SKATEBOARD PARK
Alameda Naval Air Station

510/748-4565

This facility, set on the bay in a former U.S. Naval station, is the state's largest facility of its kind designed for and by skateboarders. Thrashers will find a tasty array of tabletops, pyramids, and vert ramps all transitioned nicely to allow maximum trickery. Open dawn until dusk. (Oakland)

Swimming

HEARST GYM
Bancroft Ave.
Berkeley
510/642-3894

Ignore those outdated signs that say Hearst Gym for Women. This pool went coed years ago, so now both genders can swim their laps here. This classically styled temple for the body was designed by Julia Morgan, the same person responsible for the stunning Roman pool at San Simeon. For eight dollars a day, anyone can swim past all the noble statuary, the black marble pool deck, and the Campanile rising in the distance. (Berkeley)

STRAWBERRY CANYON
Centennial Dr. (above UC Stadium)
Berkeley
510/643-6720

This pool is set in a beautiful woodland area in the lush cleavage of a Berkeley canyon. The two near-Olympic-size pools get jammed on hot summer days because a good portion of each is roped off for romping kids. It's surrounded by beautifully maintained lawns ideal for sunbathing. Visitors are welcome. A day pass also gets you parking privileges. Adults $5, children $4.50. (Berkeley)

TEMESCAL
371 45th St.

Oakland
510/597-5013

Children's swimming classes are offered at this hidden neighborhood pool (voted "best" by San Francisco's *Bay Guardian* newspaper), but otherwise this facility is for serious lappers only. It's very old but well maintained, with a nice, low chlorine level. There's not a lot of room to loll around on the sides. Most swimmers just come, do their laps, and go. Hours change every season, so call ahead. $2.50 adults, $1 children. (South Berkeley/North Oakland)

Tennis

DAVIE TENNIS STADIUM
198 Oak Rd.
Oakland
510/444-5663

There are 50 public courts in Oakland and 10 in Berkeley, but this woodland site is a bona fide gem. In the '30s, WPA workers converted a former rock quarry into this five-court facility and clubhouse. Today, the sheer 100-foot-high quarry walls are dense with foliage, and bay and eucalyptus trees perfume the air and all but eliminate wind interference. Fees are $5 an hour and reservations are recommended. Ask for directions because it's well off the beaten path. (Oakland)

ROSE GARDEN TENNIS COURTS
Euclid and Eunice
Berkeley
510/644-6530

Players facing south have a direct, dazzling, and distracting view of the city's Rose Garden. Because these four courts are cupped in Berkeley's Northside hills, you have to compensate for the sometimes

Local legend has it that several years ago a Stanford professor—a rabid A's fan named "Crazy George"—led his fellow fans in a series of bizarre cheers. One of those cheers became the rise-and-fall crowd movement that later swept the country as "The Wave."

capricious winds. It's easy (on the weekends, especially) to just bring your racket and, without much of a wait at all, find yourself in a pick-up doubles match. (Berkeley)

Water Sports

BERKELEY MARINA
Cal Adventures
124 University Ave.
Berkeley
510/642-4000
Those whiplike bay winds can be as strong as 15 knots in the afternoon, but mornings are somewhat more tranquil. That's a good time for beginners to take advantage of the activities here. Sit-on-top sea kayaks rent for seven dollars an hour. So do regular sea kayaks, but first you have to prove that you know how to do a self-rescue. Anyone who's sailed before should be able to pick up windsurfing quickly. Boards go for $10 an hour plus deposit. Hours vary wildly by season, so be sure to call ahead. All rental equipment is doled out on a first-come, first-served basis. (Berkeley Waterfront)

CAL SAILING CLUB
124 University Ave.
Berkeley
510/287-5905
www.cal-sailing.org
Even sailors on the world's tightest budgets can enjoy the local waters. From one to four on the first full

weekend of each month you can board one of this group's 26 sailboats (from 14 to 25 feet long) for a free ride into the bay. This entirely volunteer organization offers sailing and windsurfing classes to anyone who buys a three-month membership for $45. Open daily year-round. (Berkeley Waterfront)

LAKE MERRITT BOATING CENTER
568 Bellevue Ave.
Oakland
510/444-3907
Without the heavy bay winds, the boating in the middle of this city lake is relaxing and less rugged. Canoes, rowboats, kayaks, and paddleboats are generally available without a wait except on the warmest summer weekends. There's a $10 deposit and rates run from $6 to $8 per hour. If you bring your boating certification with you (or pass a quick oral and/or practical exam), you can rent anything from an El Toro to a catamaran. Deposits range from $10-$20; hourly rates are $6-$12. (Oakland)

OAKLAND ESTUARY
California Canoe and Kayak
409 Water St.
Oakland
510/893-7833
The flat, unruffled water conditions and easy access combine to make the Oakland Estuary very popular with paddlers. One of the best ways to explore the estuary is to rent a

boat from California Canoe and Kayak. Canoes at this well-stocked shop can be borrowed for $15 per hour; sea kayaks, on the other hand, go for $12 per hour, but you can't take one until you've convinced the staff that you know how to self-rescue. If you want to take a private lesson, call 800/366-9804. (Oakland)

OLYMPIC CIRCLE SAILING CLUB
1 Spinnaker Way
Berkeley
510/843-4200
The Olympic Circle Sailing Club may be your best bet if you want to get out on the challenging, chilly waters of the bay and you have little or no experience operating a boat. Their 30- to 40-foot sailboats cruise every Wednesday night (except during the winter) for $35 per person. The first Wednesday of the month, they include a special barbecue at club headquarters behind the Radisson Hotel. For longer, more ambitious (and more expensive) sails past the Golden Gate Bridge, ask about their skipper charters. Reserve your spot at least two weeks in advance. (Berkeley Waterfront)

11

THE PERFORMING ARTS

Sooner or later, everything comes to Berkeley. On any given evening, for example, you might find a staging of last season's most provocative off-Broadway play, a recital by a pianist fresh from a debut in Carnegie Hall, or a riveting performance by a trend-setting French ballet company. Thanks to the area's reputation as an intellectual community with citizens that are as culturally fine-tuned as they are insatiable, the East Bay is never short on performing arts.

Homegrown artists are treated well here. The demand for local talent is so great that these modestly sized cities proudly possess two symphony orchestras, two ballet companies, eight chamber groups, and several established troupes that concentrate on everything from Baroque violin to politically charged modern dance. For whatever reasons, however, music has more of a grip on the East Bay than do theater or dance. Devotees of early classical music are treated to a couple of concerts every month. Chamber groups and soloists are in such demand that they play in churches almost every weekend. Internationally recognized artists regularly include UC Berkeley's Zellerbach Hall on their concert schedules.

Still, local theater and dance troupes cover a lot of ground. The solidly established Berkeley Rep might do Oscar Wilde one month and David Mamet the next. An annual outdoor Shakespeare festival is always popular. Every December, Berkeley and Oakland are treated to at least two, if not three, Nutcrackers, and all year long there's a steady parade of internationally acclaimed ballet companies, from Mexico's Ballet Folklorico to New York's Alvin Ailey. Modern dance is firmly grounded here, at least from the time Isadora Duncan danced in a Greek temple up in the hills. In fact, you might say that the East Bay, a small city with high cosmopolitan standards, still considers itself a kind of Athens.

THEATER

AURORA THEATER COMPANY
Berkeley City Club
2315 Durant Ave.
Berkeley
510/843-4822

Berkeley's most dramatic venue is the Berkeley City Club, the Moorish palace/hotel designed by Julia Morgan. Its 67-seat chamber theater is tucked away in a space slightly bigger than a large walk-in closet. The Aurora Theater Company performs five plays a year here. Many of the performances are literary orientations, such as a dramatization of the letters of Flaubert and George Sand or an evening of Emily Dickinson. But they also do Shakespeare and contemporary works, such as the recent West Coast premiere of Woody Allen's play *Central Park West.* & (Berkeley)

BERKELEY REPERTORY THEATER
2025 Addison St.
Berkeley
510/845-4700

Awarded a Tony in 1997 for its consistently high production standards and wide-ranging menu of plays, this company has avoided the easy route to popularity. You might arrive in town to see the latest sensation from Ireland's current l'énfant terriblé playwright, last season's best off-Broadway drama, or the world premiere of an original work. They have two theaters, and their season runs from September to July with seven performances a week (including matinees). A vast and loyal subscription audience means that many shows sell out, so it's best to book tickets in advance. & (Berkeley)

BLACK REPERTORY THEATER
3201 Adeline Ave.
Oakland
510/652-2120

Danny Glover is only one of the stars who have appeared at this long-running local theater that's now approaching its fourth decade. The season extends from November through July and focuses on uplifting works by great twentieth-century black writers such as Langston Hughes, August Wilson, and Lorraine Hansberry. The company is very professional (they've staged a vivacious *Bubbling Brown Sugar*) and maintains an out-there New Artists program. The plain but comfortable venue seats 250. Unlike most of the city's theaters, parking here is not a problem because the huge Ashby BART lot is just one block away. & (South Berkeley/North Oakland)

CALIFORNIA SHAKESPEARE FESTIVAL
Bruns Amphitheater
Orinda
510/548-9666
www.calshakes.org

On nearby hills, cows gaze at the antics of two gentlemen from Verona. From June through September, four of The Bard's plays are presented outdoors in this 521-seat theater just over the hill from Berkeley. Sight lines are great from either the front seats or the terrace area, where you can lay down a blanket and picnic during the performance. One word of caution: If the fog rolls in, whichever play you're seeing could turn into a winter's tale. Dress warmly. Shuttle buses to and from the performances pick up and drop off at the Orinda BART station. & (Hills)

CENTRAL WORKS
510/558-1381

This experimental troupe has traveled around the East Bay for the past decade to stage their unconventional plays at unconventional locations. *Rux,* a stark drama about women who kill, was performed in the former Berkeley Women's City Club. *IRS, I Want You,* a political satire, was staged in a banquet room at the Santa Fe Bar and Grill. All of their works are collaborative, and they gestate over months of workshops and rehearsals. Unfortunately, that limits the troupe's productions to two or three a year. But it also makes them sharper and more fully produced. The *Oakland Tribune* called their work "impeccable." (Zone varies with venue)

LAVAL'S SUBTERRANEAN THEATER
1834 Euclid St.
Berkeley
510/234-6046

Strange things can happen when you go underground. Descend the stairs of this off-campus pizza parlor and you'll find yourself in a cave-like 75-seat theater that showcases ambitious, full-length productions of Shakespeare, Tennessee Williams, and David Mamet, among others. Several part-time troupes use this venue, including the Subterranean Shakespeare Company. Some shows are wickedly elaborate considering the space limitations, but the venue's real strengths are found in its stripped-down performances and high-intensity actors. The troupes that appear here do an excellent job of keeping the avant-garde alive in the East Bay. (Berkeley)

LIVE OAK THEATER
1301 Shattuck Ave.
Berkeley
510/841-5580

Berkeley's Actors Ensemble is the city's oldest stage company. They tend to favor lighter fare, especially from recent American playwrights

Berkeley Repertory Theater

Ken Friedman 1998

like A. R. Gurney and classic ones like George S. Kaufman. When ambition strikes, they even do musicals, such as a memorable version of Stephen Sondheim's *Company.* Their home, this intimate 142-seat theater in the woodlands of Live Oak Park, is, with its small and high stage, a lot like a grammar school auditorium. Tickets are generally available on the day of the performance. & (Berkeley)

SHOTGUN PLAYERS
3280 Adeline
Berkeley
510/655-0813

This decade-old troupe presents stripped-down productions in their new 99-seat theater for some of the most reasonable prices in the city— $8 to $10 a ticket. They've done smart versions of Greek tragedies and Shaw, but they lean toward modern writers like Mamet, and pride themselves on West Coast premieres. Monday nights they have readings of new plays, and sometimes they do live radio dramas for local station KPFA. In August and September they perform Shakespeare for free in East Bay Parks. (Berkeley)

WOODMINSTER AMPHITHEATER
3300 Joaquin Miller Rd.
Oakland
510/531-9597

The back rows in this 1,500-seat open-air theater give you a free second show in addition to the perky Broadway musical that's on stage— an IMAX-size vista of San Francisco. The season runs all summer long and is family-friendly. They tend to present American classics like *South Pacific* and *Grease.* Nearby picnic tables are available for pre-theater dining. Dress warmly because you never know whether the fog is going to make an entrance during Act II. Kids age 16 and under get in free with every adult ticket. Only the top row is wheelchair accessible. (Hills)

MUSIC AND OPERA

BELLA MUSICA
510/525-5393

This ambitious five-year-old orchestra and chorus leans on the orchestra more than it does the chorus, as evident in such pieces as Beethoven's *Violin Concerto* and Bizet's *Symphony in C.* Still, they do a stellar job on the *Magnificat* and *Carmina Burana.* Recently, they have become more adventurous and play new and commissioned pieces, even stirring Gregorian chants. The chorus is tight and professional sounding, with up to 80 voices. Many performances take place at Berkeley First Congregational Church at Dwight and Dana Streets. Tickets run from $10 to $15. Their five CDs are available at Hear Music on Fourth Street and the Musical Offering on Bancroft Way. (Zone varies with venue)

BERKELEY CHAMBER PERFORMANCES
Berkeley City Club
1800 Dwight Way
Berkeley
510/525-5211
Sometimes the right location can make a big difference, and this—early-twentieth-century architect Julia Morgan's magical City Club—is the most enchanting musical venue in Berkeley. About five times a year, this group holds chamber concerts in either the lounge or the ballroom. The rooms are intimate and the acoustics warm and "alive." You will hear local or nationally known ensembles performing Baroque pieces or Beethoven, Stravinsky, even Gershwin's *American in Paris* arranged for two pianos. The audience is invited to stay for a re-

Woodminster Amphitheater

Gail Geetler

ception afterward and meet the performers. (Berkeley)

BERKELEY COMMUNITY CHORUS AND ORCHESTRA
510/528-2145
This may be the East Bay's best musical bargain—a full orchestra and chorus that performs for free. They give seven concerts a year at various churches around town, but they can usually be found at St. Joseph the Worker Church at 1640 Addison Street. For 30 years, they have presented large-scale classical works, including all the major requiems and a generous mix of Bach, Haydn, Shubert, and Beethoven. In the summer they offer a "Gems of Broadway" series. During major events, the chorus swells to 200 thrilling voices. ₺ (Zone varies with venue)

BERKELEY OPERA
Julia Morgan Theater
2640 College Ave.
Berkeley
510/841-1903
Some operas, like Mozart's, deserve more intimate theaters. This 20-year-old company puts on two to four scaled-down shows a season (February through July) at the 350-seat Julia Morgan Theater. Most are fully, if not elaborately, staged, with a 28-piece orchestra. The singers are quite talented semiprofessionals. The repertoire tends to run from the familiar, like *Don Giovanni* and *Otello,* to the rare, like Berlioz's *Beatrice and Benedict.* ₺ (South Berkeley/North Oakland)

BERKELEY SYMPHONY
Kent Nagano, conductor
510/841-2800
When Maestro Nagano isn't con-

ducting orchestras in Berlin, Manchester, England, or nearly anywhere in the world, he may be heard in Berkeley, most often at Zellerbach Hall. This risk-taking group specializes in neglected or rarely performed works, like Bruckner's difficult Ninth Symphony, for example. They balance these pieces with explorations into the challenging world of new music, including many world premieres and performances of work by local composers such as John Adams. Edgy and avant garde, these programs are not for listeners who like to hum along to Tchaikovsky. Tickets are generally available the night of the performance. & (Zone varies with venue)

KITKA WOMEN'S VOCAL ENSEMBLE
510/444-0323
www.kitka.org
This nine-woman Eastern European a cappella choral group doesn't need any instruments to send chills through its audience. Their deep, open-throated harmonies can be heard on weekends, mostly in local churches, but they also perform at Mills College and Berkeley's Freight and Salvage Club. Their vibrant renditions of Balkan folk songs are even more rich and haunting in light of the recent tragedies in those countries. If you can't believe what you've heard, you can find their two CD recordings in Berkeley at the Musical Offering and Hear Music. (Zone varies with venue)

LOVE CENTER CHOIR
10400 International Blvd.
Oakland
510/729-0680
This highly charged choir secured

a firm spot on the musical map when Edwin Hawkins recorded the joyous "Oh, Happy Day" several years ago. Today his sister leads this 60-voice ensemble at the Love Center Church every Sunday as well as on their tours across the country to Chicago, Atlanta, and New York. They also make local appearances at venues like the Paramount and the Berkeley Community Theater. They have been sending audiences to their feet for 25 years, and they are now on their fifth CD in the *Love Alive* series. & (Oakland)

MUSIC SOURCES
1000 The Alameda
Berkeley
510/528-1685
The East Bay has an obsession with elegant, early Renaissance music—the stately and precise melodies played on recorders and clavichords. Every month from October to April, this umbrella organization offers chamber concerts that are both entertaining and educational. During the first hour, artists from around the country and the world perform several short works, including, on occasion, a dance or two. The second hour is a reception, during which a discussion of the work and the unusual instruments is held. The group prides itself on musical rarities and once gave a concert of music published during the Gold Rush. (Berkeley)

OAKLAND EAST BAY SYMPHONY
199 Harrison St.
Oakland
510/446-1992
Glorious Mahler, earth-shaking Beethoven . . . the most epic works of classical music fill the delirious

Cal Performances

One of the sources of Berkeley's high cultural self-esteem is Cal Performances, 510/642-9988, www.calperfs.berkeley.edu, a richly programmed music, theater, and dance series. Most events are staged in Zellerbach or Hertz Hall on campus, or occasionally in the First Congregational Church. The range is awesome. Regular visiting dance companies include Merce Cunningham, Alvin Ailey, the Dance Theatre of Harlem, and Mark Morris. Internationally acclaimed soloists such as James Galway and Fredericka von Stade return yearly. From Irish folk singers to African drummers to Latin American guitarists, the lineup is stellar. Every other June they present the premier early-music festival in the United States. Most performances occur during the school year, not during the summer. Single ticket prices range from $18 to $50.

Art Deco halls of the Paramount Theater every month from November through May when Maestro Michael Morgan conducts this highly polished 55-player ensemble. But classics aren't the only things you'll hear from them. They also take off on more adventurous musical paths when they perform the works of emerging composers. For the full effect of this magnificent 50-year-old orchestra, attend one of their large-scale choral concerts. Tickets are generally available on the day of the performance, but avoid the last rows of the balcony because the Paramount was built for movies and the sound fades out up there. &. (Oakland)

OAKLAND INTERFAITH GOSPEL CHOIR
510/848-3938

They give 25 to 30 concerts a year, but if you can make it to only one Interfaith Gospel Choir concert, it should be the first Saturday in December at Oakland's Paramount Theater. This event features a shimmering, soul-stirring selection of classic holiday carols and soaring gospel songs. The choir's 65 members represent a true cross-section of East Bay religious groups, including all Christian denominations as well as Jews, Buddhists, and Sufis. Their CD is available at Tower or Nu Revelations Records at 10700 MacArthur in Oakland. (Zone varies with venue)

OAKLAND LYRIC OPERA
4618 El Centro
Oakland
510/531-4231
Who's afraid of grand opera? Fewer

and fewer people if this ambitious organization has its way. Since 1992 they've been presenting classics to the community—sometimes with full orchestra and chorus, most often in concert form—with minimal staging. They offer three or four series a year at locations like Oakland's Scottish Rite Temple and Holy Names College. The performances last about an hour and a half. After that there is a lively question-and-answer period. During the summer, they perform free every other Tuesday at noon in the City Center Plaza downtown. (Oakland)

OAKLAND SYMPHONY CHORUS
510/428-3172
If you're in the mood to hear large-scale vocalizing, especially the symphonic masterworks, this 100-voice ensemble will blow you away. Although composed entirely of volunteer singers, the chorus' ability to tackle epic works (Bernstein's "Chichester Songs," for example) is unmatched. Each year they give two concerts with the Oakland Symphony at the Paramount Theater and one with the Oakland Youth Orchestra at Calvin Simmons Theater. They also stage a separate a cappella event on their own. The 40-year-old organization is highly regarded, and programs frequently sell out. Order tickets in advance. (Zone varies with venue)

OAKLAND YOUTH CHORUS
510/287-9700
Tapping into the wellspring of adolescent musical energy, this organization gives exuberant concerts around the Bay Area during the school year. The 50 or so teenagers from every ethnic and racial group in the community perform a varied repertoire with influences from around the world, from Kenyan hymns to love songs by Babyface. Their talent and high spirits are on display each year during their holiday and spring concerts, held in the magnificent, 600-seat First Presbyterian Church in downtown Oakland. Tapes and CDs are available. (Zone varies with venue)

PACIFIC MOZART ENSEMBLE
415/705-0848
www.pacificmozart.org
After singing the entire Mozart chorale repertoire more than a few times throughout their 20-year existence, this 44-voice group has finally branched out into twentieth-century music. They still cover standard eighteenth-century works, however, and they are so well regarded that they have toured Europe several times. They give three concert sets a year at various venues around town, but you can also hear them with the Berkeley Symphony or on the soundtracks of George Lucas films. One of the year's highlights is their spring a cappella jazz and pop series. (Zone varies with venue)

PHILHARMONIA BAROQUE
415/495-7445
This preeminent 20- to 40-instrument ensemble plays at least seven concerts of seventeenth-, eighteenth-, and early-nineteenth-century music each year at the First Congregational Church in Berkeley. Their season lasts from September to April. Musical director Nicholas McGeegan (who also directs Germany's Gottingen Handel Festival) imports at least half the players from around the country. The period instruments and the musical arrangements re-

produce sounds that Mozart himself would have heard. Their subscription audience is quite large, so it's suggested that you call first to reserve tickets, especially if they are doing Handel's *Oratorio*. (Zone varies with venue)

SACRED AND PROFANE CHAMBER CHORUS
510/524-3611

This small, highly accomplished 24-voice chorus has been performing locally for 21 years. They give two or three concert sets annually in the fall and spring, mainly at churches in Berkeley and Oakland. Lately they've included more and more twentieth-century music from composers like Benjamin Britten. Their crystalline sound remains one of the area's musical treasures. (Zone varies with venue)

UC CHORUS AND CHAMBER CHORUS
Hertz Hall
UC Campus
Berkeley
510/642-4860

Tours from New York to Vienna have secured the reputation of these two extraordinary a cappella groups. The 70-member chorus performs five or six concerts a year on campus at Hertz Hall, scaling the heights of such masterpieces as Mozart's "Idomeneo" and Verdi's "Requiem." The 30-voice chamber chorus also gives half a dozen concerts around the Bay Area, with a repertoire that spans Monteverdi to Vaughn Williams. Competition for the limited spots in this chorus is fierce. The result is a level of musicianship that is, frankly, professional. (Berkeley)

DANCE

BERKELEY BALLET THEATER
2640 College Ave.
Berkeley
510/843-4687

The historic Julia Morgan Theater glows every holiday with the charming Berkeley Ballet Theater production of *The Nutcracker*. A cast of 140, which includes students from the theater's school and professional dancers, gives 10 to 12 enchanting, full-stage performances. Local ballet students also give recitals in the spring and at the end of the summer. Classical programs, as well as the work of outside choreographers, are featured. & (Berkeley)

DIMENSION DANCE THEATER
1428 Alice St.
Oakland
510/465-3363

Picture a dance where the featured performers are former Black Panthers. That's the kind of innovative work this eight-member ethnic dance troupe has been doing for nearly 30 years. Their season runs from January to August and includes at least one concert each month of traditional African, modern, and jazz dancing. All of the choreography is original and heavily collaborative. This troupe's spoken-word events have featured poets, such as Nikki Giovanni. When the drummers get going, the energy ratchets up and the dancers achieve total lift off. & (Oakland)

OAKLAND BALLET
2025 Broadway
Oakland
510/452-9288

Wait, was that the A's ace pitcher in tights doing *The Nutcracker*? Could be. It's a holiday tradition to include baseball stars in the annual December production by this 40-year-old, 33-member dance company. The full season pirouettes from September to December and offers three different programs. Enjoy choreography commissioned just for the Oakland Ballet; a modern classic like deMille's *Rodeo*; or a fastidious revival of a piece from the Ballet Russe, such as *Les Biches*. The setting—the golden Art Deco Paramount Theater—is extraordinary. ♿ (Oakland)

CONCERT VENUES

ALICE ARTS CENTER
1428 Alice St.
Oakland
510/238-7222
This former hotel is now an active center for multicultural dance performances, recitals, and plays. Downstairs is a 450-seat theater with an enormous stage that projects out into the audience. Resident companies include Dimensions Dance Theater, Citicentre Dance Theater, the Oakland Ensemble Theater, and the African American Theater. ♿ (Oakland)

CALVIN SIMMONS THEATER
10 10th St.
Oakland
510/238-7765
The programs here represent—much like Oakland's population—a cross section of the world. You're as likely to hear blues divas as you are a Cambodian New Year celebration. The elaborately designed concert hall seats 1,860, but the acoustics are intimate. The Peking Opera performs here, as does the Oakland Youth Orchestra. It's hosted the Black Def Comedy Jam, Tina Marie, and an endless stream of gospel concerts (including a Mother's Day show that's not to be missed). If you're here during December, catch the *Black Nativity,* a Christmas story with gospel and folk music. ♿ (Oakland)

HERTZ HALL
UC Campus
Bancroft Way/
College Ave. entrance
510/642-4864
The warm-toned, wood interior of this 700-seat, Californian suburban-looking recital hall makes many performers and audiences prefer it to the chillier acoustics of Zellerbach Hall. Summer is quiet here, but during the spring and fall semesters two ambitious series are performed. Every Wednesday at noon free concerts showcase anything from African drummers to a Bach chorale. On weekend evenings and Sunday afternoons performing ensembles include the UC Symphony, Chorus, and Chamber Chorus. On Monday evenings they often schedule concerts of new music. ♿ (Berkeley)

JULIA MORGAN THEATER
2640 College Ave.
Berkeley
510/845-8542
A big, wooden Berkeley barn of a theater, this place was originally a church designed by Julia Morgan. Now, however, the congregations come here to see and hear an eclectic schedule of artists. Both the Berkeley Opera and the Berkeley Ballet call this theater home. Expect the unexpected, from classical soloists to Third-World instruments you may have not previously

heard to concert-version Broadway musicals and even stand-up comedy nights. Weekends, they offer a children's theater festival. Because the theater is in a residential neighborhood, parking is at a premium. ⅙ (South Berkeley/North Oakland)

KAISER ARENA
10 10th St.
Oakland
510/238-7765
Elvis has left the building. The King has sung here, but nowadays you're more likely to see a barefoot karate or judo competition than blue suede shoes. Even though it's a site for concerts by well-known figures, such as Patti LaBelle, Harold Melvin, and the Foo Fighters, the really interesting ones aren't advertised in the mainstream press. Call for a schedule and ask about their Hong Kong rock concerts, Bollywood nights from East India, Ethiopian and Nigerian Independence Day celebrations, and reggae festivals. With 9,000 seats, it's not overwhelmingly large. And in the second and third balconies, the 85-year-old wooden seats have gotten even more comfortable over the years. ⅙ (Oakland)

MILLS COLLEGE
5000 MacArthur Blvd.
Oakland

510/430-2171
This 500-seat concert hall, with its exotic 1929 murals, tiles, and flamboyant lighting fixtures, sometimes comes close to stealing the show. During the school year they have one or two concerts a month that roam the history and world of music. International classical soloists such as pianist Jean-Phillipe Collard have performed here, as has the Indian master Ali Abkar Khan. Shows are modestly priced. The modern Haas Pavilion is where the Mills repertory company performs its dance season each year. Guest artists also appear there. (Oakland)

PARAMOUNT THEATER
2025 Broadway
Oakland
510/465-6400
Even when empty, this 3,000-seat Art Deco movie palace is an amazing experience. The ornate wall carvings have been immaculately restored and gilded. It is the home of the Oakland Symphony and the Oakland Ballet. In addition, 150 to 200 other performances are given here every year, including some by musical celebrities such as Bonnie Raitt and Stevie Wonder. The holiday gospel concert is a high point. And 24 Fridays a year it reverts to its original role as a film theater, showing classics from Hollywood's

Nordstrom's isn't the only place that entertains shoppers with live music. Berkeley's Cheese Board (1504 Shattuck Ave., 510/549-3183) has lunchtime piano concerts on Fridays and Saturdays. Usually, you'll find Betty Shaw playing bebop piano.

Top 10 Musical Highlights of the East Bay

By Michael Morgan, conductor, Oakland East Bay Symphony

1. Oakland East Bay Symphony (of course)
2. Oakland Youth Orchestra and Youth Chorus (two organizations, one goal)
3. The acoustics of the Calvin Simmons Theater (probably the best in northern California)
4. Jazz is almost everywhere (most famously at Yoshi's in Jack London Square)
5. The Young Musician's Program in Berkeley
6. The Festival Opera and the Regional Arts Center in Walnut Creek
7. Gospel is everywhere (but the Oakland Interfaith Gospel Choir is the best)
8. Orchestras are everywhere (California Symphony, Berkeley Symphony, etc.)
9. The East Bay Center for the Performing Arts in Richmond (where every kind of music is taught)
10. The beauty of the Paramount Theater (a shrine to Art Deco), home of the Oakland Ballet

golden age. This theater is also the site of the gala annual Black Filmmakers Hall of Fame award ceremonies. & (Oakland)

ZELLERBACH HALL
UC Campus
Berkeley
510/642-9988
Try to get over the grotty, Fred Flintstone interior of this 2,000-seat, '70s auditorium because Cal Performances presents most of its am-bitious, adventurous, and international programs here. The Berkeley Symphony also performs here, as does the Berkeley Ballet. The bigger the orchestra the better because the sounds of small ensemble groups tend to be swallowed up by Zellerbach's cavernous space. Way up in the back of the balcony the sound gets muffled, but the seats are comfy and the leg room is generous. & (Berkeley)

12

NIGHTLIFE

The Pointer Sisters, Green Day, En Vogue ... the East Bay breeds musical talent like Kentucky breeds racehorses. For years, rhythm and blues here has had its own sound—funkier, slower, and more soulful than that you'll find elsewhere around the country. Hometown players mix it up with nationally known artists in about a dozen clubs across the East Bay. Jazz venues range from sleek supper clubs to intimate little bars, and they book artists with such talent that even insular San Franciscans journey across the Bay Bridge to hear them. Clubs in the area offer everything from swing to salsa to Bulgarian folk dancing. And speaking of folk, folk music has been popular here since the '60s, and musicians from as far away as the Ozarks, the Argentines, West Africa, and even Los Angeles have no trouble keeping area clubs swaying with the sounds of their guitars. Perhaps the only drawback to the Berkeley/Oakland nightlife scene is the way the sidewalks are pretty much rolled up by midnight. If you're into late nights, you may be disappointed.

DANCE CLUBS

ALLEGRO BALLROOM
5855 Christie Ave.
Emeryville
510/655-2888
If you're one of those dancers with two left feet, come here for a quick lesson guaranteed to improve your style. Dance lessons are offered between seven and eight on weekend nights. After that the floor gets pretty jammed as ballroom and disco take over. Plenty of single people show up, so there's no need to worry if you come without a partner. A six-dollar cover charge is levied at the door, but the music is

recorded and the drinks—well, you'll find what you need in the vending machines. (Berkeley Waterfront)

MAIKO DANCE CLUB
1629 San Pablo Ave.
Berkeley
510/527-8226
Conventional businessman comes down with dance fever: It sounds like the plot of *Shall We Dance?*, the Japanese tango film. But in this case, the businessman decides to open a small ballroom where beginners can take lessons before the veterans pour in for a few hours of live music, salsa, waltzes, and foxtrots. Wine, beer, and sushi are all available. The cover charge begins at five dollars and includes lessons. (Berkeley Waterfront)

SWEETS BALLROOM
1933 Broadway
Oakland
510/893-2902
Big, brassy, and back from the dead, this '30s and '40s hotspot jumps every Friday and Saturday from 8:30 to 10. You'll find a 10,000-square-foot dance floor and, on many nights, six-piece swing, salsa, or reggae bands. The Art Deco frescoes and modern lighting give the joint a nice, faded sense of glamour. Just for the fun of

it, try arriving decked out in a period costume. There's a full bar, but seating is limited. (Oakland)

TERRACE BAR
Claremont Hotel
41 Tunnel Rd.
Oakland
510/843-3000
Swing dancing CEOs kick up their loafers on the Terrace's miniscule dance floor Thursday through Saturday nights. If you're shy about your dancing skills, classes are offered before the masses arrive on Thursday evenings. And if you don't like watching yourself do the lindy, go elsewhere—one entire wall is mirrored. The seven-dollar cover charge includes one drink. If a swing band isn't on tap for the evening, you'll likely be in for light jazz or rhythm and blues. The show goes from 9 to 11, but get there early because it can be crowded. The view of the bay is show-stopping. (South Berkeley/North Oakland)

MUSIC CLUBS

Jazz and Blues
CUCKOO'S NEST
247 Fourth St.

Theological renegade Mathew Fox is the guiding spirit behind the monthly "Techno Cosmic Mass" at Sweets Ballroom. A cross between a church service and a rave, it's juiced with ancient music, Hindu chants, gospel music, multimedia light projections, freeform dancing, and ecstatic renditions of the Western liturgy. It's the kind of event that would give Jerry Falwell a coronary. And it's free! Call 510/835-4827 for a schedule.

Oakland
510/452-9414
The loft people of Jack London Square use Cuckoo's Nest as their unofficial clubhouse. During daylight hours it's a mild-mannered, sometimes inventive restaurant that serves bargain meals. But after 6:30 Wednesday through Saturday nights, local combos play cool contemporary jazz and bossa nova. There's no cover charge, but don't dilly-dally—the music stops by 10 or 10:30. (Oakland)

DEJA BREW
5850 San Pablo Ave.
Oakland
510/652-1317
The brew is coffee. This former drugstore on the edge of high-tech Emeryville is cool, dark, and friendly. The comfortably funky setting includes lots of local art on the walls, old sofas, and multicultural chatter. The music, which usually happens Thursdays and Fridays from 4:30 to 9:30, ranges from classic ragtime to

Yoshi's at Jack London Square, p. 199

Marty Forsyth

the sounds of local bands experimenting their way through jazz-tinted, hip-hoppish bebop. (Berkeley Waterfront)

FAT LADY
201 Washington
Oakland
510/465-4996
Proudly flaunting its brothel past, this now-respectable fish-and-steak house has a miniscule stage where soloists play light jazz and blues for diners on Friday and Saturday nights. At around 10:30 the tables in the back dining room are cleared and the West Express band takes over, pumping out top 40 and rhythm and blues for bar patrons and dancers till one in the morning. (Oakland)

FIFTH AMENDMENT
3255 Lakeshore
Oakland
510/832-3242
The basic constitutional right to have a good time is enforced nightly in this dark, easygoing bar off Lake Merritt. Nobody has tampered much with the 60-year-old Art Deco décor, but that doesn't stop the dancers. It's one of the area's few venues that has live music every night of the week. Sunday is devoted to jazz, whereas the rest of the week is a mixed bag of local bands playing rhythm and blues (with a distinct emphasis on the rhythm). Get up and dance! (Oakland)

GEOFFREY'S INNER CIRCLE
419 14th St.
Oakland
510/839-4644
Once a club for well-to-do white businessmen, Geoffrey's is now a

spiffy, live entertainment complex that's perennially popular with well-heeled 20- and 30-something blacks. Occasionally a rap artist or two slips in, but more likely you'll hear contemporary billboard rhythm and blues. Wednesdays are for stand-up comedy, Thursdays bring singing competitions, and Sundays are all about live jazz. The upstairs restaurant serves until midnight. (Oakland)

H'S LORDSHIP
199 Seawall
Berkeley
510/843-2733
H's Lordship is set on the water, but the view is of the Berkeley hills, not the bay. This cute olde-English bar is used as a waiting room by people on their way to the main restaurant (which does have a good view of San Francisco), but you don't have to eat here to have a good time. Instead, just sit and devour the live jazz or rhythm-and-blues combos that play each evening until midnight. (Berkeley Waterfront)

IVY ROOM
860 San Pablo Ave.
Albany
510/524-9229
A neon martini on the sign outside is your first clue that this place is real retro. Dating back to 1948, the Ivy Room is a local hangout that serves a large, authentic, ungentrified dose of nostalgia and—on Fridays, Saturdays, and Tuesdays—live music. There's a lot of get-up-and-dance blues in addition to some jazz and rockabilly. There's some room for dancing, but it's a bit tight. (Berkeley Waterfront)

THE JAZZ SCHOOL
2375 Shattuck Ave.
Berkeley
510/845-5373
If you stretch your definition of nightlife to include happenings in the late afternoon, the groovy concerts at The Jazz School will fit into your vocabulary quite nicely. On Sunday afternoons from 4:30 to 6:30 the school showcases its best students and visiting artists downstairs in La Note restaurant. Upstairs, students are taught everything from full-body singing to salsa piano. Expect anything. General admission is $12. (Berkeley)

KIMBALL'S EAST
5800 Shellmound
Emeryville
510/658-2555
Keep your eyes peeled for the discreet "Jazz" sign, or you might miss this hip 350-seat supper club tucked away on the second floor of an

office building. It's an enormous warehouse space, but the acoustics are mellow enough for stars like Nancy Wilson and Freddie Jackson. The first few rows are good if you're looking for drinks only. Away from the stage you'll get full service on tiered dining tables. Dinner is served from 6:30 to 10 and there are two shows nightly Thursday through Sunday. Tickets range from $20 to $30. (Berkeley Waterfront)

THE OAK TREE
380 Embarcadero
Oakland
510/286-8400
This place across from Jack London Square has hotel-like polish and professionalism. Sit down for a Cajun/Creole dinner with soft live jazz in the background. Then move across the hall to the clubroom, which swings Friday and Saturday nights from nine to two with top 40

and brassy jazz and on Sunday nights to the sounds of a 21-piece big-band orchestra. The cover charge is $10 until nine. (Oakland)

VOULEZ-VOUS BISTRO
2930 College Ave.
Berkeley
510/548-4708
Soloists or duos playing light jazz with a New Age touch serenade early diners at this perky Parisian restaurant. Around 9:30, though, the background music takes the main stage, and you might hear anything from French folk songs to edgy jazz to Appalachian love ballads. (South Berkeley/North Oakland)

YOSHI'S
510 Embarcadero W.
Oakland
510/238-9200
www.yoshis.com
Ask jazz musicians, and they'll put

REALLY BIG SHOWS

During the summer, the 10,000-seat, open-air Greek Theatre (510/642-9988), on Piedmont Avenue above the UC campus, is the site of shows by performers such as the Gypsy Kings and James Taylor. The biggest theater in town is the Berkeley Community Theater (510/644-8957), with seating for 3,500, on the Berkeley High Campus at Allston Way and Grove, where Bob Dylan shows up regularly. The Network Associates Coliseum (510/569-2121), off Highway 880 near the exit to Oakland Airport, is the kind of huge arena found in most major American cities. It hosts acts such as The Rolling Stones and Bette Midler. To order tickets for major events, call BASS at 510/893-7191, or stop by Tower Records at 2518 Durant Avenue, Berkeley.

this cabaret at the top of the list of the country's premier clubs. Attached to a mediocre Japanese restaurant, this swank Upper East Side room seats 315 people intimately. The roster of stars who perform nightly is a who's-who of the jazz world. The list includes greats such as Bobby Short, McCoy Tyner, Pharoah Saunders, and several Cuban artists. The cover charge slides from $5 to $25. Check their Web site for the schedule, and book a reservation at least two weeks in advance. (Oakland)

Blues

BLUESVILLE
131 Broadway
Oakland
510/893-6215
Lower Broadway clubs open and close with alarming regularity. Cross your fingers and hope that this recent addition makes it because it's a chance to hear the whole spectrum of blues. Bluesville is committed to showcasing older West Coast blues as well as newer bands like The Resistors. The relaxed, rough-edged scene stands in contrast to the packaged evenings you'll find down the block on Jack London Square. Wed-Sun 9-1. (Oakland)

ELI'S MILE HIGH CLUB
3629 Martin Luther King Way
Oakland
510/655-6661
Any day now the city will probably confer landmark status on this home of the West Coast blues. That distinct Oakland sound, with its urban horns, has been played here for decades, even after a jealous lover shot the owner in 1979. Stop by to hear the likes of Sonny Rhodes and Jimmy

McCrackin, and plan on dancing because this is no place to sit still. Wed-Mon 9:30-1:30. (Oakland)

JIMMIE'S
1731 San Pablo Ave.
Berkeley
510/268-8445
The neighborhood is eerily empty; the entrance looks like that of a health club; and the VIP room is pretty much deejay-led dancing, but in the big, brick-lined, two-level back room, the place is pumping. Ike Turner played here, and so did Jimmie McGriff. This is where Solomon Burke recorded his last blues CD. The "Sorry, no rap" signs posted everywhere let you know where the musical line is drawn. Open nightly. (Oakland)

Rock

924 GILMAN
924 Gilman St.
Berkeley
510/524-8180
Graced by bands like Creeps on Candy and God Hates Computers, 924 Gilman may be a parent's worst nightmare. It's decorated with wall-to-wall graffiti, has more blue and pink hair than a retirement home, and five raucous bands play every night. One thing that makes mom and dad happy, however, is the fact that this teen center strictly enforces its ban on drugs, drinking, and smoking. If you're over 20, you're over the hill here. $5 admission plus $2 membership fee. Weekends only. (Berkeley Waterfront)

LARRY BLAKE'S
2367 Telegraph Ave.
Berkeley
510/848-0886

Cal students have been hanging out at Larry Blake's since before World War II. The latest incarnation of this one-time starting point for Third Eye Blind is a dark, cavelike basement so small it's hard not to feel like you're playing in the band. The musical spectrum ranges from rock to acid jazz to funk and is performed mostly by local bands. It's open seven days a week. The cover charge fluctuates between three and eight dollars, depending on the band. (Berkeley)

PORT LITE
229 Brush St.
Oakland
510/451-0600
By day a scruffy dive with décor by Budweiser, this buddy bar near the waterfront turns into a hangout for local rockers from nine to two Thursday through Saturday nights. Don't expect to hear top-40 covers—these are local players doing original, alternative, and country rock 'n' roll. There's no dance floor, but if the beat moves you, nobody's going to stop you. Sunday afternoons from four to eight it's all jazz. $3 cover. (Oakland)

Folk

ASHKENAZ
1317 San Pablo Ave.
Berkeley
510/525-5054
Lissome young revolutionaries boogie with ponytailed senior citizens at this Berkeley institution. Everybody dances, mostly to a mixture of Cajun and blues, but what really distinguishes this place is its atlas of world music, from Eastern European to African to Latin to all the dance classes that go along with it. If your appetite kicks in, Ashkenaz serves

wine, beer, and tofu sandwiches. Bring the kids. Open seven nights a week. (Berkeley Waterfront)

FREIGHT & SALVAGE
1111 Addison St.
Berkeley
510/548-1761
This is Berkeley unplugged. Seven nights a week you can hear folk music by people who hail from places as varied as Austin, Boston, and Edinburgh. It's mostly theater-style seating in this former garage, but every Tuesday the stage is open, providing a great chance for budding musicians to jumpstart their folk-singing careers. It's definitely a place for those who like to keep their nightlife as mellow as possible. Coffee, tea, and various munchies are available. Admission is around $13. (Berkeley)

STARRY PLOUGH
3101 Shattuck Ave.
Berkeley
510/841-2082
It's Greenwich Village 1965 every night here. The décor consists of revolutionary posters, and the music leans towards Irish bands, although you could walk in tomorrow night and hear sarcastic punk rock. Poetry slams are staged on occasion. There's a full bar, plus sandwiches, pizzas, and burgers. The young grad-student patrons are heirs apparent to the '60s counterculture. (South Berkeley/North Oakland)

Latin

CAPOERIA
2026 Addison St.
Berkeley
510/666-1349
Innocently stumble in for a latte or

Every June, to mark the summer solstice, an appropriately otherworldy concert is held at the Chapel of the Chimes (510/654-0123), Piedmont Avenue's haciendalike funeral parlor. Expect any and all kinds of music, from medieval to avant-garde.

a power smoothie at this coffee shop and performance space and you may be surprised by an exotic, Afro-Brazilian melange of dancing and martial arts. The acrobatic performance is a fast-moving, low-to-the-ground, tribal kind of thing whose closest U.S. cousin is break-dancing. Mon-Fri 5-9, Sat noon-5. (Berkeley)

CARIBBEAN SPICE
1920 San Pablo Ave.
Berkeley
510/843-3035

If you like your Lambada fish or stewed goat spiced with Latin music, have a late (after 10 p.m.) dinner at this bouncy island restaurant *con* club. On Friday nights a deejay spins Caribbean-Spanish music. On Saturdays it's mostly live Afro-Cuban bands, and the irresistible beat goes on until two. Sunday from six to nine you'll hear local jazz bands. There are also monthly poetry readings and occasional comedy nights. Cover charge is $5. (Berkeley Waterfront)

EL REVENTON
408 Webster St.
Oakland
510/835-1813

This downtown dance hall turns into a Mexican border-town fiesta around 10:30 on Friday, Saturday,

and Sunday nights. The name for this place is fitting: *El Reventon* means "the blast" in Spanish. The local *banda* musicians play Mexican country and western here with such electricity that if you're not up and dancing within four notes, you're probably in a coma. (Oakland)

LA PEÑA
3105 Shattuck Ave.
Berkeley
510/849-2568

A quarter-century ago, Chile's dictator, General Pinochet, sent artists and intellectuals into exile. A few who came to Berkeley started this sophisticated club. The small, concertlike space regularly features acoustic music, from folk to flamenco to Japanese jazz. The adjacent restaurant serves traditional Latin dishes at reasonable prices. Open Wed-Sun. (Berkeley)

MR. E'S
2284 Shattuck Ave.
Berkeley
510/848-2009

If you've never seen a platinum record, three stand behind the bar here as testimony to the stardom of the club's owner, Pete Escovedo (the father of another star, Sheila E.). Latin jazz is the heart and soul of this vast, slick dance club, but they mix it up with big names in

TIP Remember that the East Bay, like the rest of California, is an official No-Smoking Zone. If you want to light up at a bar, club, or restaurant, you must step outside. Even then, however, don't expect to smoke in peace. Anti-nicotine passersby have been known to harass smokers.

swing and blues. Open nightly except Monday. (Berkeley)

Country and Western

THE STORK CLUB
2330 Telegraph
Oakland
510/444-6174
If you like holiday parties, come to the Stork. This seedy club throws Halloween bashes and New Year's galas off and on all year long. The bar area is clogged with Christmas tchotchkes, and the dance floor is festooned with lights and tinsel. On Wednesday and Thursday nights local bands pound out hard-driving country music. Fridays and Saturdays it's alternative rock, and on Sundays it's open mike. (Oakland)

Indian

KAMAL PALACE
2175 Allston Way
Berkeley
510/848-9906
How would you like a classic Indian raga with your curry? North and South Indian music is quite tasty at this Indian restaurant just across from the east entrance of UC Berkeley. Musicians from the Ali Abkar Khan Music School in San Jose play hypnotic 45-minute sets on the tabla, sitar, and sarod seven nights a week until 9:30. They're just quiet enough to keep from drowning out your dinner conversation. (Berkeley)

Hawaiian

TEMPLEBAR
984 University Ave.
Berkeley
510/548-9888
Slip into your muumuu and tune up your ukulele. Berkeley's one and only Hawaiian club has shows both on stage and off. Local island musicians and dancers perform Friday and Saturday nights. Between sets, the sometimes talented customers do their own numbers. There's a luau buffet and enough plastic tiki gods to make you think—or wish—you were back in Waikiki. (Berkeley Waterfront)

PUBS AND BARS

ALBATROSS
1822 San Pablo Ave.
Berkeley
510/843-2473
This 35-year-old pub is the place to go if games are your thing. You'll find darts, chess, Pictionary, and more than 20 other favorites to keep you entertained. Albatross also offers an enormous selection of obscure English, Irish, and Belgian beers, as well as pizza, chips, and the regular assortment of bar food. Live entertainment takes the

tucked-away corner stage every Saturday but never disturbs the customers hunching over their game boards. (Berkeley Waterfront)

THE ALLEY
3325 Grand Ave.
Oakland
510/444-8505
Don't be fooled by the innocent Hansel and Gretel exterior. Inside it's out-and-out weird, a dark village with lingerie hanging like ghosts from the ceiling and walls stapled with thousands of business cards. In the corner is a massive piano bar where loyal local patrons gather to belt out everything from show tunes to golden oldies. (Oakland)

ANNA'S PLACE
1801 University Ave.
Berkeley
510/849-2622
The what's-the-hurry mellow hum of this pub/restaurant/club is too far from campus to pull in many undergraduates. But grad students and neighborhood professionals who

Jupiter

Viviana Rennella

seek a few hours without the Internet enjoy its fairly priced menu and, after 10, live jazz, blues, and folk music. The clutter of antiques may make you feel as though you're hanging out in your grandmother's attic. (Berkeley)

BISON BREWING
2598 Telegraph Ave.
Berkeley
510/ 841-7734
This place isn't hard to find: Look for a rusted buffalo sign on a brazenly modern building draped with trumpet vines on the perimeter of punkish Telegraph Avenue. Inside, this microbrewery serves its own beers and a menu of light pizzas, mussels, and tacotillas. On Friday and Saturday nights from 9:30 to midnight, local rock, blues, and jazz bands set up on the first floor and proceed to bring down the house. (Berkeley)

CATO'S ALE HOUSE
3891 Piedmont Ave.
Oakland
510/655-3349
The music isn't exactly the main attraction here, but on Sunday and Wednesday nights from six to nine you'll find acoustic players strumming out tunes in a corner. This place is as convivial a pub as any you'd find in County Clare. They pour 22 tap beers and offer the usual fare: salads, pizzas, and sandwiches. (Oakland)

JUPITER
2181 Shattuck Ave.
Berkeley
510/843-8277
A kind of graduate-student lounge that serves beer instead of coffee, Jupiter is big, dark, and brown and

For 12 Saturday nights during the summer, the Pyramid Brewery at Ninth and Gilman (510/528-9886) turns its parking lot into an outdoor movie theater to show recent and classic Hollywood fare.

has walls covered with pressed tin. At the gleaming copper bar, you'll find four or five house beers and more than 20 other local microbrews. A short but tasty menu of pizza, salads, and focaccia melts keeps appetites under control. A patio out back offers a bit of air and jazz Tuesdays through Sundays during the summers. When the temperature drops, the music moves indoors. (Berkeley)

MALLARD CLUB
752 San Pablo
Albany
510/524-8450
This 1945 landmark is happily schizophrenic. You walk into what looks like a '50s rod-and-gun club with miles of Naugahyde. Outside in the back, it's Polynesia revisited, with flaming tiki torches and smoking permitted. Head upstairs and you're in a wainscoted English club with five pool tables and one of the town's best jukeboxes. (Berkeley Waterfront)

PACIFIC COAST BREWING
906 Washington
Oakland
510/836-2739
Remember that bar on TV where everybody knows your name? This pub and restaurant has the same fake-brick walls, beveled glass, and an ornate bar saved from an 1874 Oakland saloon. Twenty beers are on tap, including some of their own award-winning brews—mostly full-bodied ambers brewed downstairs in the basement. An offbeat selection of exotic European ales and stouts is also offered. (Oakland)

SPATS
1974 Shattuck Ave.
Berkeley
510/841-7225
Proving that drinking in Berkeley isn't legally limited to beer and wine, this truly bizarre restaurant/cocktail lounge serves mixed drinks such as black vodka martinis and Burmese fog cutters. If your conversation gets dull, the walls will give you something to talk about. They're thick with old movie posters, beer ads, stuffed animals, and just about anything else you can think of. A full dinner menu is served until eleven and bar food until one. (Berkeley)

TRIPLE ROCK BREWERY
1920 Shattuck Ave.
Berkeley
510/843-2739
It's like a cowboy bar—except the cowboys are grad students and they're all watching ESPN. An ornate saloon counter is where the bartenders dispense the dozen or so beers brewed right on the premises. They've got shuffleboard and a roof deck, and dirt-cheap sal-

ads, nachos, and beer are served until midnight. Barflies here insist it's the most convivial place in town. (Berkeley)

WHITE HORSE INN
6551 Telegraph Ave.
Berkeley
510/652-3820

There aren't many drag queens or chain-rattling musclemen hanging out at the state's oldest gay bar. The White Horse Inn welcomes men and women of all ages and races. Thursday, Friday, and Saturday nights a three-dollar cover gets you into the back room, where deejays play house music and the dance floor comes alive. The first Sunday of every month from four to nine there's a tea dance with free hot dogs and hamburgers. (South Berkeley/North Oakland)

MIXED BAG

DORSEY'S LOCKER
5817 Shattuck Ave.
Berkeley
510/428-1935

You could run a couple of power plants with the energy generated in this mostly black neighborhood bar. Seven nights a week it serves everything from stand-up comedy to soul, from hip-hop to the spoken word, and from rhythm and blues to top 40. Decibels can be deafening, but it

doesn't seem to disturb the couples playing dominoes or a card game called Bid Whiz. The Wednesday night open mike is a chance to catch the untapped local talent. (South Berkeley/North Oakland)

MAMBO MAMBO
1803 Webster
Oakland
510/832-9422

Where else can you find a lineup of Cambodian, Filipino, and black comedians one night and jazz, rhythm and blues, or maybe open-mike poetry the next? The ambitious nonprofit entrepreneurs behind this two-story, warehouse-like club see it as the first step in an East Bay entertainment empire. The kitchen remains open 24 hours a day for breakfast and not-too-exotic African dishes such as braised fish with plantains. (Oakland)

MOVIEHOUSES OF NOTE

FINE ARTS CINEMA
2451 Shattuck Ave.
Berkeley
510/848-1143

A dedicated cinemagoer might recognize the titles shown at this small theater, but for most film buffs, a night here promises to be fresh and challenging. A few Bergman and Buñuel classics alternate with foreign and experimental films that are

For the star-struck, the Lawrence Hall of Science offers the use of their telescopes on the plaza on Saturday nights. Winter viewings take place between 8 and 11 p.m. In summer, the action starts half an hour before sunset.

usually seen only at obscure festivals. Most films run for three or four days. (Berkeley)

GRAND LAKE THEATER
3200 Grand Ave.
Oakland
510/452-3556
Even when this 1926 movie palace was divided into a quadplex a few years ago, it miraculously held on to its original, palatial character. The 600-seat theater #1 has incredible leg room and includes weekend pre-movie concerts on a massive Wurlitzer organ, but it's actually not as authentic as theater #2, which used to be #1's balcony. The other two theaters feature smaller, modern designs with Art Deco motifs. You'll find only first-run Hollywood movies here. (Oakland)

PACIFIC FILM ARCHIVES
2621 Durant Ave.
Berkeley
510/642-1412
www.bampfa.berkeley.edu
So you think you've seen everything? Then try this place. This nightly feast of international film includes Pakistani comedies, Finnish documentaries, and restored French silents that you definitely haven't seen anywhere else. The theater, a 234-seat temple on the bottom floor of the Berkeley Art Museum, enshrines masterworks of world cinema and video and has taken a leading role in restoring endangered classics. You'll find retrospectives, lectures, children's festivals, and world premieres. Admission is $6. (Berkeley)

PARAMOUNT THEATER
2025 Broadway
Oakland
510/465-6400
On 24 Fridays (and occasional Saturdays), this stunning Art Deco palace reverts to its original role as a film theater, showing classics from Hollywood's Golden Age in addition to cartoons and newsreels. The Paramount often hands out prizes, like gift certificates to local restaurants. You usually won't have a problem getting a seat, but some films like *Casablanca* and *Breakfast at Tiffany's* sell out. Tickets are $5. (Oakland)

PARKWAY THEATER
1834 Park Blvd.
Oakland
510/814-2400
If dinner and a movie sound good, then come here for a change of pace. This funk-a-Deco 1929 neighborhood theater goes light years beyond popcorn, offering pasta, sandwiches, 10 kinds of pizza, and, yes, beer and wine. Imbibe a rosy Preston Vineyards Faux while you catch a recent Hollywood flick from the comfort of your own '70s vintage sofa. All seats are $5. (Oakland)

UC THEATER
2036 University Ave.
Berkeley
510/843-3456
Roughly the size of a 747 hanger, this mildly Art Deco 1,313-seater changes double features almost every night. The movie matchups are wildly perfect—for example, *A Simple Plan* and *The Last Seduction*. Their repertoire doesn't dip too far back into the past, but they show restored prints of Hollywood and foreign classics, kung fu festivals, and Japanese animé. Almost every coffeehouse in town has a stack of their tri-monthly schedules. (Berkeley)

13

DAY TRIPS FROM BERKELEY/OAKLAND

Day Trip: The Marin Coast

Distance from Berkeley/Oakland: 85 miles

It's clear from the moment you reach the Pacific at **Point Reyes National Seashore** (415/633-1092, www.nps.gov/prns), a 100-square-mile pistol-shaped peninsula north of San Francisco, that you have come to the edge of North America. That, or you've suddenly been transported to the chalky coast of Scotland.

The weather is likely to be densely foggy with winds slamming in off the ocean. The landscape consists of tough, grassy, heathery hillsides punctuated by deep, soulful forests. Overhead, white gulls dip and glide. It reminded Sir Francis Drake of the Dover Coast when he harbored here in 1579.

All the information you need you can find at the **Bear Valley Visitor Center**. Detailed exhibits tell about the Miwok Indians, who once resided here, as well as the rich flora and fauna that survive this obdurate climate. Maps show the more than 140 miles of hiking trails in the area. Driving will take you to windswept **Limantour Beach** and 20 miles north to the **Point Reyes Lighthouse**. There, from January to April, you can watch migrating gray whales parade across the sea. Even on a hot summer day the water is too cold and the currents too treacherous to swim. If you're the type of person who can't go to an ocean without swimming in it, try the nearby **Heart's Desire Beach** on tranquil Tamales Bay.

Dairy farms still outnumber B&Bs in the area, but who knows for how long. Ecotourists love the local three-block towns with their craft galleries and surprisingly good restaurants. **Manka's** (415/669-1034) in Inverness offers mildly spicy Czech cooking. **The Station House** (415/663-1515) in Point Reyes Station has a fresh California menu, including oysters harvested just up the coast. Another great restaurant right nearby is **Nick's** (415/663-1033), a zero-pretense seafood roadhouse.

You could easily spend the whole day on this wild coast, but if the winds are blowing you away, drive south on Highway 1 through Olema. This highway qualifies as one of the most beautiful roads in the United States, especially as it unfurls through eucalyptus groves.

When you arrive back at the coast, you'll pass an unmarked road on your right that leads to the resolutely anonymous hippie town of Bolinas. For years, the residents have fought the state's desire to put up a sign.

Farther south is **Stinson Beach,** a long, white crescent flanked by overpriced weekend homes. Tempting as the water may be, you either need to wear a wetsuit or down a shot of vodka to enter the frigid waves. On the beach, the **Parkside Snack Bar** has creamy softies. **The Sand Dollar** (415/868-0434) is the weathered restaurant of choice for locals. On summer weekends, you can catch a night of live Shakespeare.

As you continue south, prepare to be awed. If you can't get to Big Sur, the jagged, cliff-hanging coast south of Stinson is close enough to the real thing. Its sheer, 100-foot drops strike terror into the hearts of flatland Midwesterners.

Just when you start to breathe normally again, you'll have your breath taken away. **Muir Woods National Monument** (415/388-2595, www.nps.gov/mwnm) is to forests what the Vatican is to churches. Redwoods, some 200 feet high and more than 1,000 years old, will awe you with your own relative insignificance and nature's staggering beauty.

You have spent your day on the rural, western edge of Marin County, a wealthy community much mocked for its New Age narcissism. You'll find more of it when you drive over the ridges of **Mount Tamalpais** to Mill Val-

Muir Woods

Jay Blakesberg

ley, a sweet, woody little village recently invaded by Range Rovers fleeing Hollywood. It's worth stopping to see the art and jewelry at Susan Cummins (12 Miller Ave., 415/388-1512), and Village Music (9 East Blithedale, 415/388-7400), the best source of old LPs in the Bay area.

Getting there from Berkeley/Oakland: *Take Highway 80 north to the San Rafael exit, which becomes Highway 580 and crosses the Richmond San Rafael Bridge. At the west end of the bridge, take the Sir Francis Drake Boulevard exit and continue for about 40 minutes to Highway 1.*

BERKELEY/OAKLAND REGION

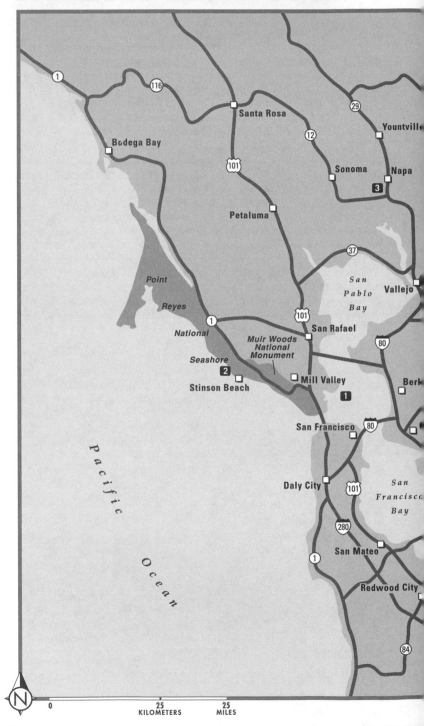

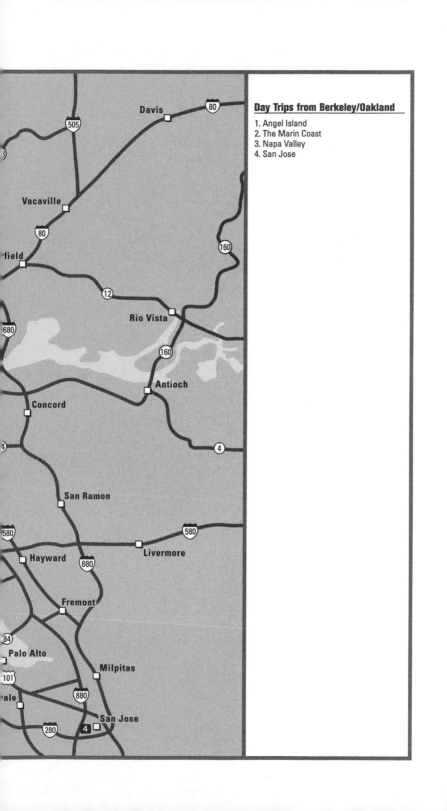

The Tech Museum of Innovation in San Jose

Day Trip: San Jose

Distance from Berkeley/Oakland: 55 miles

San Jose, the Rome of the world's computer empire, is the fastest growing city in California. Easily mistaken for a freeway-ribboned corner of L.A.'s San Fernando Valley, it's working hard to earn some respect.

The **Tech Museum** (201 S. Market St., 408/795-6100, www.thetech.org), an impossible-to-miss, hot-orange building downtown, has three floors of hands-on exhibits (largely computer stations) that detail the impact of technology on media, telecommunications, and medicine. It also has an IMAX theater. You can easily spend half a day steering a simulated submarine, starting your own earthquake, and adventuring inside the human body. Most of the exhibits are over the heads of small children.

Across the plaza from the Tech Museum is the **San Jose Museum of Art** (110 S. Market St., 408/294-7787, www.sjmusart.org). Thanks to a clever arrangement with New York City's Whitney Museum, it regularly displays work by great American artists like O'Keefe and Hopper. The amazing Gilhooly glass chandeliers inside the entrance alone are worth the trip.

Downtown is starting to acquire a little urban snap. The theater and music scenes are active year round. The Sharks hit the ice at the **San Jose Arena** (525 W. Santa Clara, 408/999-5823). The **Hotel de Anza** (233 W. Santa Clara, 408/286-1000) has been remodeled in spiffy Spanish décor. Inexpensive ethnic restaurants downtown include **House of Siam** (65 S. Market St., 408/279-5668), **Inca Goddess** (87 E. San Fernando, 408/977-0816), and **Señor Emma's** (177 W. Santa Clara, 408/294-6785). A bit more expensive is the hugely popular **Gordon Biersch** beer parlor (33 E. San Fernando, 408/294-6785). Pricier still, and equal to San Francisco's best, is **P.J. Stumps** (163 W. Santa Clara, 408/292-9928).

San Jose's reputation as a geek magnet is nothing new. It has always had a nutty side. Sarah Winchester, of Winchester rifles fame, was told by a fortune teller in 1884 never to stop building her home. She never did until the day she died, and today tourists can see the result. It's possible to tour 110 rooms of her 160-room **Winchester House** (525 S. Winchester Blvd., 408/247-2101).

The **Rosicrucian Museum** (1342 Naglee Ave., 408/247-2101) is the home of an international reincarnation cult. It makes a stab at respectability with carefully preserved Egyptian funerary artifacts, but its circa 1920s buildings are pure de Mille.

If you expect **Silicon Valley** to be a 21st-century show on wheels, you're in for a disappointment. Unless you decide to live here, the excitement is all virtual. You have to work 140 hours a week in an Internet start-up company to experience the biggest local thrills. From the road, this place is identical to a million other industrial parks.

Traffic, of course, is hellish. Avoid it and head up to the hills. The tasteful, old-money towns of Los Gatos and Saratoga are chock-a-block with charm-drenched antiques stores. These towns also host summer music festivals at the **Villa Montalvo** (15400 Montalvo Rd., 408/961-5800). Higher up the steep, scrubby landscape you'll see sprouting grapevines. Two of the best-regarded wineries are **Ridge Winery** (17100 Montebello Rd., 408/867-3233) and **David Bruce** (Bear Creek Rd., 408/354-4214). Even higher up, **Skyline Boulevard** is a twisting, shadowy road pierced by shafts of light that slice through the redwoods.

You can take Skyline Boulevard all the way to San Francisco if you have the time, but you will have missed **Stanford,** one of the world's preeminent and most beautiful universities, a wide-open rancho grande of Spanish colonial architecture. Stop at the half-classic, half-contemporary **Cantor Museum** (650/723-1216), with its sun-drenched **Rodin Sculpture Garden.** Up the road, visitors can check out the **Stanford Linear Accelerator** (2575 Sandhill Rd., 650/926-2204), where research is done on particle physics and other obscure subjects.

Palo Alto is the Beverly Hills of university towns. You can watch wealthy locals get rid of their cash at the **Stanford Shopping Center,** and partake of a gentrified deli meal at **Max's** (650/323-6297). Or swing into downtown Palo Alto for an outdoor meal at the **Empire Tap Room** (651 Emerson St., 650/321-3030) or the less yuppified **China Delight** (461 Emerson St., 650/326-6065). Summer nights are usually warm enough for a slow stroll down the brain-clogged sidewalks of University Avenue to see a Hollywood classic at the restored **Stanford Theater** (221 University Ave., 605/324-3700). Strung along the peninsula, from here to San Jose, are a wild assortment of pubs and clubs. Pick up a copy of the local *Metro* weekly paper for all the listings.

For a final dose of floral flamboyance, pull into the magnificent **Filoli** estate (650/364-2880) at the Edgewood Road exit off Highway 280. There you'll find acres and acres of French and Spanish gardens amidst the million-dollar estates of Woodside. Afterward, as you head north on Highway 101, you'll spot **Heller Aviation Museum** (601 Skyline Rd., 650/654-0200). Its exhibits of early aircraft are brilliant.

Getting there from Berkeley/Oakland: Take Highway 880 to Highway 280 south. Turn off at the Guadeloupe Parkway and follow the signs to the Tech Museum and downtown. To get to Los Gatos or Skyline Boulevard, jump back on Highway 880 and head west. To get to Palo Alto, just retrace your steps, take Highway 17 back to Highway 101, and go north. Exit at University Avenue.

Day Trip: Angel Island

Ferry time from Berkeley/Oakland: 50 minutes

Leave your cares and your car behind. Take the ferry from Jack London Square directly to Angel Island and back any weekend from May to November. The rest of the time you'll have to brave the hordes at Pier 39. The brisk Bay boat ride is the first stage in detaching yourself from the cares of the modern world. The second stage begins when you land on this 740-acre chunk of golden California hillside off Tiburon.

Just up from the **Ayala Cove** landing dock is a large patch of lawn where you can sit down and partake of the elegant picnic you packed in Berkeley/Oakland. There are also dozens of tables scattered around the island. When you're ready to walk off your meal, choose from more than 13 miles of easy trails that circumnavigate the island. For the best views, take the **Northridge-Sunset Loop** to 781-foot-high Mount Livermore. If you brought your bicycle, you have eight miles of road at your disposal. Bikes are also available for rent. If you miss your car, take the guided tram tour.

You can thank the National Park Service for keeping this place as unspoiled as possible. For centuries, the Miwok Indians used Angel Island for hunting and fishing. Consisting mostly of grassy fields and oak trees, it's home to a surprisingly varied population of deer and raccoons, a large number of birds, and, on summer weekends, a steady parade of Bay-area families. Educate yourself on what poison oak looks like because the itchy weed runs rampant here during the summer.

You can relax on a couple of decent beaches on Angel Island. **Quarry,** on the island's protected eastern side, is the best. The water, however, is just for looking. The currents are dangerous, the temperature is Alaskan, and no lifeguards are on duty. Don't be surprised to see seals and sea lions romping offshore.

This idyllic little isle's history is almost as grim as that of neighboring Alcatraz. It's home to **Fort Reynolds,** a Civil War-era prison for suspected confederate sympathizers, and to the **Immigrant's Station,** where at the end of the nineteenth century more than 175,000 Chinese were detained as victims of the state's draconian anti-immigration (more specifically, anti-Chinese) laws. A museum now stands on the site of so much suffering. If you look closely, you can see the poems carved by immigrants into the wooden beams. There are remnant wooden structures all over the island, but most of them are in bad shape and have been closed for safety reasons.

If you work up an appetite, snacks are available at the **Cove Café.** If you're up for some recreation, a kayak tour can be arranged by calling

415/488-1000 in advance of your visit. It's also possible to reserve a campground and spend a night under the stars. Where else in the world can you pitch a tent and gaze out at the glittering skyline of one of the world's great cities?

Getting there from Berkeley/Oakland: Take the ferry from Jack London Square (415/773-1188) directly to Angel Island and back any weekend from May to November. The roundtrip excursion costs $13.

Day Trip: Napa Valley

Distance from Berkeley/Oakland: 70 miles

Remember those progressive parties where you'd migrate among friends' homes, eating and drinking for hours? Picture partying like that all day long and you've got a good idea of what life is like in Napa Valley.

More than 250 wineries spread across the valley floor and up into the lower foothills. All told, they produce more than 9 million cases of wine a year. Some of the wineries, like **Clos Pegase** (1060 Dunweal Lane, 707/942-4981), are great architectural experiments. Others, such as **Chateau Montehelena** (1429 Tubbs Lane, 707/942-5105), which has its own lake, are shamelessly romantic. Tastings are occasionally free, but more often they cost from three to five dollars per person. Case prices are not any better than those at your local retailer, but you can pick up special reserve wines that are not available in stores.

Save up for at least one knockout meal here. The quality of cooking is astonishing. In Yountville, **The French Laundry** (6640 Washington St., 707/944-2380) is a multi-starred little farmhouse that's a temple of haute cuisine á la Française. In Saint Helena you could eat out for a week or two

Napa Valley vineyards

John Weil

without going to the same restaurant twice. The country Italian villa that houses **Tra Vigne** (1050 Charter Lane, 707/963-4444) is cool even in Napa's roasting summer heat. The spa town of Calistoga is also blessed with great restaurants. **Catahoula** (1457 Lincoln Ave., 707/942-2275), for instance, has a hearty menu rooted in Louisiana. Even the more modest restaurants aim high. Try the all-American **Bergman's** (1234 Main St., 707/963-1063) in Saint Helena or the friendly **Red Hen Cantina** (1591 St. Helena Hwy., 707/255-8125) in Napa. But a great option is to stock up at one of the gourmet emporiums like **Dean and Deluca** (607 St. Helena Hwy., 707/967-9980) or **Oakville Grocery** (2875 St. Helena Hwy., 707/944-8802) and simply make your own picnic to eat at one of the wineries.

If your cares haven't melted away by now, dip into a bath of volcanic ash (more like mud) or a mineral whirlpool at one of Calistoga's spas. **Nance's Hot Springs** (1614 Lincoln Ave., 707/642-6211) runs about $80 per night. Other recreational offerings include hot air ballooning, horsebacking, and bike riding.

Grapes aren't the only things cultivated here. The valley's art is nearly as popular as its wine. The **Hess Collection** (4411 Redwood Rd., 707/255-1144), attached to a mountaintop winery, is modern and international. The **di Rosa Preserve** (5200 Sonoma Hwy., 707/226-5991) is a 200-acre art park full of works by leading Bay-area sculptors.

Napa Valley is B&B country. Rooms are expensive—$150 or more per night—and reservations must be made far in advance. Still, there are camping grounds and funkier (and cheaper) accommodations like Calistoga's **Triple S Ranch** (4600 Mt. Home Rd., 707/942-6730), which offers doubles for $70. If you want to avoid the crowds, don't visit in the summer. Rather, come in the spring when wildflowers are rampant; or, if you want to experience the "crush," arrive in the fall during harvest.

Getting there from Berkeley/Oakland: Take Highway 80 north to Vallejo. Exit on Highway 37, then turn right on Highway 29 and continue north.

EMERGENCY PHONE NUMBERS

Police, Fire Department, and Ambulance
911
Poison Control
800/876-4766
Battered Women
510/536-7233
Suicide Hotline
510/849-2212 (North County)
510/889-1333 (South County)
Parental Stress Service
510/893-5444
Child Protective Service
510/259-1800
AAA Emergency Road Service
800/AAA-HELP

HOSPITALS & EMERGENCY MEDICAL CENTERS

ALTA BATES
2450 Ashby Ave.
Berkeley
510/204-4444

CHILDREN'S HOSPITAL OAKLAND
747 Summit St.
Oakland
510/428-3240

SUMMIT MEDICAL CENTER
350 Hawthorne Ave.
Oakland
510/869-6600

RECORDED INFORMATION

Local Forecast
510/251-6000, x1112
Time

510/767-8900
Air Quality
800/435-7247
Road Conditions
800/427-7623

VISITOR INFORMATION

Berkeley Chamber of Commerce
510/549-7000
Berkeley Convention & Visitors Bureau
510/549-7040
Oakland Chamber of Commerce
510/874-4800
Oakland Convention & Visitors Bureau
510/839-9000

CITY TOURS

Oakland Walking Tours
510/238-3243

POST OFFICE

BERKELEY MAIN
2000 Allston
510/649-3100

OAKLAND MAIN
1675 7th
510/251-3360

CAR RENTAL

Alamo
800/327-9633
Avis
800/831-2847
Dollar

800/800-4000
Enterprise
800/736-8222
Hertz
800/654-3131

DISABLED ACCESS INFORMATION

Center for Independent Living
510/841-4776 (Berkeley)
510/763-9999 (Oakland)

MULTICULTURAL RESOURCES

Spanish Speaking Unity Council
510/535-6900

Asian Cultural Center
510/893-8795

OTHER COMMUNITY ORGANIZATIONS

Gay Switchboard
510/841-6224
Senior Resources
800/510-2020

BABYSITTING/CHILDCARE

Bananas
510/658-0381

NEWSPAPERS

Berkeley Monthly
510/658-9811
Berkeley Voice
510/339-8777

Urban View
510/645-1330

The Daily Californian
510/548-8300
East Bay Express
510/540-7400
Montclarion
510/339-8777
Oakland Tribune
510/208-6300

AM RADIO

560	KSFO	Talk
610	KFRC	Sports/Oldies
680	KNBR	Sports/Talk
740	KCBS	All news
810	KGO	News/Talk/Sports
960	KABL	Pop
1260	KOIT	Adult contemporary
1510	KIOI	Adult standards
1640	KDIA	Talk/Catholic family

FM RADIO

88.5	KQED	NPR
90.7	KALX	College radio
91.1	KCSM	Jazz
91.7	KALW	NPR
93.3	KYCY	Country
94.1	KPFA	Progressive, listener sponsored
96.5	KOIT	Adult contemporary
97.3	KLLC	Adult contemporary
99.7	KFRC	Oldies
100.7	KJOI	Adult standards
102.1	KDFC	Classical
102.9	KBLX	Adult contemporary
103.7	KKSF	Smooth jazz
104.5	KFOG	Adult alternative rock
105.3	KITS	Alternative rock
106.1	KMEL	Urban contemporary
107.7	KSAN	Classic rock

TELEVISION STATIONS

(note: cable channels may vary from Oakland to Berkeley)

KTVU	2	Fox
B-TV	25	Public Access
KRON	4	NBC
KPIX	5	CBS
KGO	7	ABC
KQED	9	PBS
KBWB	29	Warner
KBHK	24	UPN

OAKLAND BOOKSTORES

BARNES & NOBLE
Jack London Square
98 Broadway
510/272-0120

THE BOOK MARK
721 Washington St.
510/444-0473

THE BOOK TREE
6121 La Salle Ave.
510/339-0513

DIESEL A BOOKSTORE
5433 College Ave.
510/653-9965

LITTLE BOOKSHOP
3403 Fruitvale Ave.
510/530-3946

PENDRAGON FINE BOOKS
5560 College Ave.
510/652-6259

RENAISSANCE BOOKS INC.
7700 Edgewate Dr., Ste. 647
510/444-2665

SECOND EDITION
6120 La Salle Ave.
510/339-8210
WALDENBOOKS
Oakland Square
501 14th St.
510/839-1983

BERKELEY BOOKSTORES

AVENUE BOOKS INC
2904 College Ave.
510/549-3532

BARNES & NOBLE
2352 Shattuck Ave.
510/644-0861

THE BEAR STUDENT STORE
University of California
Bancroft Way at Telegraph
510/642-7294

BLACK OAK BOOKS
1491 Shattuck Ave.
510/486-0698

CODY'S BOOKS, INC.
2454 Telegraph Ave.
510/845-7852
1730 Fourth St.
510/559-9500

COLLECTED THOUGHTS BOOKSHOP
1816 Euclid Ave.
510/843-1816

MOE'S BOOKS INC.
2476 Telegraph Ave.
510/849-2087

PANDORA'S BOOKS INC.
1223 Eighth St.
510/528-3254

PEGASUS DOWNTOWN
2349 Shattuck Ave.
510/649-1320

SHAKESPEARE & CO. BOOKS
2499 Telegraph Ave.
510/841-8916

INDEX

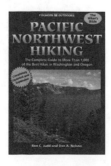

MOON HANDBOOKS

provide comprehensive coverage of a region's arts, history, land, people, and social issues in addition to detailed practical listings for accommodations, food, outdoor recreation, and entertainment. Moon Handbooks allow complete immersion in a region's culture—ideal for travelers who want to combine sightseeing with insight for an extraordinary travel experience in destinations throughout North America, Hawaii, Latin America, the Caribbean, Asia, and the Pacific.

WWW.MOON.COM

Rick Steves shows you where to travel and how to travel—all while getting the most value for your dollar. His Back Door travel philosophy is about making friends, having fun, and avoiding tourist rip-offs.

Rick's been traveling to Europe for more than 25 years and is the author of 22 guidebooks, which have sold more than a million copies. He also hosts the award-winning public television series Travels in Europe with Rick Steves.

WWW.RICKSTEVES.COM

ROAD TRIP USA

Getting there is half the fun, and Road Trip USA guides are your ticket to driving adventure. Taking you off the interstates and onto less-traveled, two-lane highways, each guide is filled with fascinating trivia, historical information, photographs, facts about regional writers, and details on where to sleep and eat—all contributing to your exploration of the American road.

*"Books so full of the pleasures of the American road,
you can smell the upholstery."*
~ BBC radio

WWW.ROADTRIPUSA.COM

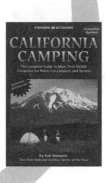

www.travelmatters.com

User-friendly, informative, and fun:
Because travel *matters.*

Visit our newly launched web site and explore the variety of titles and travel information available online, featuring an interactive *Road Trip USA* exhibit.

also check out:

www.ricksteves.com

The Rick Steves web site is bursting with information to boost your travel I.Q. and liven up your European adventure.

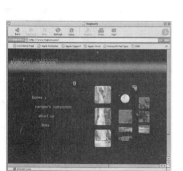

www.foghorn.com

Visit the Foghorn Outdoors web site for more information on the premier source of U.S. outdoor recreation guides.

www.moon.com

The Moon Handbooks web site offers interesting information and practical advice that ensure an extraordinary travel experience.

ABOUT THE AUTHOR

John Weil is a creative director at an Internet company, following a career in advertising. In the last few years, he has reviewed restaurants in Oakland and Berkeley, written and produced a musical in San Francisco, and created a documentary on deaf education. A UC Berkeley graduate and fifth generation San Franciscan, John lives in Berkeley with his wife, Jane.

AVALON TRAVEL PUBLISHING
and its City•Smart Guidebook
authors are dedicated to building
community awareness within
City•Smart cities. We are proud to
work with Berkeley Reads of
Berkeley as we publish this guide
to Berkeley/Oakland.

AVALON
TRAVEL
publishing

Berkeley Reads is the adult literacy program of the Berkeley Public Library. Our program offers free tutoring to English-speaking adults who want to improve their basic reading and writing skills. We train volunteer tutors and match them one-to-one with adult learners. Together, tutoring pairs design literacy lessons that address the individual learning goals and needs of the adult learner. Volunteers in Berkeley Reads play a key role in helping adult learners function more effectively at home, at work and in the community.

For more information, please contact:
Berkeley Reads
West Branch – Berkeley Public Library
1125 University Avenue
Berkeley, CA 94702
Phone: 510/644-8595
Fax: 510/549-3057
http://www.infopeople.org/bpl/

Berkeley Reads